The Rodfather

The Rodfather

*Inside the Beautiful
(Ugly, Ridiculous, Hilarious) Game*

RODDY COLLINS
WITH PAUL HOWARD

SANDYCOVE

an imprint of

PENGUIN BOOKS

SANDYCOVE

UK | USA | Canada | Ireland | Australia
India | New Zealand | South Africa

Sandycove is part of the Penguin Random House group of companies
whose addresses can be found at global.penguinrandomhouse.com.

First published 2022
001

Copyright © Roddy Collins and Paul Howard, 2022

The moral right of the copyright holders has been asserted

Set in 12/14.75 pt Bembo Book MT Pro
Typeset by Jouve (UK), Milton Keynes
Printed and bound in Great Britain by Clays Ltd, Elcograf S.p.A.

The authorized representative in the EEA is Penguin Random House Ireland,
Morrison Chambers, 32 Nassau Street, Dublin D02 YH68

A CIP catalogue record for this book is available from the British Library

ISBN: 978–1–844–88595–4

www.greenpenguin.co.uk

There is only one person to whom I could dedicate this book, and that's the person who has dedicated so much to me – my wife, Caroline. I love you, pal.

Prologue

I was watching football on television not so long ago when the supporters of Drogheda United, one of the teams involved, launched into a spontaneous chorus: 'Roddy Collins – is a wanker, is a wanker!'

I can tell you this – it's a very strange feeling to be sitting at home with your wife, sipping a glass of wine at the end of a week, and to suddenly hear a crowd of people calling you a wanker on the telly.

Welcome to my life.

I've never managed Drogheda United and most of the fans doing the singing would have been far too young to remember me playing for the club when we got relegated in the mid-1980s. But 'Roddy Collins is a wanker!' has become a sort of generic terrace standard – a bit like, 'He wears a suit, he wears a tie – fuck Delaney and the FAI.'

And God knows, I've beaten that drum once or twice myself.

I started wearing glasses a few years ago after I hugged a man who was running towards me in the Phoenix Park. I thought it was John Toal, who'd played football for Shamrock Rovers.

'Toaler!' I said, throwing my arms around him. 'How are you, me old pal?'

It turned out it was just a fella from the country out for a jog.

So glasses have become part of my life, although I'm too vain to wear them all the time. Instead, I carry them around with me in a little man-bag with a cross-body strap and I pull them out whenever I need them. One day I was walking along the quays when a fella in a lorry shouted, 'Collins, you wanker – what are you doing with that drug-dealer bag?'

And that was the first time it occurred to me. I turned to my wife and I said, 'Do you know what, Caroline? Maybe I *am* a wanker.'

I've been hearing it for so long now that I wouldn't be human if I didn't occasionally wonder.

But I've also been around football long enough to know that most of the people who say they hate me don't really hate me at all. About ten years ago Shamrock Rovers played Tottenham Hotspur in the Europa League and I was asked by RTE to do co-commentary on the match. I arrived in Tallaght early and went across to the Maldron Hotel to meet a mate of mine for a 7-Up.

The bar was full of Rovers supporters, who had more reason to dislike me than the fans of Drogheda United. I was the manager for most of the season when they got relegated for the only time in their history – although I still say I would have kept them up if they hadn't got rid of me.

I hadn't even reached the bar when the singing started. All the old favourites. I could have taken the easy option and walked out. But I decided no, I'd brazen it out. I ordered my drink. The chanting stopped. And soon the fans started drifting over to me.

'Fair play to you for staying,' they said, shaking my hand. Soon we were having a laugh and talking about the thing we all had in common – our love of football.

I'm not an innocent. A lot of the abuse I got over the years I brought upon myself. When I was a manager, I enjoyed the notoriety. I'd throw on my most expensive Louis Copeland suit and a nice overcoat with a pair of spats and it drove people mad. I was an actor, hamming it up for the audience. Football grounds were my stage. And the people who screamed and roared abuse at me were booing a pantomime villain. Too often we forget that football is about entertainment. It's supposed to be enjoyable or else what's the point?

Looking back over the course of my life, I used to focus a lot on the unlucky breaks I had, especially the broken legs I suffered during my playing career.

But I also had the luckiest break of all. I met Caroline when I was fifteen years old. She was my first girlfriend. I fell in love with her and I got to spend my whole life with her.

Caroline sacrificed everything while I pursued my dreams in football. Wherever football took me, she upped roots and came with me. We lived in bedsits. We ate baked beans for dinner. And when it didn't work out, and my confidence was on the floor, she urged me on, telling me, 'Rod, keep going,' even as we were packing everything we owned into the back of another removal lorry to return home yet again. 'I believe in you.'

So how unlucky have I been, really?

We have five beautiful children and four equally beautiful grandchildren. And I love my wife as much today as I did the first time I laid eyes on her. I hug her every day. I can't help myself. And when we go to bed at night, I say to her, 'I love you, pal,' and she says the same back to me.

That's not a bad bottom line in the audit of any man's life.

We go out walking a lot. Our first date when we were teenagers was a stroll through the Phoenix Park. And now we're in our sixties, it's still our favourite place in the world.

Most days we walk from our home in Castleknock into Dublin city centre, through Cabra, Smithfield and all the old haunts of our childhood, stopping and talking to people along the way, old friends and, yes, sometimes football fans.

Usually, I buy a few packets of cigarettes and I give them out to homeless people that I see. It's not the healthiest thing to give them, but the cigarettes aren't the point. The cigarettes are just an opener – to social contact. I've known loneliness in my life, especially when I was a kid, living in London, when I was a triallist with Fulham and Arsenal. It's a horrible, corrosive thing that eats you up inside. You might be surprised to discover how many people who spend their days on the streets just want someone to talk to, if only to make them feel seen.

So I always ask, 'Where did you stay last night?' or, 'Do you have anywhere to stay tonight?' and if the conversation progresses any further: 'So, where are you from originally?'

Sometimes I'll see a flicker of recognition in a face: 'Ah, you're the boxer's brother.'

'That's right,' I'll say. 'Stephen's my little brother.'

'I remember he beat your man Eubank. How's he doing?'

'He's doing brilliant.'

Or sometimes it'll be: 'You're your man — the fucking *Rod Squad*!'

The TV programme that made me sort of famous is still following me around nearly twenty years later. The internet has given it an unexpectedly long half-life. Every so often a clip from it will do the rounds on social media, introducing me to a brand-new audience. Kids who are far too young to remember the reality TV series about my time as the manager of Carlisle United point their phones at me now and ask me to quote lines from it:

'Just say, "I'll tell your ma on ye!"'

The line from the show that has, mercifully, so far stayed off the internet is the one where I said I was going to manage Manchester United and Ireland one day.

I was going to do a lot of things in life. When I was in my twenties, I was going to be a famous professional footballer, just like my brother was going to be the middleweight champion of the world. Stephen's dream came true. Mine didn't. But I do wonder sometimes how happy I would have been if it had.

I used to be great friends with the late Albert Gubay, the billionaire supermarket tycoon. When he opened a Total Fitness gym in Blanchardstown, I used to call in to see him once a week for a scone and a pot of tea and he'd attempt to pass on to me the benefit of his wisdom.

'Roddy,' he said to me one day, 'if I gave you a million quid for one year, what would you do with it?'

'I'd spend it in six months,' I told him.

Albert just laughed. He thought I was off the wall. But I was telling the truth. Money has never interested me — which goes a long way towards explaining why I don't have any today.

But I got something else. A lifetime of experiences in football, the game I loved from the time I was a child.

I can't say I've no regrets, but I've none that I can't live with. Tony O'Connell, my great friend who brought me up North to Crusaders and gave me some of the happiest days of my footballing life, has a good line of thinking when it comes to life's what-ifs. I used to be one for dwelling on what might have been, but Tony taught me to look at things differently:

'If you could live your life over again,' he said, 'you wouldn't make the same mistakes. But you'd make different ones. So the trick is to come to terms with the ones that are your own.'

I've done that now. And I can honestly say that I've loved my life, every happy, mad and sad moment of it.

I

Where do I start? It could be that there's only one story you need to know about my childhood: that when I was four years old, I walked out of school for the first time, but definitely not the last time. I stood up from my tiny desk and I was out of there as fast as my skinny little legs could carry me, crossing two main roads on my way back to 12 Annamoe Terrace, our home in Cabra. My ma tells me that she had nightmares for years afterwards – about what could have happened. And although I've no memory of it, it's clear to me now that my personality was set very early on. I wasn't going be controlled. There would be a lot of teachers, building contractors, football managers and club chairmen who would learn all about my problems with authority over the course of my life. It's why I'm not a multi-millionaire today. It might be why I never played for Manchester United, or managed Ireland, or did any of the things that I said I was going to do in football. I couldn't be told what to do. Couldn't at four years old. Still can't today.

I was born in the summer of 1960, the second of six children, and was christened Roderick, an affliction of a name that, in keeping with family tradition, I have since passed on to one of my own sons. Growing up, I felt like the character in Johnny Cash's 'A Boy Named Sue', saddled with an embarrassing name to either 'get tough or die' among the Bistos, Whackers and Blackies of my childhood. When I was a teenager, I remember standing in the dole office on the Navan Road, looking to sign on after failing to make it as a footballer in England for the first or maybe second time. In a posh voice, the hatch clerk called out, 'Roderick Collins!' Everyone in the room burst out laughing. I did what had, by then, become a habit for me. I headed for the door.

We grew up within earshot of Dalymount Park. From our back

garden you could hear the *ooohhh*s and *aaahhh*s of the crowd on match days. I was a kid who liked attention and I spent my childhood listening to the famous Dalymount Roar. How could I *not* want to be a footballer? The atmosphere was electric on midweek nights when Bohemians were playing in Europe, or when Ireland had a European Championship or World Cup qualifier. That was when the feeling of missing out became too much. I'd say, 'Ma, I'm going down to Dalyer,' and she'd roll her eyes and say, 'Don't you tell your father,' which she said so often that it became a sort of catchphrase. Once I was out of the house, I could run to Dalymount in two minutes, then pester a grown-up – 'Mister! Mister! Mister!' – to lift me over the stile, before outrunning the stewards and disappearing into a forest of legs.

My entire childhood was like that, a time of fun and adventure, and the streets of Dublin's north inner city were a playground to me.

As with most kids, the older I got, the further I journeyed. There was a laneway that connected Cabra to the North Circular Road and it was known as The Daf. That was where we hung out and divvied out the apples that we stole from the gardens of the posh houses on the North Circular. They were tiny, sour things that gave you stomach cramps, but the thrill was in robbing them.

There was a barn just off The Daf with an old Clydesdale horse belonging to Ollie Brocken, the local coalman. We slept in the loft of it one night when we were all supposed to be camping somewhere else. Ollie came home flutered and started roaring at the horse and we lay on the hard floor for the whole night, too terrified to sleep.

Sometimes our walk home took us through the grounds of St Brendan's Hospital in Grangegorman – or The Gorman, as we knew it – where we frightened the life out of each other with stories about escaped lunatics and tried not to look at the pale faces of the patients staring out of the windows at us.

There were games of street football that went on for hours. We played the ball off kerbs and walls, improvised our way around parked cars and told ourselves that we were George Best, and Don Givens, and Johnny Giles, and even Gerry Daly, who played football on our road and had just been signed by Manchester United, where I told myself that I was headed too. Afterwards, we drank cold bottles of milk from the Annamoe Dairy up the road.

Once or twice a year, Fossett's Circus arrived and pitched up on the site next to St Dympna's, a hospital for alcoholics on the North Circular Road. We were drawn there to look at the elephants and monkeys, then we crawled under a gap in the tent and climbed up the back of the scaffolding into the seating area to watch the show.

There was a cattle market and an animal auction house up at Hanlon's Corner at the end of our road. When I was eleven, I used to earn money helping to drive the cattle through Cabra to the City Abattoir on Blackhorse Avenue, waving a hankie and a stick to usher the terrified animals to the slaughter. The job paid sixpence per day, half of which had to be placed on the mantlepiece when I got home. My ma sometimes slipped the money straight into her purse and said, 'Don't tell your father.'

We did anything and everything for a thrill. At Hanlon's Corner, the foundations of the old orphanage had filled up with rainwater, ten feet deep, and we swam in it every day for an entire summer. We even dived into it from the shell of a half-demolished building that towered over it. There was a crane on the site and I watched in awe as my younger brother Stephen clambered up the ladder to the very top.

As kids, we knew no fear, except the sound of my da's whistle that summoned us home and the leather strap that was taken out whenever one of us veered off course.

We lived – nine of us – in a tiny two-bedroomed terraced house. It was the home of my nanny Collins and we were really just squatting there. My ma nursed and cared for her until the day she died. Like many homes in Dublin's inner city, it had no bathroom and the toilet was out in the back yard. The house was so cold in the winter that ice formed on the inside of the windows and sometimes I wonder was it just our collective body heat that saved us from hypothermia. The children – four boys and two girls – slept in one bedroom. The second bedroom was partitioned into two spaces. My ma and da slept on one side and my nanny on the other. There was so little room that, when there was housework to be done, my ma left the young ones in the front garden in our prams with a Staffordshire bull terrier named Gyp Collins standing guard and showing his teeth to any passers-by who got too close.

At some point in my childhood, my da built an extension onto the back of the house, after deciding that what his growing family needed more than anything else in the world was a boxing gym. It was a wooden structure and he built it with his own hands. Then he hung a heavy bag from the ceiling. It was there that all four of his sons learned how to fight. Every Sunday afternoon was the same. It was boxing, boxing, boxing. Even family gatherings ended with the men slipping out to the extension to throw punches at each other.

Mr Nelson, a skinny man with glasses from the Royal Liver Assurance company, called to the house sometimes to talk to my nanny. One day, he brought two pairs of boxing gloves with him. I remember the first time I pulled them on – and I remember Da, down on his knees, holding up his hands for me to hit them with all the force that was in my puny little arms. When we were old enough, we were taken to Corinthians Boxing Club, which was then in a basement on Gardiner Place, to test ourselves against kids from even tougher parts of the Dublin inner city.

Boxing was a family obsession. My da was in the ring the night he found out he'd become a father for the first time. 'Paschal,' his brother Terry shouted through the ropes, 'you've a little boy.'

We grew up listening to the story of how Uncle Terry battered Reggie Kray around the ring as an amateur, and I even saw him fight, at a carnival behind the Cabra Grand picture house on Quarry Road, steeling himself with a nip of whiskey before he ducked through the ropes.

Boxing was on both sides of the family. My ma's brother was Jack O'Rourke, the former Irish heavyweight champion, who spent a lot of his time in England. But two or three times a year he would suddenly appear in our lives. To us, he was like Jack Doyle, this ruggedly handsome man who could box and sing and tell funny stories. He'd throw around money, take us to the shop across the road for ice creams or anything we wanted. He'd work the heavy bag over with his enormous, shovel-like hands that we knew had done work – real work – in the mines. He'd stay up half the night telling stories and singing songs. Then he'd go back to England, leaving us all just shaking our heads.

I grew up in a macho environment, where the greatest compliment someone could pay you was to say you were 'a *man*'.

My da often stayed up all night to listen to fights on the radio from America. If Muhammad Ali was fighting, he woke me up to listen with him. Later, after we got our first black-and-white TV, he called me in from a kickabout on the street to show me a scraggy-bearded lightweight who threw bombs like a heavyweight. My poor da. I know I broke his heart when I chose football over boxing, but he still held out hope that I might yet be turned. 'Come and see this fella,' he said. 'He's called Roberto Duran.'

Years later, in the spring of 2007, I was in Las Vegas for the fight between Oscar de la Hoya and Floyd Mayweather Jr when I spotted Duran walking through the MGM Grand in the middle of the day. Remembering how much he meant to my da, I grabbed him by the shoulders and told him that I loved him – I can't even begin to describe the fear on the man's face – before a security guard arrived to drag me away.

Every night at six o'clock without fail my nanny said the Rosary in the scullery, where she also washed herself down once a day in a tub while we made ourselves scarce. She was a lovely old lady. She was frail and walked with the aid of two sticks. If she had a party to go to, I'd bring her into town on the number 22 bus to get a new frock from the Silk Mills on Dorset Street. She wasn't a drinker but she liked the odd glass of sherry, which made her cheeks flush red. Every November she made Christmas puddings, which she loaded with whiskey and stout, then wrapped in cloth and hung from the ceiling to be sent to her two sons, James in Birmingham and Dixie in Glasgow, but not before we'd reduced them to mush with uppercuts, jabs and left hooks.

My ma and da were the best-looking couple in Cabra. On Saturdays, my da would send me over to Tom Creen's shop across the road, where we had an account, for a Gillette blade and an *Evening Herald*. Then they'd get dolled up for their night out in the pub at Hanlon's Corner. My ma looked like a film star. As they left the house, the waft of perfume and Old Spice followed them down the terrace.

There was always music in the house. It was Tom Jones and Frank Sinatra and Dean Martin. My ma and da both had beautiful voices and every social occasion became a sing-song. They loved 'Green, Green Grass of Home'. And 'Strangers in the Night'. And 'Little Old Wine Drinker, Me'.

Gilbert O'Sullivan was my favourite. I knew every word of every song. And then, after I saw him on *Top of the Pops*, it was Gary Glitter. On Saturday nights, my ma and da would come home from the pub and my da would say, 'Come on, let's get him up to do Gary Glitter.'

I'd roll out of bed, then pull on my ma's leather jacket and her knee-high boots. I'd use a mascara brush to draw hair on my chest. Then I'd walk into the living room, clapping my hands over my head, singing, 'Come on, come on! Come on, come on! Come on, come on, come on!'

That was another part of my character that was formed early on. I never minded making an exhibition of myself.

'Colette,' my da would say, 'where did we get him?'

We didn't have much money, but we weren't poor in the way that many of our friends understood the word. We knew that we were different on account of the fact that our da had a job in Guinness, first in the brewery, shovelling grain, then later as a truck driver.

We had a car, nothing flashy, a boxy little Triumph Herald, in which we set off for our summer holidays every year. All of the children were crammed into the back, the younger ones perched on the knees of the older ones as we headed for Tramore or Salthill or Ballybunion or Clogher Head. We loved when the road took us through Termonfeckin because it was the only time in our lives when we could get away with cursing in front of our da.

'Look,' we'd say when we saw the signs, 'it's TermonFECKIN! Da, I need the toilet – can we stop in TermonFECKIN?'

Mick was the eldest of us and the star of the family. Blond, blue-eyed and handsome, he looked like Johnny Logan in his prime and the girls all fell at his feet. He had a silver tongue, the voice of a tenor and the soul of a poet. And he was hysterically funny.

There was just a year and a few weeks between us, but Mick always seemed like an adult to me. From the time he was thirteen, he presented himself as a man. Physically, he was built like a heavyweight champion – whereas I looked like a skinny little whippet – and he spoke and dressed in a way that was far older than his years. At fourteen, he was going to fashion shows in the Shelbourne Hotel and coming home with the smell of Courvoisier on his breath. Da, who was innocent in many ways, would say, 'Has he drink on him?' and Ma, who always covered for us, would say, 'I didn't smell anything.'

As a teenager, he worked as a waiter in the United Arts Club on Fitzwilliam Street, where he got me a job in the kitchen as a pot-washer. I watched him move from table to table, making easy conversation with Micheál Mac Liammóir and all these other stars of the Irish theatre, whom he spoke to on equal terms. My da would come and collect us and we'd bring home whatever food was left in the fridge. We were the only family in Cabra eating roast pheasant and braised duck on a Tuesday night.

Stephen was four and a half years younger than me, which might as well have been a whole generation. He was always my baby brother and still is to this day. Every night, I'd tell him to go upstairs to warm up the bed that I shared with Mick, then I'd go up after him up and tell him to get into his own bed, which he did obligingly.

As a kid, he was utterly fearless, heavy-set and strong as an ox, but he had a soft heart, especially for animals. When he was twelve, he swapped a pushbike that he had put together from parts for a little donkey, which he kept in a field by the railway line at the back of Faussagh Road. The poor animal was malnourished and injured, but Stephen nursed it back to health again, bringing it turnips and carrots and spending hours with it every day.

He was very good at school, a pleasant surprise to his teachers, whose expectations can't have been high, having already had the pleasure of teaching me. He was quiet, not shy in the way that my da was shy, but a deep thinker who liked his own company. You wouldn't have had him pegged as a future world champion boxer. Such was the air of solemnity he gave off that the entire family was convinced he was headed for the priesthood.

I didn't really know the other members of the family – not then. They were just babies to me and I was too old to relate to them. It was only when we all became adults that I got to know them. Colette, the older of my two sisters, was named after my ma. She's the funniest person I've ever met. Like Mick, she has a singing voice that can silence any party and her version of 'Don't Cry Out Loud' would bring tears to a snowman's eyes. She's quiet and thoughtful like Stephen with a heart of pure gold. I can talk to her about absolutely anything – after Caroline, she's the person I would feel most comfortable confiding in.

Audrey was my da's pet. She was a gorgeous-looking child. But, again, there was a separation between us, not just because of the age difference, but because she moved to America and spent a lot of her adult life there. She's very different from the rest of us. She likes tattoos and had an *Alice in Wonderland*-themed wedding that was pure California. She's strong-minded and principled, as well as smart, funny and loving. And she's a straight talker who has no time for my nonsense. Recently, she asked me for a lift to my ma's house. I rolled up half an hour late and she let me have it: 'Who the hell do you think you are, leaving me here waiting, then turning up like a film star in your Merc and your Louis Copeland suit?'

Typical me, all I heard was that she thought I looked like a film star.

Paschal was the baby of the family. He was a son to me as much as he was a brother. I used to take him on as many holidays as I could to make up for the absence of our da. Like him, he flies as straight as an arrow. In many ways, he's the brains of the family. Education is his thing. He's single-minded and good-natured and fiercely loyal.

There was another brother named Paschal, who was born after Mick and me, but he died shortly after he was born. He was never forgotten and always spoken about as the brother we never got to know. My da and Uncle Terry went out and bought a tiny coffin to put him in. For years we all believed he was buried in the Angels Plot in Glasnevin Cemetery, where unbaptized babies were laid to rest. But years later, Paschal discovered that my da had bought a plot for him in the main graveyard.

That was the measure of my father. He was an old-fashioned gentleman in lots of ways. He never used bad language and he impressed upon us every day the importance of family loyalty, being chivalrous towards women and not 'acting the bowsie', which was one of his favourite phrases.

He was a very reserved man. Tommy Cooper and Laurel and Hardy cracked him up, but even the way he laughed was modest, almost apologetic, his mouth closed and his eyes shut tightly, like he was trying to hold it in.

He was, in every respect, a *man*. Cabra was a tough area. You only survived by standing your ground and often that meant using your fists. One afternoon, a man called to the door to tell my da that his best friend, Christy Gilligan, was getting a hiding from a gang of cattle drivers up at Hanlon's Corner. He put on his coat and left the house without a word. What happened next, according to an apprentice barman I knew who worked there, was like something out of a Kenny Rogers song. My da walked in, locked the door behind him, then banjoed three men – all with body shots.

That was how disputes were settled in our neighbourhood – with what we called a straightener. One Christmas, my da bought me a dog, a gorgeous little puppy that I called Nell. I only had her a day or two before she was stolen from the back garden. Word reached us that someone had her in a house on St Attracta Road. By the time my da got there, Uncle Terry had already arrived in his Mini-Minor and was knocking lumps out of two men in the garden. The puppy came home with him.

There was another time when I was playing football in the school yard. I put the ball between the legs of an older lad, who kicked me in the face. I had a cyst on my cheek, which burst, and I went home with my face covered in blood. My da asked how old was the boy and I told him two years older than me. When Mick arrived home, my da sent him out to find the lad. Not long afterwards, there was a big man in an overcoat and a small woman in a hat standing at the hall door, shouting at my father that their son had been beaten up.

'And who do you think did that to my son's face?' my da asked. He smoked these slim panatella cigars, which he cut in two with a razor blade, then smoked one half at a time. The roaring continued until he handed me his cigar, then said in a cool voice, 'Are you going to go down that passage, or am I going to put you down that passage?'

To us it was like having King Kong as our da. As long as he was around, we feared nothing except the leather strap, or – worse than that – one of his looks of disappointment.

Only twice in my life did I ever see him cry. The first time was when Gyp died. He went out the back of the house to do it because he didn't want his children to see him crying over a dog. But I saw him through the window, sobbing his heart out, before he dug the hole to bury him. The next time I saw him cry was when his mother died.

One of the other things you needed to survive in Cabra was a sense of humour. My ma was funny – a natural comedian. There was a woman who lived a few doors down who was known as T-Bone Steak, because when she called her husband for his dinner, she made sure the entire road knew what they were having: 'Are you wanting onions with your T-bone steak?'

My ma would respond by opening the door and shouting, 'Kids, your roast turkey is on the table!'

In Cabra, you developed a thick hide as a defence mechanism.

It was an area bursting with interesting characters. Sometimes it was like they were auditioning for parts in a TV show. There was a man who modelled himself on Dean Martin and another who walked around all the time dressed in cowboy boots, a bootlace tie and a Stetson hat. There was a man who fixed televisions, although never quickly, so you could barely move in his house for tripping over the things. There was a bald man who suddenly took to wearing an oily black pompadour of a wig that he told people was his own hair grown back and another man who was known as Pope because he went to Mass three times a day. There was a man who heated his house by feeding eight-foot-long scaffolding planks into his fireplace six inches at a time. There was a barber who was known as Shakey on account of his delirium tremens and he always gave you the same haircut no matter what you asked for.

Directly opposite us, in number 36, lived Frankie Grimes, the famous Irish actor. We watched him walk up and down the terrace with our mouths slung open. In those days, anyone who appeared on television was presumed to be a multi-millionaire and we couldn't understand why he never moved to Castleknock, which was the end of the rainbow for people in Cabra.

Living on top of each other as we did, you never had any secrets from your neighbours and you certainly didn't have any from your family. But there was darkness along with the light and you saw a lot of things that you wished you hadn't. There was a woman who went to the off-licence every day to buy large bottles of stout for her husband, then he used to beat her. I saw it happen in the garden one day and it turned my stomach. Another day I stood with a crowd outside a burning house, yelling at a man at the upstairs window to jump. But he didn't. He moved away from the window and we never saw him again.

I saw a lot as a child. That was part of what it was to come from Cabra. You figured out how the world worked quicker than most. By the time I was thirteen I was – as the saying goes – as wide as a gate.

I have this strange habit that you'd know about if you'd ever shared a cup of tea or a glass of wine with me. For no reason, and without even thinking, I'll move your cup or glass right to the edge of the table. A psychiatrist could probably offer a good explanation for it. A metaphor, Caroline calls it. And it's true. There are many things I push right to the edge.

One time, in the mid-1990s, when I was enjoying my last hurrah at Bohemians, I told Caroline that we'd won the National Lottery. Worse, I let her find out that we'd 'won' for herself. One morning, before I left for Dalymount, I said to her, 'Would you ever check Saturday night's numbers? I never got a chance,' and I handed her our docket. She found the winning numbers on Aertel – and we'd matched all six. The jackpot prize was £3.2 million and there was only one winner. Roddy, our eldest son, was still a baby at the time and Caroline was holding him on her hip as we danced around the kitchen. Our days of struggling to make ends meet were over for ever.

Caroline was too excited to check the date on the docket and see that I'd taken the previous weekend's winning numbers and used them to do the following Wednesday night's lottery. I probably should have told her the truth before I left the house.

But, typical me, I didn't. I headed off to Dalymount and Caroline couldn't but admire my dedication. I mean, there we were, multi-millionaires, and I was off to work as usual.

I collected Ricky McEvoy in the car. He was playing for Glentoran at the time but training with us. Twenty minutes had passed and I was wondering had the penny dropped back home. I handed Ricky my giant brick of a mobile phone and I said, 'Ring Caroline – see does she know yet.'

A party was in full swing back in the house. Caroline had phoned her sisters, her brother and my ma and told them that we'd won £3.2 million and they'd all descended on the house. All Ricky could hear when the phone was answered was people singing Cliff Richard's 'Congratulations'. He handed the phone back to me and said, 'Whatever's going on, you're on your own, Rod.'

Pushing things to the edge. I've always done it. I suppose that's the best explanation I can offer for what I was like as a teenager.

When you stepped out of our front door on Annamoe Terrace, you could turn left and head towards Hanlon's Corner, where the good kids hung out, or you could turn right towards the Cabra Road, where you were guaranteed to find a different kind of company. Mick and Stephen turned left. I turned right. I'd be letting myself off too lightly if I said that I fell in with a bad crowd. I *was* the bad crowd, one of the bowsies that my da warned me about.

School wasn't for me. I wasn't temperamentally suited to following instructions. I twigged that at the age of four. The idea that you had to put up your hand and ask for permission to go to the toilet was something I just couldn't get my head around.

When I was twelve, I was sent to O'Connell's on the North Circular Road, a secondary school run by Christian Brothers who were big on discipline and quick to twist your ears, or pull your locks, or hit you over the head with a blackboard duster, if you displeased them. The problem was that all kinds of things displeased them, from walking around with your shirt untucked to not having the Irish version of a word on instant recall. One day I was caught playing shove-penny in a shed at the back of the school by a Brother, who tore the crest off my school blazer, then slapped me hard across the face. That was when I decided they were going to see as little of my ugly mug as I could get away with.

I left the house every morning, dressed in my uniform, then took a long detour somewhere else. Unfortunately, I was always getting caught. Once, I persuaded a friend of mine named Sid Daly to come mitching with me. We were in Coolmine, riding around on the back of a donkey, when we saw a man making his way across the field towards us with a big angry head on him. I realized that it was my da. He chased me across the field and grabbed me so hard by the legs that he tore the trousers clean off me. The walk home took us through the grounds of the school where Mick went, and he still remembers the sight of me being frogmarched back to Cabra in just my underpants to get the strap. Knowing how vain I was about my looks, my da then took me up to Billy Wright's barbershop on the Cabra Road and told him to give me a bowl haircut, which I had to hide under a woolly hat for weeks.

It didn't stop me mitching – just made me more cautious. I started venturing further afield, into the city centre, sometimes alone, sometimes with a crew. A school day never seemed longer than when you weren't actually there, but it was easier to fill the hours with company. I was obsessed with clothes and loved walking around the shops, looking at the threads. I used to pass the Louis Copeland shop on Capel Street and see Old Louis standing in the doorway, a dapper man with a measuring tape draped around his neck.

We sat in the restaurant in Arnott's on Henry Street and ate scones with jam and cream and drank tea from china cups. We went to the Garden of Remembrance, took off our shoes and stockings and rolled up our trousers to pick coins up out of the fountain. Then we headed for Barney's Amusements on Marlborough Street to play pinball. When we ran out of money, we sold our schoolbooks – or someone else's schoolbooks – for a shilling a throw in a second-hand bookshop off Talbot Street.

In the afternoon we went for chips in Woolworth's on Henry Street. Or if it was May or September, and the weather was fine, we'd sun ourselves in Stephen's Green or the Phoenix Park.

I still got caught from time to time. My da's friend, Christy, worked as a ganger with the P&T and I never knew where he'd pop up.

'How was school, son?' my da would ask.

'Yeah, good, Da,' I'd tell him, no idea that I'd been spotted stretched out on the grass in front of the Wellington Monument. 'Learned loads today.'

'You've a lovely tan on you.'

'Yeah, we were playing football in the yard at lunchtime – it was roasting.'

Then the truth would come out and so would the strap.

There was one day when I knew I'd been caught and I didn't want to go home to face the music. I wandered the streets of Dublin until it was dark, then I headed for the docks, where the Guinness boat sailed for Liverpool at midnight every night. I climbed into one of the lifeboats, pulled the canvas over me and lay there shivering in the dark, thinking about what I'd do when I arrived in England. At eleven o'clock, I decided to go home and take the strap instead.

I'm grateful now for every lash of the strap that my da gave me because he could see that I was going wrong. I wanted to be with the wide boys. Paddy and Seaner Coleman. Johnny Kenna. Pat Masterson. That was my crew. We hung around outside the shops, acting the maggot. Hard chaws with smart mouths. One night, I remember, Dickie Rock's da walked past with a corgi.

'Here,' I said, 'what breed of a dog is that?'

He put his hand on my shoulder and said, 'A better breed than you, son.'

I went with Pat Masterson to my first disco – it was the Lord Eccles on Eccles Street. I left the house looking like an altar boy, but changed into my skinhead gear – Docs, parallel trousers and a bomber jacket – in the grounds of the church. I stashed my clothes in a bush, then necked two bottles of Harp before walking through the door. All the hardmen from the Grenville Street flats were there – blokes who were up to no good in their lives, but they impressed me because they had coats with velvet collars and shiny shoes.

There was another disco on Bachelor's Walk. I was in there one night, aged thirteen, when a lad from Finglas called Ryano walked in looking for Mick Collins. I told him that I was his brother and he invited me outside. I put my two fists up, ready to have a go off him, when he pulled out a big hunting knife. I panicked and threw my coat at him, then escaped through a snooker hall, went through the back door and out the front, before jumping onto a moving bus. I found Mick in a pub on Dorset Street with his mates and told him what happened. We all went charging down O'Connell Street in search of Ryano. We found him in a youth club, run by some religious order, where they played music and served Bovril. There was a big mill, then the air was filled with the scream of sirens and everyone scattered. I ran across O'Connell Bridge and stood outside McBirney's department store as police cars and ambulances arrived on the scene. I walked home and told my da that a lad from Finglas had come looking for Mick with a knife. He took us to my nanny O'Rourke's house in Martin Street in Portobello, where Mick and I stayed until things cooled off.

By then, two of my friends were already dead. Paddy Coleman was stabbed in the stomach one night in a row outside a chipper. I'd been with him earlier in the night but went home early. The next morning, my da woke me and asked, 'Where were you last night? Something happened down at Boland's Corner.' I wandered down there. There was yellow scene-of-crime tape everywhere. That's when I found out that Paddy was dead. I was numb. Not long after that, Pat Masterson stepped out on the road one day and was mowed down by a car. Like Paddy, I'd seen him just hours earlier. It was a lot of death for a young lad of my age to take in.

I was pushing my own luck. One night, a hard-nut Republican I'd fallen in with invited me to go on a stick-up with him to raise funds for 'the movement'. He had a replica gun, which he was planning to use to hold up an off-licence on Blessington Street. There was a third lad with us who drove the getaway car. When we walked into the shop, the driver lost his bottle and fled in a squeal of tyre rubber. We scarpered. I hid under a park bench for two hours, too frightened to come out, shaking with the adrenaline, listening to the sound of distant sirens belonging to ambulances travelling to and from the Mater Hospital. In my imagination, it was the police searching for me to put me away.

By then, I had finally been expelled from O'Connell's – or indefinitely suspended, as it was called. The final straw came when one of the Brothers took me out of another teacher's class to hit me with a strap. I was older now, and starting to fill out, and I wasn't going to take a beating from anyone who wasn't my da. So when he leathered me across the hand, I chinned him with a right hammer and there was no way back from that. My ma went down to the school to try to sort it out. The Brother said to her, 'Is your husband not man enough to come and face me?'

Little did he know. On the way home, my ma said the usual: 'Don't tell your father.'

My ma and da tried to find a new school for me. Cabra Tech agreed to take me. It was a different kind of school. There was no leather strap. We were spoken to like adults. I never mitched again and left there at fifteen with a grand total of three passes in my Group Certificate, though what use they were going to be to me I hadn't a clue.

I started to straighten myself out. I had a moment of enlightenment one night when a gang of us were throwing snowballs at the windows of The Gorman. A carer came out to chase us off and got a smack in the face with a ball of ice. I saw the blood pouring from his wounds and I thought, 'That's not right.' The others ran, but I stayed to help him. I said goodbye to the wide boys for ever.

Then two things happened to me around that time that helped set me on the righteous path. The first was that people started to talk about me as a useful footballer. The second was that, for the first – and I'm happy to say *only* – time in my life, I fell in love.

2

It was the thunderbolt. For me, anyway. It may have taken a bit longer in Caroline's case, but I loved her the very first time I saw her. She was standing at a bus stop on O'Connell Street. We were both fifteen years old. I'd just turned off Henry Street and there she was in her school uniform – one sock up and one sock down – and this long brown hair that I couldn't take my eyes off. My face got hot and my heart was going like the clappers. I thought, Jaysus, what's that?

I was with a few heads – messers, I'd say, more than bowsies. As it turned out, we were all getting on the same bus. I sat there and stared at the back of her head.

One of the fellas took out a cigarette.

'Here,' he said, acting the maggot, 'have you got a light, love?'

'Leave the girl alone,' I said.

She told me afterwards that I made her feel safe and that when I got off the bus at Hanlon's Corner she had a good long look at me. It was a while before I saw her again.

I'd left Cabra Tech and I was managing The Tap bar on North King Street, which was owned by Pat Walsh, who was a Garda, and Tom Darwin, who was a rep for Beamish. The working day started for me at nine in the morning, when I stocked the bar, then I'd throw open the doors at 10.30. The first crowd in were always the winos and drunks coming off an all-nighter. They were mostly easy to manage. A lot of detectives came in during the day. Usually, they were attending one of the courts in the area. There was trouble from time to time. The door burst open one day and a man walked in with a tomahawk. I went over the bar, wrestled him to the floor and threw the tomahawk down into the cellar. At seven in the evening, I'd hand over the keys to Tom or Mick and that was me finished for the night.

There was a lad who drank in The Tap called Nollaig O'Connor and he was going with a girl called Marian Donegan from O'Devaney Gardens, the flats off the North Circular Road. She had a friend – 'a gorgeous mate', as Nollaig described her – called Caroline Hanney.

'Not Mick Hanney's sister?' I asked.

I was friendly with Mick, who was from O'Devaney as well.

'Yeah,' Nollaig said. 'I'm meeting Marian and her after work. We're heading into town. Would you meet her friend and maybe walk her home?'

I wasn't going with anyone and I didn't mind being paired up. So I was standing with Nollaig outside The Tap when Marian and Caroline turned the corner. And it was *her*. The girl from the bus stop with the brown hair. And she was wearing a pair of white, tight-fitting jeans. I don't have the words to describe how happy I was in that moment. It was the kind of feeling you could spend the rest of your life chasing but never, ever experience again.

Like me, she came from a big family, except hers was dominated by females, not males. She had five sisters and three brothers. Unlike me, she loved school, especially history and bookkeeping. She was about to sit the Leaving Certificate, which was unusual for anyone from our social background, especially a girl, in the 1970s.

I walked her home every Sunday for six weeks. I wanted to ask her out, but I was worried she'd say no. But I finally got the courage from somewhere and she agreed to go on a first date with me – a walk in the Phoenix Park. I was way out of my depth and I knew it. I did my Mick Jagger impression, which had always been popular in the yard of Cabra Tech, and it made her laugh. She said yes to a second date, a proper date, which was a night at the pictures. She told me to pick her up from O'Devaney and we'd get the bus into town. That meant I was going to meet her family for the first time and I was determined to make an impression. Nollaig had a black, almost ankle-length, leather coat, which I'd always admired on him.

'Nollaig,' I said, 'I'm out of me depth here. You wouldn't lend me the leather coat, would you?'

I threw it on me. I thought I was gorgeous. I turned up at the flats to find Caroline's sisters staring down at me from the balcony. The next thing I heard was all this screaming:

'Ah, Jaysus, no! Not *him*! Ma, get rid of him!'

My reputation had gone before me.

'It's your man Collins! And he's wearing Nollaig's leather coat!'

Caroline wanted to see *The Omen* in the Plaza on Granby Row. I was terrified of horror films. But I couldn't let myself down in front of Caroline, so I put a brave face on it and in we went. Five minutes into the film, I realized I'd made a terrible mistake. I tried not to look at the screen, just stared at the head belonging to the man in front of me. I'd my arm around Caroline's shoulder and very quickly it went numb. I sat through the entire film – scared stiff, unable to feel my arm and sweating buckets in Nollaig's leather coat, which I was afraid to take off in case it was stolen.

Afterwards, trying to act the big man, I took Caroline to a pool hall just off Dorset Street, where the hard chaws hung out. All of Gerry Hutch's crew were in there. They were known as the Bugsy Malone Gang. There I was potting balls and shooting the breeze with them.

'All right, Rod? This your bird, is it?'

'Yeah, this is Caroline, lads.'

Caroline swore that she wasn't going to see me again. Happily for me, she changed her mind. Her sisters got over whatever reservations they had about me – I'd given the leather coat back to Nollaig, and I was welcomed into the family home.

Caroline's da, Billy, was a big, jolly man who worked hard to support his family. For eight months of the year he was a coalman, then in the summer he parked cars in Dublin Zoo. He'd arrive home with a bag full of coins, which he'd spill out onto the table, then Caroline and her sisters would sort it into piles and count it.

Billy's ma was in Grangegorman. After her husband died, she couldn't cope with life on her own. She was admitted to the hospital, where she lived for the rest of her life. She had a daughter, Bernie, who lived with her there, in private accommodation in the grounds of the hospital. They came to O'Devaney for dinner every Sunday.

Billy was a man of high moral principles. A lot of coalmen ended up with arthritis in their shoulders because of the damp bags they were forced to carry on their backs. Billy took part in a protest to try to get waterproof bags as standard issue for all coalmen. There was a photograph of the protest in the *Evening Press*. Fearing victimization, many of the men put their heads down. Billy looked straight into the camera.

He was a man of firm convictions, but he was also a gentle soul with a lovely childlike quality about him. He always carried around peanuts in his pockets for the birds, and they would come down and eat them out of his hands – not just robins, but sparrows, too. Like Caroline, he didn't see badness in anything or anyone. He thought the world was great.

As if to balance him out, Caroline's ma, Ellen, was sharp as a tack. She was kind and caring – and an absolute lady – but she was nobody's fool.

I started spending more time in Caroline's home than I did in my own. One of her brothers, Liam, was at sea with the Irish Navy and I claimed his bed. There was a great buzz about the flat. There were always six or seven people crammed into the tiny living room and it was full of laughter and slagging. Caroline's sister Sandra was going with a lad called Alan, who told us that he was an office worker and he talked and dressed like he was a few postcodes posher than the rest of us. Then I spotted him one morning pushing a trolley around a scrapyard up at Hanlon's Corner.

'An office worker?' I said to him. 'You bleeding spoofer!'

'Ah, Rod,' he said, 'please don't say anything!'

He was a great lad and we loved winding each other up. He arrived at the flat one night wearing a pair of gloves made from the softest goat's leather. When he made the mistake of leaving them down, I gave them to Caroline's da. I said, 'There you are, Billy – got you a pair of gloves.'

Billy loved them. He wouldn't take them off. He sat there watching *Charlie's Angels* in them and poor Alan hadn't the heart to ask him for them back.

I broke my da's heart more times than I could ever count, but never more so than when I chose football over boxing. To him, boxers were *men*, while footballers were – in the language of the times – nancy boys. I had a moment of clarity when I was about twelve years old, sitting in school one morning with dried blood up my nose, my jaw sore and my ears still ringing after a sparring session the night before. I thought, Why am I doing this?

Around the same time, I saw George Best on TV, sitting in an E-type Jag with a fur coat on him, and I made up my mind that football was the game for me. When I was eight, Manchester United won the European Cup and Best was the star of the final against Benfica. I remember watching it with my da and even he agreed that there was something special about him. The way he played. The way he dressed. The way he lived his life. He was like some kind of exotic creature from another world.

Two neighbours named Joe Webb and Tommy Myles, who'd seen me playing football out on the street, asked me to represent Annamoe at the Mini Olympics in Walkinstown, which might as well have been on the other side of the world. We wore green hoops like Celtic. I was about three years younger than the other kids on the team, but I managed to score a goal and I remember Joe standing in the garden and telling my ma and da that I was a great little footballer.

Then I joined my first club, Villa United, who played in what's now called John Paul II Park but was then known as The Bogies. We were coached by George Corcoran, whose brother Eddie was a scout for Wolverhampton Wanderers and later worked as the FAI's logistics man. They were some of the best days of my childhood. I had a part-time job in Hogan's butchers in Cabra, which kept me fit. Every day after school I scrubbed the blood off the chopping block with a wire brush, then swept the sawdust and animal guts off the floor. On Saturday mornings I did deliveries on an old boneshaker of a bike with a basket on the front. When I was finished, I left the bike in the dressing room while I played a match, then went back to work, turning the corned beef in a bath of salt, or boiling fat, then straining it to make dripping. I'd bring some home and we'd eat it on bread, which probably explains why, by the time I was forty-five, I'd arteries like a sewer main.

My ma's brother – my uncle Pat – was a Drumcondra FC fan and he started to bring me to League of Ireland matches at Tolka Park. But I always had to contain my excitement when I got home because I still felt that I was letting my da down. I never even told him when I moved from Villa United to Shelbourne on the other side of the city. At twelve years old I was taking a bus from the Cabra Road to Dorset Street, then a second bus to Ringsend to train or to play. He never knew.

A little bit later I joined Stella Maris in Drumcondra. The manager was a man from North King Street named Jimmy Brannigan, who gave me a tin of white paint and a brush and told me to paint a spot on the wall behind the goals. He told me that if I wanted to score, I should aim for that. It was the best bit of coaching advice I ever got as a kid.

I loved Stella Maris. On those mitching days when I couldn't find a partner in crime to come into town with me, I headed for the ground in Drumcondra and mowed the grass, trying to copy the patterns I'd seen on *Match of the Day*. Then I marked the pitch with the paint roller and gave the goalposts a coat or two. In return for my efforts, I was given the David O'Leary Award for Clubman of the Year. One day I used the paint to write 'R Collins' on a wall inside the ground. It was only removed recently. Someone put a photograph of the freshly painted wall on Instagram and said, 'It's finally gone – that Cabra madman's name.' I nearly shed a tear.

I was impressing a lot of people with my performances as a big, physical centre-forward. I'd played in midfield for Shelbourne, but now I was modelling myself on Joe Jordan of Leeds United. Tall for my age, and strong from all the years of sparring, I was good at letting defenders know I was there.

I was invited to go for a trial for the Ireland under-15 team. At that point my da had never seen me play football before, but he wanted to see me succeed. On the morning of the trial he woke me up early and took me to Mass in Christ the King and we said a prayer that I'd be picked. It was snowing heavily. He gave me a bottle of horse liniment to rub into my legs to warm up my muscles. Then he drove us to the Trinity College Sports Grounds in Santry. There was about a hundred kids there.

A coach asked, 'Does anyone play right-full?'

Worried that I wasn't going to get a chance to show what I could do, I threw my hand up and shouted, 'Yeah, me!'

I spent the next hour being tortured by Paddy McCarthy, a Stella Maris teammate of mine and a neighbour of Caroline's from O'Devaney Gardens, who turned me inside-out and upside-down. The snow really started coming down then. All of the other parents scarpered to the dressing room for cover – all except my da. When I close my eyes now, I can still see him on the sideline, in his fawn overcoat, through a blizzard of white. I was having an absolute nightmare, but he wanted me to know that he was there for me.

To the surprise of absolutely no one, I didn't make the Ireland squad. But from that day onwards my da went everywhere to see me play. I played in a cup final against Home Farm in Inchicore and he took Stephen with him. There's a photograph of the three of us standing around after the match with our arms around each other's shoulders.

One day I was playing a match and there was a man in the crowd wearing a sheepskin coat. A buzz of excitement went around the ground. The only people who wore sheepskin coats to football matches were talent scouts for English clubs. When the match was over, Jimmy Brannigan called me across and introduced me to the man.

'This is Gordon Clark,' he said. 'He wants you to go over to Fulham.'

I couldn't believe it. It was 1977. Fulham was where George Best was making his comeback to English football after walking out of Manchester United at the height of his fame. I was thinking something like this couldn't happen to a sixteen-year-old kid from Cabra.

Gordon Clark put his hand in his pocket and pulled out a wad of cash. He said to me, 'That's what you're going over for, son – it's all about money!'

That Sunday, my da sailed up to Hanlon's Corner to tell the relations. To see his face, you would have thought I was already in the first team. He bought me a 7-Up while I tried to remember the names of some of the other players who were at Fulham. I knew that Rodney Marsh had just joined them on loan. And they had Bobby Moore, who captained England when they won the World Cup in 1966.

I really believed that I was going to make it as a professional footballer. There were more technically gifted players than me, but I was tough and determined. I was the best header of the ball in

Ireland – or so I believed. I wasn't the quickest player in the world, but I was quick enough. My first touch wasn't great, but it wasn't bad either. And I was tough. You could kick me all day long, but I'd keep going and I had a great instinct for goals.

I went to bed that night thinking about what Gordon Clark said about money. There was a cockney character who'd just come into *Coronation Street* called Mike Baldwin and he drove around in a big Jag. I knew my da loved that car. I told myself that Fulham would only be a stepping stone for me. Where I was heading was Manchester United. I was going to be a millionaire – if only to get my da a car like Mike Baldwin's.

It broke my heart to leave Caroline, but she knew what an incredible opportunity this was for me. The night before I left, my da sat me down and tried to warn me about the temptations I was likely to face on the other side of the water. 'Caroline's your girlfriend,' he said, 'but some women over there don't drink their tea with their little finger sticking out.'

David O'Leary's da, Christy, arrived at the house with the tickets for the journey. It was my first time ever on an airplane. On a scrap of paper, I had the address of a house in London that was going to be my digs. It was a huge pad in Richmond, an upmarket part of the city. The couple who owned the house told me they took in lodgers to help them pay for their annual winter holiday and I wasn't to think of myself as part of their family. And under no circumstances was I to use the phone.

I shared a bedroom with Paddy McCarthy, my Stella Maris teammate who'd also gone over on trial. We trained with the youths, but one day we were told to join the first team – two Dublin yahoos sharing the same pitch as Best and Marsh, with their big hair and their American suntans. It was brilliant. But Bobby Campbell, the manager, didn't even grunt at us, and the next day we were back with the youths, wondering did we do something wrong.

The club paid us £50 per week, which was an absolute fortune to a sixteen-year-old from Dublin. But Paddy was desperately homesick. He missed his ma. We'd lie in our beds at six o'clock every night, bored out of our minds, listening to the TV downstairs, our stomachs full of red cabbage, which seemed to accompany every meal, and he'd say, 'Tonight would be stew night if I was back in O'Devaney.'

After a week or two he went home. Maybe he'd already twigged that we weren't going to make it.

Every Tuesday night, Caroline and her da said a Novena for me in the Church of the Immaculate Conception on Merchant's Quay, praying that I'd get signed by Fulham.

I poured out my feelings to her in letters, a sixteen-year-old boy, heartsick and desperate not to lose the girl he loved. In one, I wrote:

I can't stop thinking of you. I told you the last time how I missed you and loved you and I am telling you again. I know you miss me too but it won't be for long because if I don't come home you'll come over here to me. Because if I sign [for Fulham] it wouldn't be the end. It would only be the beginning. Because I could do all of my football in the day and forget it at night. I sometimes want to forget football and go home to you. I want to get it [a contract] for us because it would make you happy too. You would be with me all the time. I want you to think of me all day and night because I am thinking of you. On Saturday night, I was thinking of you in the Celebrity Club with some dope. It sounds possessive but I am asking you to keep away from dopes. I swear I will not go off with any girls . . . I hope you are studying hard because if I don't get the football, you will have to get the Leaving.

There was a red phone box at the end of the road that provided my only other connection to home. There was no phone back in Annamoe or in O'Devaney, but I had the number of two payphones, one in Heuston Station and one on the North Circular Road, where my da would go at a certain time and wait for my calls.

'How's it going, son?' he'd ask.

'I'm doing great,' I'd tell him, not wanting to let him down. He promised he'd come over to see me soon.

After training one day, Teddy Maybank, the Fulham striker, offered me a lift back to my digs. When I got into the car, Best was sitting in the front passenger seat. I was struck dumb. As we crossed Putney Bridge, the car conked out. While we waited for a tow, passers-by spotted Best and surrounded the car, banging on the windows. I sat in the back thinking, Can life get any better than this?

But the club still hadn't offered me a contract. I thought I was doing OK. I remember I played for the youth team against Watford and scored a goal. There was a thunderstorm after the match. We were on the coach on the way back to Craven Cottage and the radio was playing '2–4–6–8 Motorway' by the Tom Robinson Band. We were all singing along and I was on a high. As we drove through Putney, I saw my da walking along in the lashings of rain, carrying a small holdall. He hadn't even told me he was coming. I lost it. I shouted, 'Da! Da! Da!' I told the driver to pull over, but he wouldn't. He said he had to drop us back to Craven Cottage. When we got there, I jumped off the bus and ran up and down the Fulham Palace Road looking for him. I couldn't see him. When I got back to the ground I found him sitting in the stand waiting for me. He had a shocking flu and he was drenched to the skin. I just burst into tears. It was like meeting God.

He stayed with me in Richmond, sleeping in Paddy's old bed. I took him to see Fulham play that Saturday and he sat with 'Diddy' David Hamilton, a famous DJ with the BBC. The next day he went looking for Spooky Kelly and Richard Felin, two old mates of his from Cabra. In the years after the war they'd all worked as stokers together on the steam train service between Birmingham and Carlisle, shovelling coal into the burner. When the steam trains stopped operating, his two mates had moved to London but struggled to find work. My da found them in a pub called The Wellington Arms in Shepherd's Bush and he gave them a few bob.

On Monday I took him to training and I asked George Best if I could introduce him to my da.

'Of course,' he said, 'where is he?'

He didn't just shake his hand. He spent ten minutes talking to him. My da was so impressed by him. But the man he really wanted to meet was Gordon Clark, the chief scout who'd brought me over. My da had come to find out for himself whether or not the club was going to offer me terms. Clark said they still weren't sure. My da said if they weren't sure after six weeks, then they never would be.

Outside the ground that day, my da told me that it wasn't going to happen for me. I broke down. He took me to the Golden Gloves pub in Hammersmith, which was run by a brother of the former Ireland player Terry Mancini. The walls were covered in boxing paraphernalia. He said to the barman, 'Give him a pint of whatever he wants.'

I had a pint of lager and a whiskey to chase it down.

'It's not the end of the world,' he said. 'We'd love to have you home. Your brothers and sisters miss you. They're all growing up without you.'

The next morning I walked him to the Tube station in Richmond and I said I'd see him soon. He caught the train to Liverpool and the boat back to Dublin. I arrived back at the digs and the landlady asked me for money for the two nights that my da stayed over. That was it for me. A sure sign that it was finished.

A few nights later I arrived back in Cabra. I remember walking around the side of the house and catching the smell of apple cakes, which my ma was baking especially for me. I heard her telling Stephen to get out of bed because his big brother would be home soon. I was so happy that I thought my heart would burst.

The dream didn't end when I walked out of Fulham that day. There were one or two other clubs who were interested in me. A few months earlier we'd had a knock on the door one night and there was a man standing there in a Russian hat. It was Bill Darby, the scout who sent Liam Brady, Frank Stapleton and David O'Leary to Arsenal. I invited him in. It was Pancake Tuesday and my ma had cooked a stack of the things. I watched him tuck in while he explained that he'd seen me playing for Stella Maris and had told the Arsenal manager, Terry Neill, about me. Stephen walked into the kitchen and said, 'Where's me pancakes?' Bill had eaten the lot. He was welcome to them. He could have eaten the table for all I cared because I was going to Arsenal. Before he left the house he took out a pound note and pressed it into my hand. 'Hold on to that,' he said, 'and you'll never be hungry.'

I'd only been home from Fulham a few weeks when I was back in London again.

Arsenal was friendlier than Fulham. It was April 1977 and the training ground was full of Irish accents. Frank Stapleton and John

Devine went out of their way to make me feel welcome. They knew what it felt like to be a young lad from Dublin living on his own in the big city.

Devine was the fittest man at the club. Liam Brady sauntered around the training pitch, saving himself for the weekend, when he'd flick a switch and become a completely different player. I never felt out of my depth. I was looking at Stapleton, thinking to myself, There's nothing he can do that I can't do.

The only problem was that I rubbed Don Howe up the wrong way. Howe was the head coach. He was English football royalty and didn't appreciate it when I started questioning some of his ideas. I'd never been coached in my life. At Stella Maris we just went out and played, eleven players confident in their own individual abilities. It turned out that, having been the assistant manager when Arsenal won the double in 1971, Howe had little or no interest in how Jimmy Brannigan did things at Stella Maris.

The final act came one afternoon after training when I walked into the dressing room – angry and frustrated with myself – and got in a row with Paul Vaessen, an apprentice who was destined for big things.

I pointed to the shower next to his and asked, 'Is there anyone using that one?'

He said, 'I don't see anyone, Paddy.'

My da always told me in these situations to try to count to ten. But I always struggled to get beyond six.

'What did you call me?' I asked, squaring up to him, the two of us standing there naked as the day we were born.

'I called you Paddy,' he said.

So I stuck the head on him. His nose burst open and suddenly the shower looked like an abattoir. Terry Neill summoned me to his office and confirmed what was already obvious to me – they weren't going to sign me. Too aggressive off the pitch and not aggressive enough on it was the verdict.

Vaessen was a centre-forward just like me. Soon after that, he became the youngest player ever to play for Arsenal, at the age of sixteen. I followed his career with a vague sense of what might have been. In 1980 he came off the bench to head an eighty-eighth-minute winner against Juventus in Turin to put Arsenal into the European Cup Winners Cup final. But then he seemed to fall off the face of the earth. He ruptured ligaments in his knee and was forced to retire from football at the age of twenty. Years later he was found dead from a heroin overdose in a bathroom in Bristol. I'd just started managing Carlisle United when I heard the news and I thought to myself that I'd been the lucky one after all.

But back then I returned to Dublin with my tail between my legs. Fulham didn't want me and Arsenal didn't want me. I had one more crack at it, though. Eddie Corcoran did some scouting for Wolverhampton Wanderers and he told them that it might be worth their while seeing me up close. So suddenly I returned to England for the third time in a few months. The trial went well – so well that they took me with them to an end-of-season tournament in Haarlem in the Netherlands. I played in a couple of friendlies, but I played badly and I knew I'd blown it. A few of us went to a nightclub one night. John Jarman, one of the senior coaches, walked in. The others left their pints and scarpered. I was drinking a glass of Britvic orange so I stayed where I was. If I'd banged in a couple of hat-tricks in the two games, I'm sure nothing would have been said. As it was, the following morning I got a polite 'don't call us', and I was on the next flight home from Amsterdam.

I was just happy to get back to Caroline. I'd missed her so much. I remember that summer – it was 21 August 1977, according to the internet – we went to see Thin Lizzy, who were headlining Dublin's first ever open-air rock festival at Dalymount Park, with the Boomtown Rats as the main support. We swung into Annamoe on our way to Dalymount. I was wearing a long Afghan coat and Caroline was wearing jeans and a denim waistcoat that showed off her figure. I remember looking at her talking to my ma and knowing with absolute certainly that I wanted to spend the rest of my life with her.

But that was about all I knew. I had just turned seventeen. I had no job, no trade, no qualifications. All I had was my three passes in the Group Certificate and a girlfriend who I loved and who loved me in return. And, with the exception of the three passes in the Group Certificate, that was all I was ever going to need.

3

If I wasn't going to be a millionaire professional footballer, then I needed some other way to earn a crust. Johnny Kenna, one of my oldest friends, was working as a labourer for G&T Crampton and he got me a job in Windmill Lane, on the site of the famous studio where U2 would one day record most of their albums. The wages were £100 a week, which was good money for someone who'd just turned seventeen. I was told to report to the site at eight o'clock in the morning with my mug and my lunch.

In 1977, number 22 Windmill Lane was a disused factory that had turned out soles for shoes and had recently been used in the filming of *The First Great Train Robbery*. When we walked through the door there were movie scripts scattered all over the floor and we saw the big double bed with the brass headboard that was used in the famous bedroom scene. One of the fellas, a Ringsend character named Jock Donoghue, started rolling around on the mattress, pretending that he was Sean Connery making love to Lesley-Anne Down. It was my day one introduction to building-site banter.

Practical jokes were part of every hour of every day and you learned quickly to always be on your guard. There were two toilets in an outbuilding that we were allowed to use. Flush toilets on a building site were a rare luxury – but you used them at your peril. There was a good chance that as soon as you sat down on the bowl with your newspaper, a bucket of water was going to be thrown over the door on top of you. I was a fast learner. I came up with a new twist on the toilet trick, climbing down a manhole to connect the compressor for pumping the jackhammer to the sewage outflow pipe. The foreman went into the toilet and I switched on the pump. I may have underestimated how much power was in the thing. There was a loud boom – it was more like, BADOOM! – and the foreman came running out showered in, well, I didn't even want to think what. Every night I walked home to Annamoe Terrace with pains in my jaw from laughing.

There was one Friday afternoon when everyone had clocked off early and I was on my own on the site. A lorryload of plasterboards was delivered. I could see that it was about to rain and the boards were going to get saturated, so I humped them all inside, fifty or sixty of the things, just to cover for the two plasterers, who'd scarpered at lunchtime.

They appreciated it and started bringing me with them on their nixers. One Saturday we were working in a house next to the old Lemons Sweet Factory in Drumcondra. I was given a sledgehammer and a lump hammer and told to knock a hole in the gable wall for a window. The woman of the house made me a mug of tea and we got chatting. I told her about wanting to be a professional footballer, but the dream was over. In that case, she said, I needed to get myself a trade. I told her I wanted to be a bricklayer but a small number of families had it all sewn up.

What I didn't know was that she was married to a director of G&T Crampton, who was a friend of Willie Power, one of the company's main subcontractors. A few days later Willie showed up on the site. I was down a hole with the jackhammer, drilling away, when he was suddenly looking down at me.

'Are you the young fella who brought them plasterboards in for the lads?' he wanted to know.

'Er, yeah,' I said, thinking I was in trouble.

'Have you got your Inter Cert?'

'No, I've three passes in the Group.'

'Do you want an apprenticeship?'

'Er, yeah,' I told him, because I presumed it was the answer that was expected of me.

'Good man. Get yourself over to AnCO – it's just over Baggot Street Bridge – and register as an apprentice plasterer.'

I got washed up and headed for Baggot Street, where I filled in the relevant forms and was given an ID card with my name, address and date of birth on it, as well as my trade – plasterer. I went home and told my da. He was delighted that his son was going to be a tradesman. I was far less delighted when I found out that I was now on an apprentice's wage. My pay had been £100 per week – now, I was on £30.

The way I was treated changed overnight. The plasterers no longer treated me as an equal. Now, I was their lackey, fetching and carrying for them for what suddenly felt like starvation wages. After a few months I realized that I couldn't live on what I was earning, so I went to Willie and told him that my girlfriend was pregnant. Which, of course, she wasn't, but Willie agreed to put me on a third-year apprentice's money. The word got around the site then that Rod was going to be a daddy. The fellas all chipped in and bought me a pram, which I had to push all the way back to Stoneybatter. A man pushing a pram was a very unusual sight in Dublin in 1978. I ended up running into practically everyone I knew on the way to O'Devaney.

One of Caroline's neighbours got a gift of the thing, but I felt terribly guilty about it, especially when the fellas started tracking the progress of the pregnancy, asking me how many months along my girlfriend was now and what names we were considering.

Willie was still asking me about the baby nearly two years later.

'How's the child?' he'd say. 'Must be walking now – am I right?'

I spent six months on the Windmill Lane site, then I was told to take my hawk and trowel and report to Grafton Street, where the company was converting an old picture house into a Peter Mark hairdressers. One of the labourers on the job was Jackie Cummins, a pigeon man from Donnycarney.

'I'm Roddy Collins,' I told him, full of enthusiasm. 'I'm the new apprentice.'

'I don't give a bollocks,' he said – and he meant every word of it.

The main plasterer on the job was Seamie Dunphy, who was one of a family of plasterers from the inner city. He was the one who taught me the basics starting off.

The work was hard, especially early on when I hadn't a clue what I was doing. I was given a bag of filler and a plastic bucket and I was told to tape and joint a wall to prepare it for plastering. I mixed the filler in the bucket, but half an hour later it had set hard. I was too embarrassed to tell anyone. That night, I went home and explained the problem to my da, who could do absolutely anything with his hands.

The next day, he came into Peter Mark's with me and he showed me where I was going wrong.

'You have to put a handful of that one in,' he told me. 'It's called finish. That will retard it and stop it from setting in the bucket.'

Not for the first time in my life, my da saved my skin.

I said 'Fuck that!' to Johnny Giles around that time.

It wasn't the smartest move I ever made, especially when I still had hopes of becoming a professional footballer and he was the manager of Ireland. But how we got to that point was a long story.

I met Giles for the first time in the summer of 1977, just after I was rejected by Fulham, Arsenal and Wolves. As well as managing the national team, he was involved in an ambitious plan to turn Shamrock Rovers into the country's first full-time professional football club. I was trying to find the fastest route back to England and I thought that might be it.

I trained with them in Milltown for a few weeks that summer. Ray Treacy and Eamon Dunphy were the coaches. One day I went in hard on Dunphy. We had a few angry words. He told me that he'd see me after training. I waited behind for him but he never showed up.

I didn't sign for Rovers in the end. Eddie Corcoran told me that Wolves hadn't completely thrown in the towel with me despite what had happened in Haarlem. They wanted to continue to monitor my progress, so he suggested that I sign for Bohemians. At the same time, Jimmy Brannigan wanted me to go back to Stella Maris, so for the 1977–78 season I played for both, lining out for the Bohs reserves on a Saturday and Stella on a Sunday. I was scoring a lot of goals for both teams and Giles called me up to the Ireland under-18 squad for a match against Belgium at Dalymount Park.

This had been the dream for me since I was a child – playing for my country under the floodlights of Dalyer. And when I was made the focus of all the set-pieces in training, I was sure that I was about to win my first underage cap for Ireland. I arrived at the Maples House

Hotel, a small guesthouse in Glasnevin that was our base. I threw on my Ireland blazer and slacks. But when the team was put up on the board, I was only a substitute.

'Why amn't I in the team?' I asked Giles.

'I've decided to start Tossie Brennan instead,' he said.

'But I was involved in all the corners and the free-kicks and the throw-ins in training,' I said. 'Why did nobody pull me and say it?'

I'd told all my workmates off the Windmill Lane site that I was going to be playing for Ireland. I had a load of mates from Cabra who were coming to the match just to see me.

'You're the twelfth man,' Giles said.

'Fuck that,' I told him, then I walked out of the hotel and headed back to Cabra.

'What are you doing home?' my ma asked.

'Giles decided to go with Tossie Brennan,' I said, for all it meant to her, 'so I said "fuck that" to him and I walked out.'

'But your da and all your uncles are gone down to Dalymount,' she said.

I suddenly felt terrible. I changed out of my blazer and slacks, then I walked back to Dalymount. I paid 50p in and stood on the terrace to watch it with them.

It was one of the stupidest things I ever did. As a triallist in England, you were always asked how many times you'd played for your country. International caps were a currency that everyone recognized. I had none. The squad was going to Brussels to play Belgium in the return match the following week. I might have come on against Belgium and scored the winner. It might have reignited interest in me in England.

I didn't see Giles again for another twenty years. Then, in 1997, I ran into him at the launch of Radio Ireland, now Today FM, in the Jervis Street Shopping Centre. Enough water had passed under the bridge for us to laugh about it.

'Johnny,' I said, 'you destroyed my life.'

'Ah, Roddy,' he said, 'you were full of yourself.'

He wasn't the first person to say it – he wasn't even the hundred-and-first – so I had to take his word for it.

If Wolves really were continuing to monitor my progress they were doing it very discreetly, because I never heard a word from them again. Then Jimmy Brannigan persuaded me to dedicate my last year in schoolboy football solely to Stella. He told me I wouldn't regret it and I didn't. It was one of my happiest years in football. We won the Pepsi Cola Cup and I made a lot of great friends – some of whom are still talking to me today.

At the end of the season, just after I turned nineteen, I signed for Bohemians. There was no decision to make, really. I went to see Billy Young, the manager, in his office in Dalymount Park. I remembered being drawn to the ground as a kid by the sound of the Dalymount Roar. I passed it on my way to school every day – or those days when I decided to go in – and I thought, I'm going to play there one day.

I was only coming out of schoolboy football so there would no wages until I'd established myself. But I knew I'd made the right decision when Billy put me straight into the first team. Working on building sites had helped me add a bit more muscle to my bones. I scored a hat-trick in a pre-season friendly, then my first competitive match was against St Patrick's Athletic in a FAI League Cup match on 26 August 1979. The game was decided by a penalty shoot-out. I grabbed the ball to take the first penalty and missed. We lost the match. I said sorry to Billy.

'Don't apologize,' he told me. 'There's grown men here who didn't have the courage to pick the ball up.'

Money or no money, the competition for starting places at Bohs was fierce. Like everyone else, I was thinking about the big European match that we had coming up and doing my best to work my way into Billy's thoughts. We'd been drawn to play Sporting Lisbon in the UEFA Cup, with the first leg away from home in the Estádio José Alvalade.

We all understood that this was the chance of a lifetime. Jim Fitzpatrick, a club stalwart who I love to this day, had his own shirt company. Every member of the European squad was to be supplied with a white shirt, a navy jumper, grey slacks and a red-and-black club tie. On the wall of the dressing room a list was put up of the players who were to report to him for a fitting. My name was at the very bottom of the list. I went to Jim for my fitting. I remember he squeezed my hand and said to me, 'You've cracked it, Rod.'

I'd never been in a hot country in my life. Stepping off the plane in Lisbon, I was already sweating in my jumper. There was a crowd to greet us at the airport and about a dozen press photographers in the arrivals hall. We thought we were superstars, when in fact we were tourists.

We weren't due to train until the following day, which meant we had the afternoon off. We all set off to explore the city. Some of us went shopping for souvenirs, while others went for a few beers. When we got back to the hotel at six o'clock, there had been a change of plan. There was a heavy rainstorm forecast for the following day, so we were going to train tonight instead. This was a problem because two or three of the boys were half-locked.

We arrived at the training ground and discovered that we'd forgotten to bring the training equipment with us. We had to borrow footballs. There was a crowd of about 4,000 people at the ground. They must have thought we were having them on when they saw all the balls going wayward during shooting practice.

I roomed with Anto Whelan, a brilliant bloke who would soon be off to Manchester United. We were staying in a hotel next to a twenty-four-hour printing works, which kept us awake half the night, but I was probably too excited to sleep anyway.

On the day of the match, Billy told me that he was going to start me at number nine. I wasn't nervous. I made up my mind to enjoy it. On Friday morning I was going to be back on a building site in Dublin. At the time, I was working in Ringsend on a development of local authority houses, which were all different colours and which we called Smartie Land. I was on the lump, which meant I was being paid according to how much wall I plastered. It was hard work. But there I was on a Wednesday night about to walk out in front of 50,000 fans in the Estádio José Alvalade. I knew I might never experience anything like it again.

We lined up in the tunnel before the match, with the Sporting

Lisbon players standing a couple of feet to our left in their pristine green-and-white hooped jerseys. They were like gladiators next to us, whereas we were pale and sickly looking. Most of them were Portuguese internationals. Manoel, one of their forwards, had played for Brazil. Standing directly in front of me was our midfielder John McCormack – The Count, as we called him, after the famous tenor – who worked in the Semperit tyre factory in Ballyfermot. Behind me was Paddy Joyce – or Joycey – who I'd been drinking with in Sloopy's nightclub on Fleet Street a few nights before, when he was wearing a pair of leather trousers and throwing shapes to Sister Sledge's 'He's the Greatest Dancer'.

We were entire leagues out of our depth, but at the same time we were going to have a go. We were a decent team. We had Fred Davis in goal; Eamonn Gregg, Austin Brady, Tommy Kelly and Joe Burke in defence; Anto Whelan, Gino Lawless, John McCormack and Terry Eviston in midfield; then me and Joycey up front.

We walked out onto the pitch. The noise from the crowd was like a jet engine during take-off.

'Oh fuck, oh fuck, oh fuck,' Joycey said. 'The fucking crowd, Rod.'

I said, 'Fuck them, Joycey. You're never going to see them again – and they're certainly never going to see us!'

I played out of my skin that night. I spent the entire match just running, running, running. But I also got a sharp lesson in the difference between professional and amateur football. The game was still 0–0 when a ball dropped in front of me. I thought I'd let it bounce while I made up my mind what to do. The ball was stolen from me and a few seconds later it was down the other end of the pitch. Later, when I became a manager, it was something I always impressed on players. When you're playing at that level, you have about half as much time to make a decision as you think you do.

Manoel, the Brazilian lad, scored twice and we lost 2–0. It was a fair result and far from a disgrace. Walking off the pitch, I asked Billy if he was happy.

'Fantastic,' he said – and he was absolutely beaming.

Peter Byrne wrote something about me in the *Irish Times* that I can still rattle off more than forty years later: 'European debutant Roddy Collins was unperturbed by the magnitude of the occasion and is going to have a fine future in the professional game.'

That was the night I started to believe it again. I'd proven that I could more than hold my own against a top European team and I was sure it was only a matter of time before I was back in England.

I didn't start in the return leg at Dalymount, which finished o–o. I was carrying a slight strain and Billy wanted to rest me for the league. He asked me to play twenty minutes for the reserves against UCD the following Saturday to see if I was fit to play the next day. Still buzzing off my performance in Lisbon, my da drove out to Belfield to watch the match with my brother Stephen, Caroline's brother Mick, and Mick's friend Georgie Dillon.

With only two minutes gone, I went into a tackle. There was a sickening crack, like a branch snapping, then I found myself down on the deck. There was no pain, but I looked down at my foot and it was pointing at an unnatural angle to the rest of my leg. Billy ran onto the pitch.

'Billy, look,' I said, feeling strangely giddy, 'my leg is broke!'

I was in shock. Billy took off his coat and threw it over my leg. The pain started to kick in then. Dr Tony O'Neill – a UCD stalwart – took a look and I could tell from his reaction that it wasn't good.

My da, Stephen, Mick and Georgie carried me on a stretcher to the dressing room. All of the colour had drained from my da's face. An ambulance took me to the Meath Hospital, where I was given a pain-killing injection. Billy was there with me. Before my leg could be X-rayed, my shorts, my boot and my stocking had to be cut off. The nurse was about to take the scissors to my Bohs jersey when Billy stopped her. We had no replacement gear. He said, 'Sorry, Rod, but Joycey's going to need it for tomorrow.'

My leg was X-rayed and my worst fears came true. It was a horrific break. Both my tibia and fibula had snapped. My da spoke to Mr Pegum, the consultant, and the prognosis wasn't good. I'd suffered the kind of injury that finished careers.

Caroline visited me every single day. She brought me a copy of a poem called 'Keep Going' by Edgar Guest. She said, 'Keep reading that, Rod,' and she kissed me on the cheek.

When I left the hospital after six weeks, I could recite every word of it. I was still on crutches and I was wearing a plaster cast from my ankle to my hip. It stayed on for another six months. The bones didn't heal properly. A cavity had opened up in my tibia.

I asked Mr Pegum if I'd ever play football again.

'You will,' he said.

'When?' I asked him.

'I don't know the answer to that one,' he told me.

As part of my rehabilitation I was told to put my foot on a weighing scales and apply exactly two pounds of pressure. It was pure agony for me. But I eventually got to the point where I could throw away the crutches and walk around with just a limp.

Most days I went to the Polo Grounds in the Phoenix Park with Caroline. I'd lie down on the grass and she'd throw a ball to me and I'd sit up and head it back to her. One day Turlough O'Connor – the former Bohs striker, who was now at Athlone – happened to walk past.

'How are you doing?' he asked.

I'd never met him before, but he was an absolute superstar to me.

'Great,' I told him, trying to put a positive spin on things.

The road back was longer than I ever imagined it would be, even in my lowest moments. When I broke my leg, I'd just turned nineteen. I'd made my European debut in Lisbon and felt like I was on the verge of my breakthrough as a footballer. By the time I came back, I was twenty-two years of age – and by then the world looked like a completely different place.

The sideboard in Annamoe was starting to groan under the weight of Stephen's boxing trophies. My little brother grew up fast. It felt like one day he was a little boy, then the next he was a man. Around the time I broke my leg, the age difference that had once separated us suddenly felt like nothing at all. He was fifteen in 1979, but he was so mature and independent that we talked to each other like two adults.

Everything he did, he took seriously. He worked for Noel Chance and Liam Kavanagh, the horseracing trainers, mucking out the stables and feeding the horses. On Saturdays and Sundays, and any other days he wasn't at school, he was out of bed and gone at five o'clock in the morning, then he'd be back home in the evening, smelling like Fossett's Circus. Noel took him off to race meetings and Stephen would travel in a little compartment in the horse trailer to make sure the animal was OK.

He was a steady Eddie – the same as my da. He applied himself in school as he applied himself to everything. He was good at drawing and there was talk of him becoming an architect. But my ma was absolutely convinced that he was going to dedicate his life to God. It was just his quiet, serious manner that sometimes came off like priestliness.

He played everything close to his chest – unlike me and Mick, who were talkers and couldn't keep anything to ourselves. Even when he was working, I could never find out how much money he earned. I turned the bedroom over, looking for his payslips, but I could never find them. He was a great saver. He always seemed to have money and he always seemed to have a plan.

He was a great little scrapper. He was unnaturally strong for his age. I remember once he carried a roll of lino on his shoulder from James Street to Annamoe Terrace – a thirty-minute walk through the Liberties, across the Liffey, up through Smithfield and back to Cabra. The thing must have weighed about the same as I did. And his pain threshold was unreal. But I still wouldn't have believed that he had it in his head to become a professional boxer. Boxing always seemed like a labour for Stephen because he was such a slow starter in his fights. He was a thinker and he approached every opponent like a problem to be solved.

Stephen always came to see me play football. After I broke my leg I had a lot more time to follow his boxing career. On Friday nights me and Caroline would go to the National Stadium on the South Circular Road to watch him fight. He had eighty fights as an amateur and lost only eight. The one that hit him the hardest was a defeat to Sam Storey from Belfast. It was one of those nights when he took too long to figure his opponent out and it would bother him for years afterwards.

In 1981 he won the Irish youth heavyweight title. My da was so proud of him. Afterwards, he took Stephen, me and Caroline to the Wimpy Bar in Phibsboro for burgers and chips and I remember Stephen sitting at the table with the medal hanging around his neck. The next day I was playing for the Bohs reserves against Tullamore in the League of Ireland reserve league as part of my slow return to football. I asked him to come into the dressing room and show off his medal. As it turned out, we were short a player or two and Stephen was asked to sit on the bench for us. He came on with ten minutes to go and we played on the same football team for the first and only time.

My da loved that he'd made a boxer out of one of us. But the proudest day of his life was the day that summer when Stephen was offered an apprenticeship as an electrician in Guinness. There was a lot of snobbery in the brewery. The children of labourers didn't usually get offered valuable apprenticeships. Not even a world title would have made him as happy.

My comeback from injury took longer than I imagined even in the worst-case scenario. It was eighteen months before I could kick a ball again. I kept up my aerobic fitness using a contraption that was like a bicycle for your arms. By the summer of 1981 I had biceps like grapefruits. But I'd lost what little pace I once had and Billy Young thought I was finished as a goal-scorer. I was playing now as a centre-half.

One day, out of the blue, I got a call from Dave Bacuzzi, the Englishman who won the League of Ireland as player-manager of Cork Hibs ten years before. He was now the manager of Home Farm, where he'd helped to discover and bring through some great players, including Ronnie Whelan, who'd just moved to Liverpool. He said he wanted me to play for him, so I went to see him in the office of the travel agency he ran, opposite Kielys in Donnybrook. I told him that I still saw myself as a centre-forward. He said that was fine by him and we did the deal there and then. I was going to be on the same money I was on at Bohs – which was zilch.

But things were finally looking up for me. I was back playing football again. I was earning good money lumping for Crampton's. And my relationship with Caroline couldn't have been better. Then life dealt us a surprise bounce of the ball, as it often does. I was standing at the bus stop outside O'Devaney Gardens one afternoon, waiting for Caroline to come home from work. When the bus pulled up, she stepped off it and said to me, 'Rod, I'm pregnant.'

My first thought was, How am I going to tell my da? Followed shortly afterwards by, How am I going to provide for a child? And, Is it too late to ask for that pram back?

We weren't exactly – as the saying goes – babies having babies. I was nearly twenty-one. We'd been together for five years and neither of us had any doubt that we were going to spend the rest of our lives together. I told Caroline that I was delighted. Inside, I was in a panic. We didn't have a house. I was still living in Annamoe and Caroline was still in O'Devaney.

Caroline's ma didn't take the news well. We went into her bedroom to tell her and she went as white as a sheet. This was 1981, not 1951, but there was still a big social taboo about being an unmarried mother, and the word 'illegitimate' was still in official use to describe babies born outside of wedlock. Caroline was the sensible one in the family, the one who'd stayed on at school to sit the Leaving Cert. She was the last one they expected this to happen to.

'You'd better look after her,' her ma said, pointing a warning finger at me.

'Mrs Hanney,' I said, 'I promise – I always will.'

Later on, during the Celtic Tiger years, we'd be drinking Veuve Clicquot out of a set of Waterford Crystal glasses that I bought in the market, and which turned out to be dessert bowls, and I'd say, 'There you are, Caroline – didn't I tell your ma I'd look after you?'

I went home to Annamoe to break the news. My da was building a new extension onto the house for my brother Mick and his wife, Bernie, who'd been living in Canada and were planning to move back to Dublin. I was helping him to put the roof on.

We were sitting in the kitchen taking a break when he said, 'Caroline's looking great, son. She's put on a bit of weight and she looks brilliant for it.'

I said, 'Ma, put the kettle on,' as if tea was going to make the news easier to swallow.

'Caroline's pregnant,' I said. 'We're going to have a baby.'

'Right,' said my father – he was a very conservative man and he was struggling with it. 'And when are you getting married?'

'We're not getting married.'

'Don't worry about money – I can get it from the Guinness loan book. All you have to do is pick a date.'

'Da, we don't want to get married until we have our own money.'

Caroline never accepted the shame that was supposed to come with being an unmarried mother-to-be. One of the neighbours in O'Devaney was heard to say, 'That'll sort that snob out,' but Caroline walked around showing off her bump, as proud as punch.

I started saving for a wedding. It says something about where my head was at that the first thing I bought was two crates of Carlsberg Special Brew off Mick Tynan, a lad I knew from Blackhorse Avenue, which I hid under my bed for the big day.

I was going to Anfield. That's what I was saying to myself that summer. By the time the baby arrived, I'd be a millionaire and I'd be playing for Liverpool. The same Liverpool that had just beaten Real Madrid to win the European Cup. The Liverpool of Kenny Dalglish and Alan Hansen and Graeme Souness. One of the reasons I was so keen to sign for Home Farm was that they had a friendly against them arranged for Tolka Park. It was part of the deal that brought Ronnie Whelan to Anfield. I was only a year older than Ronnie and I saw this as my chance to get back to England again. The plan was to play so well that the Liverpool manager, Bob Paisley, would want to sign me.

But first we had a holiday to go on. Before Caroline was pregnant, we'd booked two weeks in Mallorca. It might be the last holiday we went on for a while. So off we went, me with my ghetto blaster and my two cassettes – *Desire* by Bob Dylan and *Exodus* by Bob Marley and the Wailers.

The holiday was a disaster. We'd only been there a few days when I went swimming, forgetting that all of our traveller's cheques were in the pocket of my trunks, until Caroline spotted them floating out to sea. We had to get a bus back to Palma airport to go to the Thomas Cook office and try to get the cheques reissued. Caroline was suffering from morning sickness and she puked on the man in front of us on the bus. I was trying to wipe his head with a towel while everyone on the bus was just staring at us. Embarrassed, we decided to get off and walk the rest of the way, which turned out to be a distance of several miles. When we got there, Thomas Cook couldn't do anything for us, because I didn't have the receipt with the cheque numbers on it.

A few days after that, we were relaxing by the pool – listening to Bob Dylan's 'Hurricane' for about the hundredth time – when Caroline noticed a flood of water cascading from one of the apartments above us.

'Someone must have left their tap running,' she said.

We had a good laugh about it.

And then I stopped. Because I realized that it was our apartment. I'd tried to fill the sink earlier, but there was no water coming out of the tap. I left it turned on and when the water came back on the apartment ended up getting flooded.

We were never so happy to see Dublin again.

The match against Liverpool, which I'd been dreaming about all summer, was very nearly called off at the last minute. Someone broke into Tolka Park and dug a massive H into the pitch in support of the Republican prisoners in the H-Blocks in Belfast. They were in the sixth month of a hunger strike that would see ten men starve themselves to death for the right to be treated as political prisoners. The pitch was returfed overnight and the match went ahead as planned.

Dave Bacuzzi gave us our pre-match team talk and it was based on stopping Kenny Dalglish.

'When Dalglish makes a run, follow him,' he said. 'Don't give Dalglish time on the ball. And be careful of Dalglish when he drops the shoulder.'

Frank Brady, the older brother of Liam Brady, was our centre-half and one of the funniest men I ever met in football.

'Dave,' he said, 'how will we know this Dalglish?'

The Liverpool players brought the European Cup out onto the pitch before the match. I remember seeing them in the glow of the brand-new Tolka Park floodlights and thinking how beautiful they looked. Ray Kennedy. Terry McDermott. Alan Hansen. Phil Thompson. Mark Lawrenson. Phil Neal. Ronnie Whelan. Bruce Grobbelaar. I was staring at Graeme Souness and his legs like tree trunks.

My plan to catch Bob Paisley's eye went nowhere. I had three touches of the ball that night, one of which was a nutmeg on Alan Kennedy, the full-back who'd scored the winner in the European Cup final. It was such a rare thing for someone to put the ball between his legs that he still remembered it when I met him nearly thirty years later – 'Over at the corner flag! Was that you?' – and I was able to put him out of his misery by telling him that it was a complete accident. The crowd cheered anyway, but the next time I got the ball he went straight through me.

Never have I seen a group of players who moved the ball around like that Liverpool team. It was a stroll for them. It finished 5–0. But four of those goals came in the first half. If they'd wanted ten, they could have scored ten.

From that day on I could never see the point of playing pre-season friendlies against top English teams. They generated a lot of revenue, but they also demeaned the players and taught you little or nothing. The only thing I learned that night was how far away I was from ever playing in the First Division in England. And the only thing Bob Paisley learned was that he could probably plan for the future without Home Farm's crocked number nine.

4

I had a row with Mick. It was over something stupid. He and Bernie had arrived home from Canada and we were still working on the extension for them to live in. I was carrying heavy blocks around the side of the house while he was sitting in the chair doing the crossword.

I roared at him. He stormed out.

My da said to me, 'The whole world is out there to fight with you – so don't fight with your brothers.'

I was in a fouler anyway. It was the October Bank Holiday weekend. The night before, we'd played Athlone at St Mel's Park in the semi-final of the League Cup.

I can remember nothing about the match, except it dawning on me what a terrible mistake I'd made joining Home Farm. My da was at the match with Stephen. He said to me after, 'You need to get away from these – they're brutal,' and he must have really meant it because he'd never made a comment like that before.

After every match, the two of them would sit in the car and share a cheese sandwich and a large bottle of Guinness before driving home to Cabra. Me and my da had our own little ritual. After every match, he'd stay awake for as long as he could, then I'd barge in – usually with a few shandies on me – sit on the end of his bed and we'd talk about the game. If I wasn't home by 11 p.m., he'd go to sleep all disappointed. That night I'd arrived home but I didn't go in to him. What he said about Home Farm had upset me, probably because I knew it was true.

The next day we were working away on the extension and this was hanging over us. When we finished work, he was going up to the Phoenix Park for a jog. I asked him for a lift down to O'Devaney to see Caroline, who was now five months pregnant. We stopped at a petrol station and he asked me to fill the tank for him. In those days it was unusual to see men out running – it was another one of those things that 'nancy boys' did – and he didn't want people to see him in his tracksuit.

He was going to a party in the house of one of the neighbours that night.

'Frankie's going to make me a Harvey Wallbanger,' he said, rubbing his two hands together. 'Have you ever had one? It's gorgeous. It's like a dessert.'

He let me out of the car outside the flats. I wish now that I'd given him a hug. But we weren't that kind of family. I only hugged him once as an adult and that was with a few drinks on me. I couldn't have known it was the last time I'd ever see him alive.

It was a bitterly cold day, but there was no shortage of coal in the Hanney home and the fire was blazing. A couple of hours later Caroline's da was outside fixing a light on the balcony when he came in and said, 'Your da's at the door, Roddy.' I went outside, but it wasn't my da. It was my uncle Terry, and Stephen, who was crying his eyes out. I said, 'What's wrong?' because I thought someone had hit him.

'Me da's dead,' he said.

I remember the legs going from under me. The next thing, I was in Terry's car and we were on the way to the Richmond Hospital. Stephen was sobbing his heart out but no one said a word. We were all in shock.

After dropping me off at O'Devaney, my da had gone off for his run. My ma was getting ready for the party and she was worried when he didn't come home. By 9.30 p.m. there was still no sign of him, so Stephen borrowed a scooter from someone on the road and went down to the Phoenix Park to look for him. While he was gone, the gardaí called to the door and said there'd been an accident.

But it wasn't an accident. My da had suffered a massive heart attack due to a blocked artery. He must have been feeling unwell because he'd pulled the car over just outside the Parkgate entrance and got out. He was found by the side of the road.

Because he was in his tracksuit, he had no identification on him. When he was wheeled into the hospital on a trolley, his friend Mick

Monaghan just happened to be there. He told them that it was Paschal Collins but he couldn't believe it. He kept saying, 'He's the fittest man in Cabra.'

Because the gardaí had mentioned an accident, my ma arrived at the hospital expecting to find him sitting up in the bed. It was only when she was directed to the mortuary that she realized her husband was gone. He was only forty-nine years old.

We dressed him in a beautiful blue suit and he was laid out in the funeral home just up the road from the house. I couldn't get my head around it. None of us could. At the funeral Mass, Mick did the eulogy and I don't know how he got through it.

Only for Caroline being pregnant, I wouldn't have survived the months that followed. I fell into a deep hole of grief and despair. I stopped eating and the weight fell off me. I started to develop boils from the stress and streptococcal throat infections.

I took to wearing his overcoat and trying to walk like him. I used to get up in the middle of the night and wander for miles and miles, going nowhere. There was one time I was walking down Prussia Street at three o'clock in the morning and the gardaí pulled me over. They could see I was in an awful state. They asked me what was wrong and I told them that my da was dead.

'Do you want a lift home?' they asked – two kind strangers.

'No, you're all right,' I told them, 'I'll walk.'

The house was broken into one night when no one was home. A leather jacket was taken, and a charm bracelet that my da had bought for my ma. Stephen and I drew up a shortlist of suspects and we went out looking for them in Stephen's car, thinking we were my da and Terry. I got the leather jacket back and I banjoed the lad who had it. The gardaí came to the house and said we couldn't go around acting like vigilantes.

Christmas came and went and I realized that I needed to straighten myself out. The baby would be coming soon and I'd be no good to Caroline if I was in Mountjoy.

January of 1982 was a month of heavy snow in Dublin. There were three-foot drifts and there wasn't a car or a bus on the roads. I was working as a lumper on a new hospital called Beaumont. I went in at seven o'clock every morning, then worked through my lunch break and my tea breaks, so that I could clock off early enough to collect Caroline from her job in Cosgrave Motors on Dorset Street. Then we walked back to O'Devaney Gardens, holding hands, Caroline in the red velvet maternity dress she wore for her entire pregnancy, her head in the air, the proud mother-to-be, while my head was still all over the shop.

I got out of Home Farm. I only played five times for them and never again after my da died. I wanted to be back at Bohs, among friends like Terry Eviston.

So I went down to Dalymount Park and I begged Billy Young to take me back. Poor Billy had to give it to me straight. I wasn't good enough to play for Bohs any more. He had Paul Doolin and Jackie Jameson, who were scoring a lot of goals. Fine, I told him. Put me in the reserves. He said he would, but I was under contract with another club.

I went back to see Dave Bacuzzi in the travel agents in Donnybrook, and I begged him to release me. 'Please,' I said, crying my eyes out. 'Me da wanted me to play for Bohs.'

Dave could see that I was a broken man. He tore up my contract and I ended up back at Dalymount – playing as a centre-half for the reserves. Billy was right. I wasn't the player I was before. But I still hadn't given up on being that player again. For now, I was just happy to be back on familiar ground, the place of my childhood dreams, surrounded by old pals who cared about me.

The manager of the reserves was Ralph O'Flaherty, an absolute diamond of a man who visited me many times in the hospital while my leg was in traction. He'd watched me perform my exercises using the pulley and told me not to give up. I rediscovered my love of football under Ralph. We won the Blackthorn Cup – the League of Ireland B competition for players who were either on the way up or on the way out. Which of those I was, I still hadn't a clue.

As we got closer to the baby's due date, Caroline and I knew that our domestic situation had to be sorted out. We were still living apart, sharing our old bedrooms with brothers and sisters.

Caroline's sister Sandra and her boyfriend Alan were due to get married in February and Billy was learning 'My Irish Molly', which he was planning to sing at the wedding. You could hear him belting it out in the style of Joseph Locke when he was having his shave.

There was less than a week to go to the wedding. We were all sitting around in O'Devaney and there was the usual buzz of excitement about the flat. Caroline was due in four weeks and she was absolutely glowing. Sandra walked in wearing her wedding dress to let her da see it and she looked beautiful. Billy was fixing the hall door. He was standing there looking at her with the tools in his hand. I told him to sit down.

'Billy,' I said, 'I'll fix that for you later.'

He sat down in his chair and I sat on the arm of it. Suddenly he started making strange noises, then his chin fell to his chest. I touched his arm and asked him if he was OK and I realized that he was gone.

Caroline's brother Liam and I dragged him to the floor and we opened his shirt. The only phone in O'Devaney belonged to a blind woman in the next block. Caroline ran there to call for an ambulance while we pumped Billy's chest and told him that help was on the way. The ambulance arrived. They tried to shock his heart back to life, then they took him off to hospital. I sat in the back of the ambulance with Liam and we knew that he was dead.

Billy was a gorgeous man, a salt-of-the-earth Dub who loved life. I remember walking through Smithfield with him one day and we saw a black woman – a very rare sight in Dublin in the 1970s – carrying a sack of potatoes on her head. Billy smiled at me and said, 'Isn't the world a great place, Rod?' He really, really believed that. To him, it was full of wonder and goodness and people doing what they could with whatever hand they'd been dealt.

Sandra and Alan got married that weekend. It was a double wedding that they were sharing with Alan's sister, Angela, so they decided to go ahead with it in spite of everything.

The Hanneys and the Collinses were tough, hard-working families, for whom the important thing was to keep going. Resilience was what got you through the hard times – that and loving each other a little bit more. Losing our das so close together – and just before we became parents ourselves – made the bond between me and Caroline even tighter.

She was a rock of strength throughout that time. She'd had a difficult pregnancy. She developed toxaemia and her legs were painfully swollen. She was admitted to the Rotunda a week before the baby was due to arrive. On 2 March, a month and a day after Billy died, she went into labour. It wasn't the done thing for men to be present at the births of their children in 1982. I spent the day lumping in Beaumont and making regular calls to the labour ward from the site office. The news was worrying. The baby had gone into distress and they were considering an emergency Caesarean. Caroline told the ward sister that she wanted me there. I had no car, but I got the loan of a pushbike and I tore down Dorset Street, then left onto North Frederick Street, where the bike went from under me and I skidded painfully down the road on my side. I threw the bike against the railings of the Garden of Remembrance and into the hospital I ran. Caroline was still in labour. 'I want you to hold my hand,' she said.

I was so out of it that when I squeezed her hand I nearly broke her knuckles. The baby was born safe and healthy, thanks to the staff of the Rotunda. Afterwards, the scene in the maternity ward was like something out of *The Snapper*. There must have been fifteen or sixteen family members and friends crowded around the bed, this cast of mad characters holding teddy bears and balloons and crying tears of happiness. After a horrible time for both of our families, a little baby had brought joy to our world – just as she continues to do to this day.

We named her Sinéad. She was just like me in both her looks and her need for attention. She was never a baby in the sense that her brothers and sisters were babies. From the very start, you could see that her mind never rested. Her eyes darted around the room, sussing things out. She never seemed to sleep or even lie down. When she was three or four, and we were living in England, we left her with Maud, our landlady, so that we could have a rare night out. When we arrived home, Maud looked like she'd just ran a marathon. She said, 'I won't be doing that again.'

From the time she learned to say her first word, Sinéad never stopped talking – just like me. She had an unbelievable amount of confidence as a kid. She loved speaking in front of an audience. When she made her First Holy Communion, Caroline and I went to sit in a pew halfway down the church, but she insisted on dragging us all the way to the front.

She's still a centre-of-the-room kind of person today. A few years ago, after a Dublin game, a fella I know was in the Hill 16 pub one night and there was a girl in there telling funny stories and singing and generally getting the room rocking. He rang me up and said, 'There was a girl in the pub last night, Rod – it has to have been your daughter.'

And, of course, it was.

It was a great relief to find out that she inherited her mother's brains. Sinéad was brilliant at school. After her Leaving Cert, she decided to become a teacher. She's now studying for her Masters in Social Injustice in Education while working as the Home School Community Liaison Officer in St Kevin's College in Finglas. Her job involves encouraging kids to fully engage in school life and offering help to students who are at risk of not achieving their potential. It's a job that plays to all of her strengths as a problem-solver and also a compassionate person who cares about young people. I sometimes think how different my life might have been if I'd met someone like her when I was mitching at twelve.

At the same time, she has this mad, fun-loving streak in her. When I remember her wedding day, I think about her performing forward rolls across the dancefloor in her big white dress. I look at her sometimes and I ask Caroline, 'Where did we get her?' and of course I know the answer.

She arrived like a blessing at the end of what had been the worst six months of our lives. Caroline put a cot in the room she shared with four of her sisters and they all slept as well as you'd expect with a crying baby in the room. Night-time was Sinéad's time. Sometimes I'd call to O'Devaney early in the morning to take her out for walks just so they could all get a few hours' kip.

A month after giving birth, Caroline went back to work in Cosgrave Motors. The next year was a very happy time for us, even though we had no home of our own. I was still living in Annamoe, an arrangement that came to a sudden end that summer when me and Stephen accidentally set fire to the house. It was my da's birthday – 7 June. My ma was having a difficult time and was taking a little holiday in a mobile home that my da had bought in Courtown, along with Colette, Audrey and Paschal. Stephen and I had been down there for the weekend, but we came back to Cabra because we both had work the next day. There had been a leak in the immersion heater, so I drained the water from the cylinder before we went away. Stephen didn't know. He switched on the water for a shower, then fell asleep. I woke up in the middle of the night choking. The room was filled with thick black smoke. I shook Stephen and shouted his name, but I couldn't wake him. I was starting to wonder had he been overcome by smoke when suddenly, in what seemed like one movement, he opened his eyes, rolled out of the bed and jumped out of the window, leaving me standing there.

I had on a pair of paisley Y-fronts – Penney's ones, three pairs for a pound. A crowd had gathered outside. Twenty or thirty neighbours who had seen the smoke were shouting up at the window, 'Jump, Roddy! Jump!' But my first concern was to find a pair of trousers so that they didn't see me in my underpants. I felt around the floor in the blackness of the room, coughing and spluttering, then I felt this overwhelming urge to lie down on the bed and go back to sleep, which must have been down to oxygen deprivation.

I gave up the search for the trousers and I jumped out the window in my manky underpants, landing on my arse in the front garden. One of the neighbours, who looked like Mr Bumble from *Oliver Twist*, gave me a pair of his trousers and I pulled them on me. I had to hold them up with one hand while I watched black smoke billow out of every window, then the fire brigade arrived and flooded the house with their hoses, destroying most of what little my ma had left in the world.

I was scoring goals for fun. Or so you'd have thought if you were following the Bohs reserve team's results in the papers. There was a payphone on the wall just outside the dressing room in Dalymount Park and it would ring about five minutes after every home match. One night, I answered it.

'This is the *Evening Herald*,' the voice on the end of the line said. 'Do you know what way the match finished?'

'It was three—nil for Bohs,' I said.

'And who scored?' he asked.

'Collins,' I told him. 'A hat-trick.'

Collins didn't score at all, but a hat-trick was what went in the paper.

This went on for a couple of months. I kept answering the phone and I was suddenly a goal machine.

I was hoping that another League of Ireland manager would notice that I was banging them in and come in for me.

Plastering was just a means to an end for me and I didn't take the job seriously, certainly before Sinéad came along.

I loved the social aspect of it, wandering around and having the craic. I was a big kid moving around in a man's world and figuring out how it all worked. A day on the site didn't feel complete unless you'd been both the instigator and the victim of at least one practical joke. Forget to bring your work boots home and you could return to work the next day to find them filled with concrete. Fall asleep on the job and you could wake up with a mouth full of Colman's mustard. You were on your guard all the time. I have great peripheral vision. I call it my Cabra eye. In those days, my Cabra eye became all-seeing.

By the time I was twenty, I'd been thrown off every building site I ever worked on, mostly for messing. I was a flier with the hawk and trowel. I could get my work finished very quickly, although that didn't necessarily mean to the customer's satisfaction. Beaumont Hospital was a sort of last-chance saloon for me. John Kerrigan – or Blackpool John – was Willie Power's top foreman. He couldn't pronounce his Rs.

'Woddy,' he said to me, 'you've been barred off seven sites. You get barred off this one and you're finished.'

Beaumont was the biggest building site in Europe at the time. There were thousands of people working on it and you could go missing on it for days. I just wandered around like I was the Lord Mayor of Dublin 9, meeting and greeting people I knew from Cabra or from football.

Eventually, the inevitable happened. Blackpool John's patience ran out and I got thrown off that site as well. It didn't matter. There was no end of work at that time. The government was throwing up new local authority houses and flats everywhere. I got a start on a development in New Street in the Liberties, along with Jackie Cummins, who I worked with on Peter Mark's on Grafton Street, and the Sullivan brothers, who were a family of plasterers from Dublin. I was doing what they called 'jumping in', which meant a bit of plastering and a bit of general labouring. More importantly, for the first time in my life, I was earning a man's wage.

This coincided with Sinéad's arrival and my realization that I was a grown-up who was responsible for this tiny person that me and Caroline had brought into the world. New Street was the first time I understood the meaning of an honest day's work for an honest day's pay. I stopped slacking. I earned my wages. From then on, my attitude was that a man should be paid what he's worth – and it became a huge principle for me later on, not only when I became a boss on building sites, but when I was a football manager.

There were some brilliant characters who worked on New Street, including one lad who used to tell the most outrageous lies with so much conviction that you wondered did he believe them himself. He came back from holidays in Tenerife once and told us that the pilot had had a heart attack and he'd flown the plane himself.

'The landing was a bit bumpy,' he said, 'but I got a lovely round of applause from the other passengers.'

Another time, he said he was knocking off a married woman who'd just moved into one of the houses we were building. He told us to look in the kitchen window at lunchtime if we didn't believe him. So lunchtime came and a gang of fellas headed for the house – there he was in the kitchen, hugging and kissing this woman while pulling Benny Hill faces at the fellas over her shoulder. It turned out it was his wife.

I worked with some brilliant people on that job, like Padser Harris, who's been a mate of mine since we were kids. These days he drives tourists around Stephen's Green in a horse and cart, throwing out historical facts about Dublin off the top of his head. Back then he was the hardest working labourer I ever saw and he set the template for me for what a proper day's work looked like.

I loved the hurly-burly, law-of-the-jungle aspect of building-site life. The bricklayers kept themselves to themselves. The labourers got on well with the plasterers, but everyone hated the electricians because they were – in the language of the times – yuppies. You had to keep your wits about you because you never knew when a row might kick off. One day, the foreman told one of the boys to stand in the road and keep two parking spaces clear for a concrete truck that was coming. He went out with a brush and pretended to be sweeping. Then two bricklayers from the North arrived in a van and took one of the spaces. The lad told them to move. They said no. He went and got a shovel and cracked the two of them over the back of the head with it.

Then there were the drinkers. They'd arrive into work smelling like a distillery, stretch out on a scaffolding plank to sleep off their hangovers, then put in a full day's work in the afternoon.

Years later, when I became a football manager, I drew on all the lessons I learned about human nature and group dynamics from building sites. I learned how to deal with tricky personalities, flawed geniuses and those who were just plain work-shy. I developed an instinct for knowing who needed a bollocking, who needed an encouraging word and who should be avoided at all costs.

Life for me that year was just work, family and football. I was happy to be back at Bohs, even if I wasn't scoring all the goals that the newspapers were reporting. Caroline took Sinéad to all of the reserve-team matches. None of the other wives and girlfriends had babies and she became a sort of team mascot.

At the end of the season I decided that I was going to give football just one more year. I was about to turn twenty-two and I was going nowhere. It was nearly three years since I broke my leg and I didn't want to grow old playing in front of empty grounds in the League of Ireland B Division. So, in the summer of 1982, I decided that I was going to batter my body to get myself the fittest I'd ever been. Every day that summer I trained. Jackie Cummins was big into pigeons. He had a Honda 50 with a basket on the back that he used to transport his birds before releasing them. A couple of nights a week, he drove me out to Ballymount Lane on the bike and I'd run back to Cabra.

When I was fifteen years old I worked as a barman in the Stoney-batter Inn, where I became good friends with Paddy McDonagh, one of the regulars, who was known by that most Dublin of Dublin nicknames – Whacker. Whacker McDonagh was the best-looking bloke in Stoneybatter and he had a girlfriend named Fran Fay, who looked like Cleopatra. I've been lucky in life to have had friendships that lasted the length of a lifetime and that was how it was with me and Whacker. He was one of the funniest people I ever met and an absolute diamond of a man who would give you not just the shirt but the skin off his back.

At all of the milestone moments in our lives, we were there for each other. When Whacker and Fran got married, I was his best man, at sixteen years of age. I was godfather to their first son, Paddy, and later I helped negotiate the young lad's contract when he was signed by Luton Town. Much later, when I was the manager of Carlisle United, his youngest son, William – or 'Willo' – was my first signing.

Whacker set the bar for me for what a true friendship should be – and it was a high one. He showed me what it was to be open and generous and hospitable. We celebrated all of our happy times together. And in less happy times, when I was broke, he gave me half the dinner off his plate. When he died from cancer a couple of years ago at the horribly unfair age of sixty-three, I gave the eulogy at his funeral. I could have spoken for days about all the great times we had, including the summer of 1982, when he asked me to join a seven-a-side team he'd put together of fellas from the inner city. They were stone mad but a bunch of brilliant footballers. Bunny Kennedy. Kenny 'The Bonecrusher' Lyons. Gerry 'Mungo' Munrow. Brian 'Dicko' Dixon. And Demo McGrane. We drove around the city in an old van, sometimes playing two or three matches a night. We'd play one in O'Devaney, then one in Sheriff Street, then we'd have an hour to get to our next match in Ballyfermot. We won everything. They were some of the happiest days of my life.

Then a lad we knew called Tosh Taffe told us about an eleven-a-side tournament in Inchicore with a £300 prize. The money was put up by two painting contractors who were St Patrick's Athletic supporters. Tosh added a few players to our seven-a-side team – including Brian 'Milo' O'Shea, who went on to have a great career as a goalkeeper and worked as my goalkeeping coach at almost every club I managed. There was Harry McCue, the centre-half who'd just signed for Glentoran after winning the League of Ireland with Athlone Town.

One or two League of Ireland teams were using the competition to tune up for the new season. In the semi-final we played Harry's old club, Athlone Town, who were managed by Turlough O'Connor. I scored a hat-trick and we knocked them out.

We ended up winning the competition and the £300 prize. I was named Player of the Tournament. When we went back to the dressing room, there was a treatment table filled with cans of beer. We were locked before we got out of there. Then we headed for Ryan's on Queen Street in Smithfield, where Tosh divvied out the winnings. The party went on through the night and into the next day.

It had been the hardest year of my life. But I'd gotten through it. I had a beautiful daughter and a girlfriend I loved. I was the fittest I'd ever been and I was ready to give the Bohs reserves one more year. I was still recovering from the drinking session two days later when Harry McCue rang me up and said the words that would change my life: 'Turlough O'Connor wants to talk to you.'

5

Turlough O'Connor has always been a sort of surrogate father to me. He came into my life two years after my da died and was the strong male role model that I was missing in my life. Outside my own family, I can honestly say there was no man whose opinion of me mattered more to me. It still matters to me to this day.

I'd only met him once before and that was the day in the Phoenix Park when Caroline was throwing the ball to me to do the sit-up headers. I'd no idea what he thought of me – except maybe I wondered did he think I was a bit mad.

He was already a legend to me. When I went to Dalymount Park as a kid, he was one of the players I most wanted to see. I watched him win the League of Ireland with Bohs in 1975 and 1978 and the FAI Cup in 1976.

When he took over as the manager of Athlone Town they were an unfashionable club in the midlands whose greatest achievement was holding AC Milan scoreless in a UEFA Cup match at St Mel's Park in 1975. He set about building something bigger and more lasting. In just two years he'd turned them into the best team in Ireland. They won the League of Ireland in 1981 and again in 1983.

He was the best man-manager in the game. He would identify players that no one else wanted and find out why. Then he'd sign them and he'd coax performances out of them that no one else could.

I had a problem that I had to take care of before I met him. Caroline's ma had a bottle of peroxide in O'Devaney and she'd persuaded me to experiment with a new look. Now I had a long white badger streak running through my hair, which I had to ask her to cut out. Then I went out and bought a brand-new shirt and met Turlough in a coffee shop in Phibsboro Shopping Centre.

He said he needed a striker, and if he couldn't make a League of

Ireland goal-scorer out of me, he'd eat his hat. No one in football had shown that kind of belief in me since I broke my leg. I would have played for Turlough for nothing. But he offered me £20 per week and a signing-on fee of £150. For the first time since 1979, I felt like I was a footballer again.

I threw myself into training with the seriousness of a man who knew he was on his last chance. They were a brilliant bunch of blokes at Athlone. In goal there was Jim Grace, a steady Eddie from Baldoyle in Dublin. At right-back, we had Stefan Fenuik, who came to Athlone from Stoke and never went back. At left-back, we had Tommer Conway, a Cabra man who was hard as nails. Our centre-backs were Noel Larkin, who would win seven League of Ireland titles at three different clubs, and Padraig O'Connor, one of Turlough's brothers, who never drank and would go for an ice cream after a match when everyone else went for a pint. On the right side of midfield was Larry Wyse, who was Tommer's best mate, from somewhere around Windy Arbour in Dublin. On the left was Larry Murray, who was called 'Cakesy' because he had his own cake business. In the centre of midfield, we had Mark Meagan, a brilliant lad who worked in Dundrum's Central Mental Hospital with his da, the former Ireland and Everton defender Mick Meagan. Next to him was Eddie Byrne, or 'Poodles' as he was better known – he was in his early thirties, which seemed ancient to us. I was up front next to Michael O'Connor, or Socksy, another one of Turlough's brothers who was a brilliant player and should have played in England.

Caroline and I got married in late July, right in the middle of pre-season. That morning, Caroline's brother Liam did the grushy: an old Dublin custom where, usually, the father of the bride opens the front door and throws a handful of coins into the air for the local kids to fight over. You were judged on the quality of your grushy. We'd been saving loose change for months, not just coppers, but 10p and 50p pieces. I'm proud to say that people talked about our grushy for months afterwards. The kids would stop us in the street and say, 'I got two packets of crisps and a packet of Toffos out of your grushy, mister, and my sister got a Cornetto!'

Stephen was my best man and Mick my groomsman. We got dressed in the house in Annamoe Terrace. We had a big sing-song, led by Mick, and we ended up being nearly late for the church. The wedding was at two o'clock. At ten to two, Mick was standing in the kitchen in just a pair of football shorts, singing all my da's favourite songs. When he got dressed he couldn't find his black dicky bow. He went off to get one while me, Stephen and Paschal headed for Aughrim Street without him. He eventually showed up at the church with a dicky bow with spots on it. That was Mick – but what a send-off he gave me.

Caroline arrived fashionably late. She had a fit of the shakes outside the church. After everything we'd been through in the past two years, it was the emotion of the day. Liam walked her up the aisle with Sinéad – sixteen months old, in a white dress with little red bows – toddling behind her. The priest, Father Cahill, told us that a marriage should blossom and grow every day of our lives together and I remember thinking, That's what ours is going to be like.

George Cosgrave, Caroline's boss, had supplied us with the wedding cars free of charge. We led the convoy from Aughrim Street to the Ambassador Hotel on the Naas Road for the reception. It was the best day of our lives. Caroline and I loved each other and we were surrounded by people who loved us. We'd come through two harrowing years. We were both still grieving for our das – and would for ever – but Sinéad had brought light into our lives. I stood up and I sang 'Sweet Caroline' by Neil Diamond. Everyone joined in when it came to the chorus. 'Good times never felt so good.' And it was true – they were the best times we ever had.

We were supposed to stay that night in the honeymoon suite, but George got us to cancel the reservation. Why spend good money on a hotel room, he said, when he could let us have the use of his beautiful house overlooking the sea in Portmarnock? What George didn't tell us was that we wouldn't have the house to ourselves. My abiding memory of our first night as a married couple was George pointing out all the different species of fish in his home aquarium, then showing us to what was usually his daughter's bedroom. I was in a foul humour – 'Shush,' Caroline laughed, 'he'll hear you!' – and I took my anger out on one of his daughter's teddy bears, which got half-volleyed across the room.

The next day we were back in O'Devaney Gardens. Caroline was hanging out the washing and all the kids from the flats were telling Sinéad, 'Your mammy looked gorgeous in her wedding dress!'

That was a Friday. On Saturday I played for Athlone Town against Wolverhampton Wanderers in a pre-season friendly. After that we had our big night out in Lord John's, next door to Clerys in Sackville Place. The doorman was Jack Scanlan, a big lump of a man from Rialto who knew my da. He gave us a free bottle of wine and showed us into the VIP area, where we danced around Caroline's handbag for the night.

Instead of a honeymoon, Caroline got a trip to the Isle of Man for a pre-season tournament with Athlone Town. The other teams in the tournament were Sunderland, St Mirren and Stockport County. Against Stockport, a lad whacked me in the ear with the point of his elbow. The skin split right around it and my ear was left flapping around on the side of my head. I was badly concussed, but I refused to go off until I'd evened up the score. The next time the player had the ball, I smashed him. While I was being sent off, he was being stretchered off and we left the ground in the same ambulance, the two of us shouting abuse at each other in the back.

Turlough liked the fact that I was physical and I put myself about. I scored a lot of goals in that pre-season. After four difficult years it felt like things were happening for me at last. I was a married man, the father of a beautiful little girl and the centre-forward for the League of Ireland champions. In the first few weeks of the season we bought a house in Coolock, using my signing-on fee and £500 that Caroline's da had given us as a deposit. We moved in that September – and we hated it straight away. We had nothing against Coolock; it was just that we were used to living in small spaces that were crammed with people and filled with noise. Coolock was so quiet and we felt far removed from everyone we knew. But there was no point in complaining about it. I was a grown-up now with responsibilities. And for the first time in a long time, I could see a happy future stretching out in front of us.

We were drawn to play Standard Liège, the champions of Belgium, in the first round of the 1983–84 European Cup. They were a great team. Up front they had Horst Hrubesch, a European Cup winner with Hamburg and a European Championship winner with West Germany. In midfield they had Guy Vandersmissen, who was part of the Belgium team that beat world champions Argentina in the opening match of the 1982 World Cup. And on the left wing they had a brilliant Dutch winger, Simon Tahamata.

The first leg was played on a manky night at St Mel's Park. You could hear the rain drumming off the corrugated steel of the stand. When the Standard Liège players got off the coach, they were already wearing their gear and we knew they didn't want to be there. Tahamata went off injured after Tommer Conway stamped on his foot and you could see that one or two of their players didn't fancy it. Hrubesch scored after twelve minutes, then Vandersmissen added a second, and they seemed to breathe a little bit easier. But then a minute before half-time, we won a corner. As the ball came into the box, Zoran Jelikić, their Yugoslav centre-half, had his two arms wrapped around me. I outmuscled him, swung my foot at the ball and smashed it in.

Turlough was delighted with us. We won a penalty in the second half and had a chance of causing an upset. But Joey Salmon missed it and then Gérard Plessers scored a penalty for them. Salmoner made up for his miss with a goal two minutes later and we ended up losing 3–2. It was a great result.

The second leg in Belgium was a different experience altogether. Caroline's ma gave me a St Anthony medal. The Hanney family had a special devotion to him and I promised I'd pin it to the inside of my jersey in the hope of receiving his blessing. We arrived in Belgium. We were given a police escort from the airport to the hotel and the same treatment when we went to training. We thought we were the Beatles. You could see the fellas growing in confidence, trying out things on the training pitch. We started to feel like we were professional footballers with a chance of knocking Standard Liège out of the European Cup.

That didn't last long. Jelikić scored after one minute to kick off what would be the longest ninety minutes of our lives. The Standard Liège players just stroked the ball around and we all spent the night looking at the numbers on their backs. I must have made thirty sprints in the first half and the only time I touched the ball was when we were tipping off after they'd scored. And that was four times in the first forty minutes.

We went in at half-time embarrassed. Turlough said to me, 'Can you get closer to your man, Rod?' and I said, 'Yeah, maybe when he's celebrating the next goal, Turlough. I could try and sneak up behind him.'

The second half was the same story. When you're taking a battering in a match, you can lose all concept of time, wishing away the minutes, wanting it to be over. It felt like I was constantly standing on the halfway line with Michael O'Connor, tipping off again. At one point he looked up at the scoreboard, saw an 8 and a 1 and said, 'Thanks be to Jaysus there's only nine minutes left.'

I said, 'Socksy, that's not the time, you fucking eejit – that's the score.'

Turlough decided to throw on another forward. Fran Hitchcock was in his ear, saying he wanted to experience European Cup football. Fran came on and scored. He jumped up on the fence behind the goal to celebrate. The crowd were laughing. The stadium announcer said the Athlone Town goal was scored by Alfred Hitchcock. Until the day he retired, Fran's nickname was 'Alf'.

The final whistle put us out of our misery. It finished 8–2. All I could think about was what the fellas on the building site were going to say on Friday morning. One of the Standard players glided over to me and asked if I wanted to swap jerseys. He was stripped to the waist and his body looked like it had been fashioned using a hammer and chisel. I was too embarrassed to let everyone see my milky white body with no muscle definition, so I asked could we wait until we were in the tunnel. Once we were out of sight I pulled the jersey off over my head. As I handed it to him, he had a confused look on his face. He was staring at the St Anthony medal, still attached to the jersey with a piece of string and a big nappy pin. He was thinking, What the fuck is that? and I was thinking, Yeah, thanks for everything, St Anthony – eight fucking goals. I didn't even wait to get it back.

There was murder going on in our dressing room as I slipped quietly through the door. One or two of the boys had had a drink at the airport going out. Turlough never said anything until after the game. Now he was letting them have it, hot spittle flying out of his mouth as he told them – told all of us – what an embarrassment we were to the club. Then he saw me sitting next to Tommer Conway in this pristine red jersey.

'What the fuck are you wearing?' he asked.

'It's a Standard Liège jersey,' I told him. 'The chap came to me and asked did I want to change with him.'

'Well, you can fucking change back,' he said, 'because we've only got one set of gear.'

'I'm not knocking on that door, Turlough. No way.'

In the end Paddy Smith, the assistant coach, went in. He arrived back with the jersey but no medal. St Anthony, patron saint of lost things – including, presumably, European Cup matches – was in the bin and I wasn't going in there to fish him out. I'd tell Caroline's ma that I lost the thing. We could all say a prayer to St Anthony for it to be found.

Happily, that was as bad as it ever got at Athlone. We were a very good team the rest of the time and a tight group. Most of us lived in Dublin. We'd all meet up on Seán Heuston Bridge and get the bus to Athlone for training and matches, and a great camaraderie was built during all those hours spent on the road.

A lot of the fellas had been there the year before, when the team won the league by sixteen points. We knew it wasn't going to be another one of those years. I finished the season as our top scorer with eleven goals in the league, two in the cup and one in Europe. I was no Eugene Davis, but it was a good return given that I'd been out of top-class football for four years. Shamrock Rovers were too good for everyone that season. They had Liam Buckley and Alan Campbell up front and they scored nearly forty league goals between them. They won it easily – the first of their four-in-a-row. We finished third, behind Bohemians. There'd be no European football for us next season. But maybe that wasn't such a bad thing.

The bond between me and Turlough tightened as the season went on. During the week, he worked as a rep for Jodi, a soft-furnishings company which was owned by his friend Tony O'Connell, another former Bohs legend. Turlough would ring me on a Sunday and ask me what I was doing the next day. As the economy entered a slump, and construction work dried up, the answer was often nothing. He'd take me on the road with him, just for the company. He'd jingle coins in one hand and steer the car with the other as he talked football non-stop. So many of the things I know about the game I learned during those days on the road with him.

As a football man, he believed in keeping things simple. There was no highfalutin tactical talk. What interested him was players – and he could read a player like some people could read a racing form guide. He rated me. He liked my physicality and my honesty of effort, so that's what I gave him, week in, week out. He used to shout, 'Get stuck in, Rod!' and that's what I did. I would have walked through a brick wall for the man. He knew it too. But he also had a ruthless streak in him, as I discovered when the season ended and he told me he was selling me to Drogheda United.

I was angry with Turlough. I'd done well for him. But he bought Terry Eviston from Shamrock Rovers and he reckoned he was a better goal-scorer than me.

He was offered £5,000 for me, which was huge money at the time. I took it as a rejection, but it was just business, and a good lesson for me to learn. Years later, when I became a manager, I had to develop a similar ruthlessness when it came to business.

Drogheda United were doomed. I knew it from the start of that 1984–85 season. After ten matches we were second in the table, but I knew we were going to get relegated.

The manager, Tony Macken, had played in England and won the league with Derby County. He was very knowledgeable about football and he paid me £50 a week, which was more than double what Turlough was paying me, as well as a signing-on fee of £2,000. I scored nearly as many goals as I did for Athlone – ten in the league that year – but our results in the first few weeks of the season couldn't hide what I knew in my heart. We were going down.

I had a lot of happy times there and made a lot of friends. But we just weren't a serious team. I remember one Sunday we were at home against Limerick City. Paul Whelan – Ronnie's brother – was playing in midfield for us and he was having a nightmare.

'Whelo,' I said, 'what's wrong with you?'

'Rod, I can't concentrate,' he said. 'I'm after leaving a chicken in the oven.'

'You what?'

'I was supposed to take it out before I left – but I forgot.'

Whelo lived with his girlfriend, Jane, in a flat above a dentist's on Tonlegee Road in Raheny. But Jane had gone home to Cork for the weekend and now Whelo was having visions of their kitchen going up in smoke. Coxie Corbally was the assistant manager – a great bloke from a family of Dublin dockers. He used to wear a long herringbone coat to every match.

'Coxie,' I said to him at half-time, 'you're going to have to get Whelo off.'

'Did he hurt himself?' Coxie asked.

'No, he left a chicken in the oven and his head is all over the place.'

'You fucking dunce,' Coxie said to him. 'Give me your house keys.'

Whelo handed over the keys and Coxie drove to Dublin to see to the chicken. We won the match 4–3 and Whelo had a great second half. We were all having a shower afterwards when Coxie arrived back with an angry head on him.

'You stupid fucking eejit,' he said. 'You never turned the oven on.'

I loved Whelo. We became great friends. After every match we'd get dressed up and we'd head for Rumours nightclub next to the Gresham Hotel. Like me, he loved his clothes. He used to wear a blue suit with a lemon-coloured tie and pocket square.

One Saturday night he persuaded me to go to a do with him in Wynn's Hotel. We had a match the next day away to Limerick and we were in the thick of a relegation fight at the time. I didn't mind going out because I was suspended. But Whelo played the next day and he was terrible. At one point he somehow managed to knee himself in the face. He was lying on the ground and the blood was pouring out of his nose. I got a fit of the giggles. It wasn't a good look, sitting on

73

the bench, laughing, while we were being battered. Limerick beat us 6–0 and Tony was furious.

'They know you were out last night,' I told Whelo, winding him up.

'How?' he asked.

'Just by looking at you. You should say it to them before they say it to you.'

'But they'll fine me.'

'They won't. Just say there was a family do and you'd a few gargles and tell them that you don't deserve your wages this week. They won't take it off you.'

So Whelo came clean to Tony and Coxie. He came out of the meeting and said, 'You stupid bollocks, Rod, they took me wages.'

The drinks were on me in Rumours that night.

Four teams were going to be relegated that year to create a new Second Division. After the defeat to Limerick, it had dawned on everyone that we were going to be one of them. Most of us wanted to leave. I'd had a call from Turlough. He was gone from Athlone Town and was taking over at Dundalk.

'What are you doing next season?' he asked.

'I'm not staying here,' I told him, 'playing in the Second Division.'

'That's good,' he said, 'because I want you at Dundalk.'

We had to beat Sligo Rovers to have any chance of staying up. We were winning 3–0, but we let them back into it and they scored three goals. A lad in the crowd who'd been giving me abuse for weeks started having a go again. A ball came to me in the penalty box and I tried to take it on my chest, but it bounced out of play for a goal kick.

'You useless fucking toerag,' he shouted at me. 'You're going to be in the Second Division next year.'

'You might be,' I told him, 'but I fucking won't.'

It didn't go down well. The match finished 3–3 and it was confirmed – we were relegated. I had to stay in the dressing room for an hour after the match because there was an angry crowd outside the door waiting to talk to me.

Caroline and I took Sinéad to Torremolinos that summer and we had a brilliant holiday. There was a five-a-side football pitch in Timor Sol, the apartment complex where we stayed, and every night in the bar, during the cabaret, they gave out prizes for things like Player of the Day. I'd told everyone that I was a professional footballer and I made out that the League of Ireland was a bigger deal that it was in reality. Somehow, one or two people got it into their heads that I was a Republic of Ireland international. There was no Google in those days.

One night, the compère said, 'The Player of the Day is Republic of Ireland international, Roddy Collins.'

I went up to collect my prize of a beer voucher and noticed Alfie Hale, the Waterford United manager who really had played for Ireland, sitting there, staring at me.

I looked at Alfie and I thought to myself, Alfie, please don't blow my cover here.

I became good mates with a lad named Michael Yonkers, an absolute gent from the Netherlands. He and his wife Marleese were a lovely couple. During the course of one of our drunken evenings, I mentioned that we owned land and we kept horses. Technically, this was true. When we were in Spain a couple of days, we were told that there were two piebald ponies in the garden back home, eating the grass.

At the end of the holiday I told them that if ever they were in Ireland they should come and stay with us. For some reason they chose to take this literally. In the first week in December we got a letter to say that they were coming before Christmas. The house was far from the mansion I'd made it out to be. The front gate didn't open: when Tony Macken called to the house to sign me for Drogheda he'd had to throw his leg over it. I borrowed a few bob and I dickied it up. I took down the hallway door to use it as a wallpapering table and I only put it back up ten minutes before we went to the airport to collect them in Caroline's little Mini-Minor.

My ma laughed when I told her that our friends from holidays were coming to Coolock. 'You'd better bring them for a few drinks first,' she said. So when they came through the arrivals gate, that's what we did. We had a few drinks in the airport lounge, then we drove them back to the house in the Mini, half-locked, with their suitcases on their laps in the back.

We had five brilliant days with them. I brought Michael to see me play for Dundalk on a freezing cold Sunday afternoon. We were scraping the ice off the windscreen after the match and I asked him did he learn anything. 'Yes,' he said, 'Irish people say "fucking this" and "fucking that" and "fucking everything".'

My ma invited us all round to Annamoe for dinner one night. She ordered a Chinese takeaway, poured everything into serving dishes and hid the cartons so that they'd think she cooked it herself.

They were crying when it was time to go home. Just as we were about to leave for the airport, I touched off the door that I'd used as a wallpapering table and it fell down.

They were happy times for me and Caroline, even if work was becoming harder and harder to come by. It was now an employer's market and the exploitation was horrendous. One time, I got a start on a building on the North Circular Road. It was three storeys high and I could see that the scaffolding was wobbling. I said to the fore-man, 'You'd want to get that sorted.'

'Get up on it or don't get up on it,' he told me. 'If you don't want the job, you can fuck off.'

Then I found myself having to audition for work. I remember one morning going for a job in Tallaght. I was sitting on a garden wall with two other plasterers, two blokes from Mayo. 'We've got a cou-ple of lads working,' the foreman told us. 'I'm giving them until dinner hour to see how they shape up.'

We didn't hang around.

The last big plastering job I'd done was the National College of Art and Design on Thomas Street. We laughed all the time on that site. There was only one lad I didn't like, a crane operator from the North, an ex-IRA man who was a bit of a mouth. He used to sell things like electric blankets and sets of cutlery on the side. One day he was selling saucepans – a fiver for a set. I thought my ma would love them, so I told him I'd take a set, but made the mistake of calling him by his nickname.

'Only my friends call me that,' he said, 'and you're not one of those, bollocks.'

Somehow he managed to break his arm, so they made him the

nipper, or errand boy, on the site. We were having our lunch one day, sitting on Thomas Street, watching the world go by. He was crossing the road on the way back from the shop, a bag of messages in one hand and his other arm in a sling. The traffic had stopped. There was a jeep parked in front of him with a trailer attached to it. He went to step over the towbar. As he did, the jeep pulled away and he fell into the trailer. We were all doubled-up as we watched him being driven off down the street. I think he ended up on the Naas Road.

It was on that job that I got a sharp and painful lesson in showing initiative. I went to see one of the bosses one day to complain about something. He grabbed a handful of my chest hair and he ripped it out by the roots. 'You're a man,' he said. 'Sort it out yourself.'

It was a lesson I needed to learn. By 1985 I had to earn money any way I could. I painted. I did cobble-locking. I worked with a crew of Travellers laying tarmacadam. I installed windows. I had a market stall in Finglas selling stockings with pulled threads in them. As long as I was strong and able-bodied, I'd have done anything to put food on the table. Times were hard.

I couldn't stop scoring goals that season. Turlough said to me, 'If you can't do what Tony Cascarino does, then I'm no judge of a player.'

Turlough transformed Dundalk from a middle-of-the-table team to one that was challenging for the title. Shamrock Rovers were still better than everyone else. Their team of that era was the best League of Ireland team I ever saw. But there was only three points separating us at the end. The season turned on our visit to Milltown. We lost 1–0. Had we won that game, there would have been no four-in-a-row. But I was in no position to do anything about the result because I ended up in hospital.

I went up for a high ball and Mick Neville, the Rovers defender, accidentally nutted me in the back of the head. The next thing I knew, Father Brian D'Arcy was standing over me, giving me the Last Rites of the Church. My body had gone into spasm after I lost consciousness. At first it was thought that I was having an epileptic seizure, but it turned out that I'd swallowed my tongue. Someone fished it out of my windpipe, but they had no idea how long I'd stopped breathing for and what the impact of that was going to be.

Caroline was watching all of this from the crowd, along with her sister Ellen, who had recently lost her husband, Mick Green, in a car accident. They had no idea what had happened, but Ellen was praying that Caroline wouldn't be made a widow too. I was taken off on a stretcher. I regained consciousness while I was in the dressing room. Father D'Arcy was praying for my soul and I was begging the physio to let me back out to play. She told me to lie back down. An ambulance was on its way. Caroline wasn't allowed into the dressing room, so she had no idea whether I was going to live or die until she saw me sitting up in bed in the Meath Hospital.

It was around that time – late in 1985 – that I started to become restless. I was a plasterer at a time when no one wanted plasterers. We had a house in Coolock that we hated and a daughter who was about to turn four. I was thinking about England and wondering what our lives might have been like if I'd never broken my leg at nineteen.

I went to see John Givens in his sports shop on Blessington Street. He was a brother of Don Givens, the former Ireland striker who was playing in Switzerland for Neuchâtel Xamax. I asked him if he could have a word with his brother to see if he could arrange a trial for me. John laughed. He knew the score. I was twenty-five. It was too late.

But Caroline wouldn't hear of me giving up. She told me to write to every club in England to ask them for a chance to show what I could do. I didn't bother with the First and Second Division ones, but I wrote to all the rest. One or two letters came back saying no thank you. Then the phone rang. It was John Jarman, the assistant manager at Mansfield Town in the Fourth Division. He remembered me from my time at Wolves – he was the one who found me drinking Britvic in a Haarlem nightclub.

'How old are you now?' he asked.

'I'm, er, twenty-three,' I lied.

'That's a great age,' he said. 'Can you get over next week for a trial? Ian wants to have a look at you.'

He was talking about Ian Greaves, the former Busby Babe, who was the Mansfield Town manager.

'Yeah, I'll come over,' I said.

The only problem was that I was still contracted to Dundalk. I met Turlough in Taster's Choice, a little coffee shop on Dorset Street.

'You're not going anywhere,' he told me.

'Turlough,' I said, 'please don't do this to me.'

'If they want you,' he said, 'they can come and buy you.'

Caroline went to work on him. Turlough would often call into George Cosgrave Motors to have a coffee and a chat with her. He used her as a conduit to try to get through to me. If I was looking for an improved contract, he'd mention to her casually that there was no money in League of Ireland football, or he'd show her a letter from a supporter saying that Roddy Collins was crap. Caroline told him that I deserved this break and that if I didn't take it I'd die wondering what might have been. So Turlough agreed to release me for two weeks.

'But if you get injured over there,' he told me, 'you won't be getting paid.'

John Jarman collected me at East Midlands Airport and took me to the house that was to be my digs. There was a lad from Derry staying there called John Cunningham, although he insisted that I call him Bugsy.

Ian Greaves watched me over the course of a week. I was nervous, knowing that this was my last spin of the wheel. I didn't do well and I knew it. At the end of the week he called me into his office.

'Look, Rod,' he said, 'you've a lot going for you – just not quite enough for us.'

Bollocks, I thought.

He asked me when I was going home.

'Tonight,' I told him.

'Right,' he said, 'we've a practice game organized for this afternoon. I want you to play.'

So I played. And I scored five goals. After the match, I was back in his office. He'd changed his tune.

'How much can I get you for?' he wanted to know.

'Probably about two grand,' I told him – optimistically, as it turned out.

'Brilliant,' he said. 'We'll take you.'

I rang Caroline and told her the news. Then I rang Turlough.

'Turlough,' I said, 'Mansfield Town want me.'

'Then they can make Dundalk an offer for you,' he said. 'You were given a two-week release and now I want you home.'

A day or two later I was sitting with Turlough in his car on the Cabra Road.

'I want to leave,' I told him.

'You're not leaving,' he said. 'Not without a fee.'

'If you don't let me go, I'm going to give up football.'

'Is that right?'

'I'd give it up tomorrow.'

'And what would you do instead?'

'Become a professional boxer.'

'You'd make a great professional boxer.'

He wasn't buying my bluff. But in the background, a deal was being discussed. Christmas came and went. Greaves wanted to see me play for Dundalk before the club committed to me. On New Year's Day we had a match against Limerick in Oriel Park. He came to see it. I had one of those games you dream about as a kid. Even the things I did wrong somehow went right. We won 2–1 and I scored both of our goals. Caroline and her ma were listening to the match on the radio in O'Devaney Gardens and they knew it was finally about to happen for us.

Greaves shook my hand afterwards. Then he disappeared into a room with Enda McGuill, the chairman of Dundalk, to talk money. On Monday morning, wearing a blazer and a pair of tight grey Falmer slacks, I flew back to East Midlands Airport with Enda. John Pratt, the chairman of Mansfield Town, collected us in his Rolls-Royce Silver Shadow. He was a lovely man who'd made his fortune from manufacturing cat's eyes. It was a freezing cold January day. There were flecks of snow falling. I was sitting in the back of the car while Enda was in the front passenger seat, talking business with John. We pulled into a petrol station and parked next to the pump. Nothing happened. We sat there in silence for a minute or two, with John just staring at me in the rear-view mirror, before I realized that I was being asked to get out and fill the tank. But I remembered something that Turlough had said to me – people will treat you the way you allow them to treat you. I wasn't some teenage apprentice who was keen to impress. So I stayed in the car. An attendant eventually came out and filled the tank.

The club took me at my word when I told them that I was twenty-three. My aunt Sheila's husband, Liam, was a bit of a rogue and he knew a thing or two about forging documents. I went to see him in the Blue Lion on Parnell Street, where he drank, and he did a number on my birth certificate, changing the year of my birth from 1960 to 1962. The two years that he lopped off my life were permanently lost – even my Wikipedia entry says I was born in 1962. The deal got done and I handed over my doctored birth certificate to be registered as a Mansfield Town player with the English Football League.

'We've agreed to pay a record fee for you,' Ian Greaves told me, which turned out to be £15,000. 'Don't let me down.'

'I won't let you down,' I promised him. 'As a matter of fact, in a year's time, you're going to be selling me.'

And I meant it. My plan was that, within a year, I was going to be playing in the First Division.

He talked personal terms. He wrote something down on a piece of paper and flicked it across the desk at me. It said £150 per week. I told him that I'd get that on a building site in Dublin. He pulled the piece of paper back across the desk and he wrote £200 on it. I told him that my wife would be giving up her job and the children's allowance money to move to England and it would have to be worth our while financially. He wrote down £250.

'Let me ring her,' I said, then he left the office. I rang no one, but when he came back, I told him I'd had a chat with Caroline and we could make it work if the figure was £270.

'OK,' he said. 'And I'll give you £2,000 to put your curtains up,' which was football-speak for a signing-on fee.

We shook hands on a two-and-a-half-year deal, then I stood up to leave.

'Where do you think you're going?' he asked.

'I'm going back to Dublin to sell my house,' I told him.

'Oh, no, you're not,' he said. 'You're our player now. Go and put your fucking training gear on.'

6

I was all in. Typical me, I said to Caroline, 'Sell the house, sell the car, quit your job, then you and Sinéad get over here!'

But Caroline said, 'Get to the summer and we'll make a decision then.'

It was January of 1986. Mansfield Town were pushing for promotion to Division Three. The leading striker at the club was Neville Chamberlain, the brother of England international Mark Chamberlain, and the uncle of the future Liverpool star Alex Oxlade-Chamberlain. Ian Greaves wanted another striker who could provide a few more goals to help the drive for promotion, although it was made clear to me that I was bought as an investment for the following season. A young star for the future – if not quite as young as my birth certificate said.

On my first full day as a Mansfield player I went into training with Bugsy Cunningham. He led the way into the dressing room. I looked around me. Everyone was younger than me. Half of them looked like they hadn't even started shaving.

'What's the craic with all the kids?' I asked him.

'This is the under-21s dressing room,' he said. 'This is where *we* get changed.'

'Bugsy,' I said, 'they're after paying a record fee for me. I'm not getting changed with a bunch of fucking kids. Where's the real dressing room?'

Bugsy directed me to a room further along the corridor. I pushed the door. Every conversation in the room stopped when I walked in. I went up to the player nearest to me and I stuck out my hand.

'How are you doing?' I said. 'My name's Roddy.'

He shook my hand, then I moved through the dressing room, doing the same to everyone. In that moment, I got a sense of who my pals in that dressing room were going to be. Funnily enough, it was all the strikers. Neil Whatmore had once been the club's top centre-forward. He was almost thirty-one now and I was coming to take his jersey. He welcomed me warmly. So did Mick Vinter, who was a year older, and also coming to the end of the road, as well as Keith Cassells, another player who had scored a lot of goals for the club.

I sat down to get changed. Someone sat down beside me. It was Neville Chamberlain.

'I'm Nevy,' he said. 'If you need anything, just ask, OK?'

We've been friends since that day.

But I wasn't everyone's cup of tea. Never have been. Football dressing rooms in those days were macho environments – much more so than today, when footballers do TV ads for face moisturizers and apologize to the fans on social media when they lose a match. Back then every club had its alpha males. At Mansfield, George Foster was the top dog, a centre-half and the captain of the team, who had one of those moustaches that all football hardmen seemed to have in the 1970s and 1980s.

From the moment I arrived I could see him out of my Cabra eye, taking my measure. I suppose there was a lot about me for him to dislike. I was big and full of myself and I gave off the impression that I could handle myself in a fight. It can't have pleased him that I was earning more money than him. I was on £270 a week, which was more than some First Division players were getting at the time.

The tension between us came to a head in training one morning when I misplaced a pass to him. 'Fucking hell, gaffer,' he said, loud enough for everyone to hear, 'you paid a record fee for *him*?'

At that stage I'd been away from home for about six weeks and hadn't yet played a game. I hadn't seen Caroline or Sinéad in all that time. There was no FaceTime or Zoom back then. I had one of Sinéad's little toys with me. You pulled a cord on it and it played 'Twinkle, Twinkle, Little Star'. I'd lie in bed at night, listening to this little tune over and over again, the tears rolling down my face. I was thinking, what am I doing here? I'm nearly twenty-six years old. I'm away from my wife and my daughter. And here's the captain of the team – a club legend – going out of his way to make me feel about two inches tall.

I was fuming. We went back to the dressing room after training. Nevy was chatting to me but I wasn't listening to him. We were all having a cup of tea before our shower. I was looking at George, sitting across the room with a big smirk on his face. I snapped. I threw a cup at his head. It missed by millimetres and smashed off the wall behind him.

'The fuck are you at?' he said.

'Who the fuck are you to talk to me like that?' I said to him. 'I'm over here just trying to make a living. I've a family at home who I haven't seen in weeks and you're trying to put me down. If you spoke about me like that on a building site in Dublin, you'd get a fucking shovel over the back of your head.'

Ian Greaves sent for me. I was expecting a bollocking, or to be fined a week's wages. Instead, he told me that that was why he signed me. 'I want to see that kind of aggression out on the pitch,' he said, showing me his fist. 'Fucking give it to them – right?'

I still hadn't kicked a ball yet after breaking my little toe in training. A lad stood on it by mistake. I was embarrassed. There I was, a big number nine who modelled himself on Joe Jordan – and I'd broken my little pinky after less than two weeks.

I eventually played my first game for the club against Chesterfield in a reserve-team match in a completely empty ground. There were two other Irish fellas in the side – Bugsy and Brendan Toner, a centre-forward from Coolock in Dublin, an eighteen-year-old apprentice who was as mad as a brush. Just before we tipped off, he clapped his hands and shouted, 'Let's knock the bollocks out of these English fuckers!'

I made my first-team debut against Doncaster Rovers in the Freight Rover Trophy, a knockout competition for Third and Fourth Division teams. It was on St Patrick's Day, a viciously cold Monday night. Their player-manager, Dave Cusack – another hardman defender with a huge moustache – celebrated the occasion by calling me Paddy all night. I chinned him, knocking him out cold. We won 4–2 and I scored two goals, with Keith and Nevy getting the others.

I was off to a flying start. Two weeks later I made my league debut at home against Preston North End. In the first few minutes I got in a bit of a tangle with the lad who was marking me. 'Here, you're not

84

in Dalymount now, Collins,' he said in a Dublin accent. It was Mick Martin, who'd won more than fifty caps for Ireland and played for Manchester United. We had a great little battle of wills that day. Alan Kelly Jr was in the Preston goal, eighteen years old and following in the footsteps of his legendary father, Alan Sr. At one stage of the game I was one-on-one with him and slipped the ball past him, but it bobbled wide of the post.

I started to settle in. Home for me and Bugsy was a brown-brick house on a council estate that belonged to a woman named Maud, who washed the kit for the club. We shared the box room and slept in bunk beds. I was in the bottom one, which had been Nevy's until he moved in with his girlfriend, Ange. In an alcove, Bugsy had built an altar, with candles and a crucifix on it, along with a photograph of his brother, Diarmuid, who'd been killed in a car accident. He knelt and prayed in front of it every night.

Bugsy was a diamond of a man – the kindest man I ever knew. He had a brilliant football brain. Years later, when I became manager of Carlisle United, he became my assistant.

Nevy was brilliant to me. He was the first black man I was ever friends with. My grandchildren, who live in a truly multicultural Ireland, find it hard to believe when I tell them that everybody in the country I grew up in was white.

Keith Cassells and I bonded over boxing. He was a huge fight fan and we both skipped rope as part of our warm-up. He asked me about the green vest that I wore under my jersey when I played. I told him it was my little brother Stephen's singlet that he wore when he boxed for Ireland. Stephen had set out on his own journey not long after I joined Mansfield. After winning the Irish middleweight title at the National Stadium, he represented Ireland at a tournament in New York and decided to stay in America. He made his way up to Boston and persuaded Pat and Goody Petronelli – the brothers who trained and managed Marvin Hagler – to let him fight out of their famous Ward Street gym in Brockton. Keith bought *Boxing News* and *Boxing Monthly* regularly. After Stephen made his professional debut that year, Keith kept me posted on his progress up the various British, European and world rankings. 'The WBC have him as number twenty,' he'd tell me, 'but he's number sixteen with the IBF and the WBA.'

While I had friends at Mansfield, I never really felt like I fitted in in English football. There was a horrible culture of misogyny and casual racism that you never found in Irish football. The so-called banter I heard in English dressing rooms was far worse than anything I heard on any building site over the years. My da brought us up to treat women with respect. I didn't laugh along with the jokes, which made some people distrustful of me.

Also, I wasn't a fan of Ian Greaves – or John Wayne, as I used to call him. He exuded this ridiculous cowboy air, putting one foot up on a chair when he was giving his team talks. People were terrified of him. When he cracked a joke, everyone laughed, but it was fake laughter. He'd see me not even smiling and he thought I was going against him.

But I was still keen to get Caroline over with Sinéad to show her how well everything was going. She agreed to come over for the weekend. Nevy told me that I had to put on a bit of a show for her.

'Give her the dream,' he said.

I booked us into a country club in Nottinghamshire that came highly recommended by Billy Dearden, one of the coaches at the club. Billy lent me his Ford Capri and I picked Caroline and Sinéad up from the airport and drove them to the place. Caroline was blown away.

'Oh, Roddy!' she said, as she stepped into a suite that was three times bigger than our house back in Coolock. 'This is brilliant!'

The next morning we went downstairs for breakfast. At the table beside us was an elderly man with a straight-backed, military air and a big, bristly moustache like Windsor Davies. He was a retired British Army officer who lived in the hotel like the Major from *Fawlty Towers*. Caroline noticed that he was reading *Trinity*, Leon Uris's epic historical novel about Ireland, which she'd recently read and loved.

'It's great, isn't it?' she said, because that's Caroline – always making friends out of strangers.

'Are you Irish?' he asked, picking up on her accent.

'We are,' she said. 'We're from Dublin.'

'Bloody Irish,' he said, 'I can't stick them. Murdering bastards – all of you.'

Give her the dream, Nevy had said. Well, I gave it my best shot.

'I'm sorry,' she told me, 'I can't live among people like that.'

It was going to take a lot more persuasion – months of it, in fact – to get her to throw in her hand at home and move over.

The season played out. We went on a long, unbeaten run and secured promotion to Division Three with a few games to spare. Keith and Nevy were banging in the goals, which meant my opportunities were limited. I played seven league games, five of them as a substitute, and four in the Freight Rover Trophy.

But I'd clearly made an impression, because near the end of the season Howard Wilkinson was on the phone, asking Ian Greaves about me. Wilkinson was the manager of Sheffield Wednesday, who finished fifth in the First Division that year. He was looking for a number nine who could put himself about and he liked the look of me.

Before I went home to Dublin I decided to celebrate by splashing out on a car that befitted my status as a future First Division star. I bought a Toyota Celica coupé, custom-built, with spoke wheels. I couldn't afford it. Most of my wages were going back to Caroline in Dublin. But I signed the hire-purchase agreement knowing that I was borrowing against my future success.

And I bought a brand-new jumper. The only decent clothes shop for men in Mansfield was called Limited Edition. All the players went in there to flirt with one of the sales girls, who looked like a model. In the window, I'd seen this jumper that I liked. It was blue and yellow with a little bit of purple on it and the fabric was sort of silky, so that it shimmered when it moved. I went into the shop and threw it on me. It was £50, which was a lot of money.

'It looks good on you,' the sales girl said.

Krusty the Clown wouldn't have worn it.

'Really brings out your colour,' she said, 'and gives you a great shape.'

'OK, I'll take it,' I told her.

She put it in a bag and I counted off five £10 notes.

'No, it's, em, £175,' she said.

'The sign said £50,' I told her.

'No, that was for the tie.'

I was too embarrassed to say that I couldn't afford it, so I wrote her a cheque. Then I went to the commercial office at the club and asked for a loan of £175 to make sure it didn't bounce.

I set off for Liverpool to catch the ferry to Dublin. I was tearing along the M62 in the Toyota Celica, listening to the Sade album, *Diamond Life*. But I couldn't get past the first song on side one – 'Smooth Operator'. I'd listen to it, then I'd rewind it and listen to it again, one arm out the window, in my new jumper, thinking, You have made it, Rod!

I missed my exit off the motorway and missed the ferry. I slept overnight in the car and waited twenty-four hours for the next sailing. On the boat, I ran into John McCormack, who was coming back from a boxing show with a team from St Saviours. Stephen had trained under John and his brother, Pat – both former British champions from Sean McDermott Street – after my da died.

'How's things, Rod?' he asked. 'I believe young Stephen's training with Marvin Hagler.'

'He's in the same gym,' I said, 'but I don't think he's met him yet.'

'And how are you doing?'

'Doing great, John. Professional footballer with Mansfield Town. Just got promoted to the Third Division.'

I insisted on dropping John home, then I went cruising through Phibsboro, Cabra and Stoneybatter, stopping blokes I hadn't seen since I was at school:

'Where you headed, lads? Sure, hop in, I'll give you a lift!'

Then it was:

'How are things going over in England, Rod? Who are you with again?'

'Mansfield Town. But, er – say nothing to no one – Sheffield Wednesday are having a sniff around me.'

'Nice jumper.'

'Yeah, thanks, it's new. I'm telling you, lads, it's all finally happening for me.'

Mister bleeding Wonderful.

★

Caroline gave her notice to George Cosgrave that summer and we put the house in Coolock up for sale. I went back to Mansfield on my own for pre-season training and to find us somewhere to live. I was really revved up. This was going to be my year.

Ian Greaves thought it would help the squad bond if we all lived together for pre-season, so we moved into the mansion home of the club chairman, John Pratt, or 'Mr Pratt' to us. We trained three times a day. I'd have trained four times if they'd asked me. We worked our bodies to the point of exhaustion. Football coaches didn't know as much about the science of exercise and recovery as they do today. Most of them were just glorified water-bottle men. As a player who was coming from a part-time football background, I should have been eased into it, but I'd been training like a full-time pro from the day I arrived at the club. The weight fell off me. When Caroline's ma saw me she blurted out, 'Oh my God, you look like a Biafran!'

I started to pick up niggling injuries. Our first pre-season friendly was against Leamington Spa. I jumped up for a header and landed awkwardly. Instantly, I knew that something was wrong with my ankle, but I tried to ignore it. The next morning, the area felt tender, but I went for a light jog around the grounds of Mr Pratt's estate. That made it worse. I went for an X-ray. It turned out that I had ruptured the ligaments in my ankle. I was going to be out for six weeks. It meant I'd miss pre-season, a disaster for any player.

I said nothing to Caroline. She was about to move over with Sinéad and I was worried that she'd get cold feet. I just carried on looking for a house for us to rent. I found a beautiful four-bedroom corner house with a big garden in Dormy Close, a quiet estate in a posh part of Mansfield.

On our first night in the house I walked into the bedroom to find Caroline sitting on the edge of the bed with her back to me. Her shoulders were shaking and I knew that she was crying. 'Roddy,' she said, 'I'm sorry, but I'm heartbroken.'

I was aware of what she was giving up for me. She'd left her home, her family and a job she loved so that I could pursue my dream of being a professional footballer.

'Caroline, I won't let you down,' I told her, 'I promise you.'

Famous last words.

It took longer than expected for the ligaments to heal. It was October before I was back in full training. Even then, I struggled with my form. Then someone had the bright idea of sending all the players off to a remote forest to do fitness training. It was just macho bullshit and completely off the wall. We were running up and down hills with big logs on our shoulders. On a descent I slipped and felt a sharp pain in my groin. What happened, I discovered later, was that my pelvis had shifted and I'd sustained what's commonly referred to these days as Gilmore's Groin. Even simple acts like coughing and sneezing, or getting in and out of the car, resulted in the most excruciating pain.

Being injured is one of the worst feelings in football – second only to being relegated. When you're injured, you have this sudden sense of being disconnected from the world. As far as your teammates are concerned, you might as well not exist. Fit players don't like being around injured ones. The longer you're out, the more you start to sense the resentment of you for not being able to play. It was the habit of a lot of managers in those days to stop talking to players when they were injured. From the day I hurt my groin, Ian Greaves cut me dead.

Despite my promise to Caroline, I could feel that it was all unravelling – and far more quickly than I could have imagined. I felt so guilty for dragging her across to England, chasing what had turned out to be a ridiculous dream. But there was no going back now. The house in Coolock was sold – we'd even lost money on the deal.

Caroline still believed in me. She told me to keep going. Her favourite movie is *Gone with the Wind*. 'After all,' she still likes to say in her best Vivien Leigh accent, 'tomorrow is another day.'

Much as she tried, though, she couldn't hide how miserable she was in Mansfield.

We were fish out of water in Dormy Close. The man two doors down owned horses – and not in the same way that our neighbours back in Coolock owned horses. These were thoroughbreds. We were completely out of our element.

Caroline thought she might settle in better if she was busy.

She got a job in a leisure centre in Mansfield. It hosted a lot of big events that year, which we got to see for free. There was a snooker tournament and I remember being blown away watching Steve Davis signing autographs for hours until absolutely everyone had one. It was the heyday of professional wrestling, which was on ITV every Saturday afternoon. I took Sinéad to see Giant Haystacks. The audience screamed high-pitched, foul-mouthed abuse at him. I wouldn't see anything like it again until I became the manager of Bohemians and the abuse was aimed at me.

I rehabbed the groin several times a day throughout that autumn. I played a handful of matches for the reserves and got back into the team in December. Four days before Christmas I scored a goal – the only league goal I would score for Mansfield Town – in a 5–1 home defeat by Wigan. I felt like my luck might at last be turning and that 1987 might be my year.

On New Year's Day we played Port Vale at home. I was being marked by Bob Hazell, the former QPR defender, who'd been at Wolves when I was there as a teenager. Bob was a giant and one of the most physically intimidating people I've ever met. Somewhere, I had picked up the disgusting habit of clearing out my nostrils by pressing one closed while blowing through the other, a trick that was known in football circles as the snot rocket. At one point I felt this arm come from behind me and wipe itself across my face. It turned out I'd accidentally snotted on Bob. You did not want to snot on Bob.

The Mansfield pitch was heavy and my legs were tired afterwards. I remember getting out of the communal bath and discovering that I couldn't lift my leg to put on my trousers. The groin had flared up again. It meant more painful weeks of rehab and more silent treatment from the manager.

Mansfield were having a good season without me. They had consolidated their place in the Third Division, hovering around mid-table, and had put together an impressive run of results in the Freight Rover Trophy, knocking out Halifax Town, Rotherham United, York City and Bury to reach the semi-finals.

It was about four weeks before I made my return, in a reserve team match against Stoke City. It didn't last long. One of their players went in over the top of the ball and broke my leg – the same one I broke playing for the Bohs reserves at nineteen. At first I didn't know it was broken and I managed to limp off the pitch. I was awake all night with the pain. I couldn't even bear to have the bedsheets touching it.

An X-ray revealed nothing unusual, which explains why, when I arrived into training on crutches, Ian Greaves thought I was swinging the lead. I left the crutches leaning against the wall of the dressing room while I hobbled into the treatment room. He followed me out, threw them down the hallway after me and said, 'Get your fucking gear on and get out and train.'

After ten minutes of trying to run, I was in absolute agony and walked off the pitch. I was sent back to the hospital, this time for a bone scan, which revealed something the X-ray had missed. My fibula had snapped. The only reason I was able to walk on it is because the fibula isn't a load-bearing bone.

I went home devastated and told Caroline the news. She told me to stay positive. She said, 'I'm only here because I believe in you, Rod.'

A day or two later I began to feel a bit more hopeful. The bone would take about six weeks to heal, the doctor said, which meant that the season might not be a complete write-off. The team had made it to the final of the Freight Rover Trophy. They were going to play Bristol City at Wembley Stadium at the end of May and I targeted that date for my return.

I rested the leg and did my rehab at the club every day. March turned to April. The cast was removed and I felt excited. Then the phone rang one day and Caroline's brother Liam was on the line, telling me that he was in a police station in Chesterfield – oh, and that he was Jesus Christ.

Liam was suffering from schizophrenia, but it hadn't been properly diagnosed. He'd once been arrested for disrupting Mass. He was taken to Mountjoy Prison, then they moved him from there to the Central Mental Hospital in Dundrum. He didn't belong in there. He was harmless. He just needed medication.

Caroline and I had no idea as to the severity of his illness at the time. When he told me he was in a police station in Chesterfield, I thought he was joking.

'Go on out of that,' I said, 'you're in Walsh's! Put the lads on!'

'No, you don't understand,' he said, 'I'm Jesus Christ, Rod. I've come to heal your leg.'

I asked Liam to put someone else on the line. He handed the phone to a policeman. I gave him our address – Mansfield was about half-an-hour's drive away – and I asked him to put Liam into a taxi.

We couldn't believe our eyes when we saw him. He looked wretched. He was skin and bone. He had long hair and a scraggly beard and no coat on him: he'd given it away, along with his shoes and socks. His feet were cut to bits. Caroline helped him into the house.

'You're going to play at Wembley,' he told me over his shoulder. 'I'm going to make sure of that.'

'Just get inside, Liam,' I said.

Caroline fed him and we bought him new clothes. He told me that he'd had a vision of me scoring the winner in the final of the Freight Rover Trophy and he'd come to fix my fibula. He stayed with us for two weeks until he started to feel well enough to go home. My leg must have been healed by then because I cycled to the train station with him on the crossbar and he got the train to Holyhead.

My comeback match was against Notts County away, on a Tuesday night, the week after Easter. I had the ball at my feet and I got tackled. A pain shot up my leg. The bone had snapped again. This time I was carried off the pitch on a stretcher. Nicky Andersen, one of our full-backs, told me afterwards that I kept trying to get back onto the pitch to chin the lad who tackled me.

I was taken in an ambulance to the hospital. Again, I couldn't bear the feeling of the covers touching my leg. Worse than the pain, though, was the fear that it was all over for me at Mansfield. I'd played just four league matches that season and scored one goal. My body was crocked – as well as the broken leg, my groin was still causing me trouble – and my contract had only a few weeks left to run. Once again I was treated like I was somehow to blame. John Jarman, the assistant manager, who'd recommended me to Ian Greaves, said to me one day, 'It's my fucking fault you're here.'

Mansfield had an insurance policy on me. They offered me £12,000 to retire. I said no. I was going to have surgery on my pelvis to try to fix the ongoing problem with my groin. The club weren't happy. Nevy called to the house one day and told me that I was going to be released at the end of my contract. I said, 'Fuck that – I'm not accepting it.' I spoke to the players' union, who told me the club couldn't release me as long as I was still injured.

I wasn't allowed to travel with the team to Wembley. I travelled on a separate bus with the non-playing staff and the wives and families of the players. It broke my heart. I sat in the stand and watched the final. We drew 1–1 with Bristol City after extra time, but won on penalties. I was delighted for my team-mates. But I wasn't allowed on the open-top bus for the victory parade through the town.

The operation left me with a scar below my stomach that went from hip to hip, but it was a success. Caroline asked me what was I going to do – what was our plan? I told her I was going to get the fittest I'd ever been that summer and I'd show the club that I deserved a new contract.

I cycled thirty miles on the bike every day to an outdoor pool in Nottinghamshire, where I swam. I went to the gym three days a week to lift weights. We went back to Dublin for a few weeks that summer. Turlough O'Connor invited me to train with Dundalk while I was home. Before I went back to England, he said to me, 'That's the fittest I've ever seen you, Rod.'

We returned to Mansfield and I reported to the training ground for pre-season as if everything was normal. Ian Greaves was sitting in a deckchair in the sun. He looked at me like he was seeing a ghost.

'What are you doing here?' he asked.

'I'm still a Mansfield Town player,' I pointed out.

'No, you're not,' he said. 'You're finished.'

'Not according to the union,' I told him. 'They say I have to be medically fit to leave the club.'

He looked me up and down.

'You look medically fit to me,' he said.

'I still have a twinge,' I said.

I don't know what I was playing at. I thought if I could blag my way through pre-season, they might give me another chance. I was desperate. And out of options.

I trained with the team that morning. I returned at two o'clock for the afternoon session. Greaves called me out in front of everyone.

'Oi, Irish!' he shouted. 'Fuck off!'

'Excuse me?'

'Go and train over there,' he told me, pointing to an empty field, 'on your own.'

I knew it was all over. It was 7 August 1987. I remember the date because it was my twenty-seventh birthday.

I went home to Caroline and I told her the dream was finished. We had no home. We had no money. I owed the commercial department even more than I owed the bank.

'What are we going we do?' she asked calmly.

I told her that the club had to pay me for a few more weeks and then the money would run out. I said we probably should move back to Ireland.

A few days later, Nevy called. He was getting out of Mansfield. Cambridge United, who were in the Fourth Division, wanted to take him on a month's trial. He knew the gaffer and he'd persuaded him to have a look at me as well. It wasn't much, but I had four weeks to make an impression.

Caroline went home to Dublin with Sinéad. They were going to move back in with her ma, who'd left O'Devaney Gardens and was now living in a house in Dunard Drive, off Blackhorse Avenue. We packed up everything we owned, which wasn't much. We drove the two and a half hours south from Mansfield to Cambridge, taking a detour through Luton, where I dropped Caroline and Sinéad off at the airport.

'It's only for a few weeks,' I told them. 'I'll crack this.'

7

I've made a lot of lifelong friendships out of football. If I've learned one thing from my years in the game, though, it's that allies can become adversaries – and, occasionally, adversaries can become allies.

Chris Turner, the manager of Cambridge United, said he'd heard great things about me from Dave Cusack. I hadn't a clue who he was talking about.

'The player-manager of Doncaster,' he reminded me. 'You chinned him.'

On Paddy's Day, I remembered.

'You know what it's like in the Fourth Division,' he said. 'You have to be able to stand up for yourself. And Dave said you can definitely do that.'

A good feeling came over me. The man hadn't seen me kick a ball, but I felt like I was already halfway towards getting a contract. The club did its pre-season fitness training in an army camp – more playing at soldiers – but I threw myself into it. I remember running up a hill, bollocksed tired, thinking, This it, Rod. This is your last chance.

My big audition was to come in a pre-season friendly against Stevenage. Chris put me in the starting eleven. I was doing OK until I fell under the weight of a hard tackle, put my hand out to break my fall and dislocated my elbow. I remember sitting on the ground, looking at the bone sticking out at an angle, and bursting out laughing, feeling this strange sense of relief that nothing else could go wrong.

I was still laughing while the medical staff wrapped my elbow in sponge and I waited for the ambulance to arrive. It was a hot day and I knocked back about two litres of water. When I got to the hospital, they said they couldn't give me an anaesthetic with all that liquid sloshing around inside me, so the operation to reset my elbow would have to wait until the next day. I spent the next twelve hours in the horrors. The tablets did nothing to dull the pain and I was in the depths of depression thinking about my situation. I'd no club. The house was gone. My wife and daughter were living with my mother-in-law back in Dublin. And we were broke.

My elbow was reset and I left the hospital with my forearm in a cast. I was talking to Caroline on the phone and she burst into tears. Sinéad was sick and she had no money to bring her to the doctor.

In desperation, I did something foolish. The team had another friendly that Saturday. I got my landlord to cut the plaster cast off my arm using a pair of garden clippers and I replaced it with a light bandage. Then I rang Chris and told him that I was fit to play. He was dubious, but I persuaded him to give me forty-five minutes.

It didn't go well. My game was based on physicality – pushing and pulling centre-halves around the place. After five minutes I swung my arm to try to break free of a defender and nearly passed out with the pain. Chris spoke to me after the match. Ordinarily, he said, he would take a chance on me, but he needed someone now – not in six weeks.

It looked like I was going back to Dublin and the uncertainty of life on the building sites. Then Nevy popped up again. He said that Newport County needed someone who could score goals. Nevy had played for them. He'd replaced John Aldridge as the main striker there when Aldridge moved to Oxford United. He said it was a great club, even though they were doing badly both on and off the pitch. They'd just been relegated from the Third Division and were in serious financial trouble. But I was in no position to be choosy. John Lewis, the player-manager, was good friends with Nevy, and he'd agreed to take a look at me. I drove to South Wales that same day.

Lewie and I hit it off straight away. I said nothing to him about my arm, deciding just to wing it. I was given the address of a three-star hotel on a roundabout that was to be my home while the club made up their mind whether they wanted me. I was handed the key to room 401, but when I went in there was already someone there – a six-foot four-inch Northern Irishman who was built like a double wardrobe and was standing in front of me, stark bollock naked.

'Who the fuck are you?' I asked.

'Who the fuck are you?' the words echoed back to me in a strong Belfast accent.

This was how I became formally acquainted with Paul 'Willo' Williams, son of Betty Williams, the peace activist and Nobel Prize winner. Like me, he was a striker. The club had bought him from Preston North End.

'I was told that this was my room,' I said.

'I was told that this was *my* room,' he replied, the two of us eying the double bed – which happened to be the only bed in the room.

'Right,' I said, the sexually repressed man from the Holy Catholic Ireland, 'I'll sleep at that end of the bed on top of the sheet, and you sleep at that end underneath the sheet.'

After that introduction, it really is a miracle that we became the great friends that we remain today. We spent a month in that room, rubbing along like Jack Lemmon and Walter Matthau.

One night Willo had a date and he asked me to make myself scarce just in case it went well.

'It's all right for you,' I reminded him, 'you're already in the first team. I'm on trial. I need to sleep.'

Before I left the room I ordered a prawn sandwich from room service and stuffed the prawns into my pillow case. Willo went on his date, then brought the girl back to the room, while I sat in the hotel bar, drinking Britvic and listening to the piano player slaughtering Billy Joel songs. An hour later Willo arrived down and said his date was over. The girl had run out of the place. 'There's a funny smell in our room,' he said, 'and she thought it was my feet.'

After a few weeks we were thrown out of the hotel because of unpaid bills – the first sign I saw that the club really was in financial trouble. Willo got his own place, while I was moved into digs – a room in the house of yet another little old lady. She was the nosiest person I'd ever met and would sit and listen to my phone calls.

Newport County registered me as a player for one month to see how I got on. I made my debut in the first week of September in a home match against Halifax, who had the former Ireland and Manchester United goalkeeper Paddy 'Chicken' Roche in goal. I scored the only goal of the game. My arm was still in bits, but I got away with it.

After the match Lewie invited me to go for a beer. We got locked and ended up in a nightclub in Newport that was owned by a lad from Sligo. Lewie asked me how much money I wanted to sign and I wrote down my terms on the back of a beermat: £270 per week, the same money I was on at Mansfield. When he went to the chairman, however, he was told that they couldn't afford it. He offered me £200 instead.

That afternoon, while I was in the digs, I had a call from Noel King, who was the assistant manager to Jim McLaughlin at Derry City. They were absolutely flying it, having joined the League of Ireland, and were a full-time professional club.

'We'll pay you £500 a week to come home and play for Derry,' he said.

I was suddenly very excited. It was almost twice as much money as I'd ever been paid to play football.

'Where's the nearest airport to you?' he asked.

'It's either Bristol or Cardiff,' I said.

'Right,' he said, 'I'll get Jim to give you a ring.'

I packed my bags, then I walked down to the club: it was only a couple of hundred yards from my digs. I told Lewie that I'd had an offer of £500 per week from Derry City. Thanks for everything, I told him, but I was going back to Ireland. I went back to the digs and waited for Jim McLaughlin to ring. The call never came.

At five o'clock, Lewie rang with an improved offer. It was nothing like the money that Derry were talking about, he said, but they could stretch to £240 per week plus appearance money. With no other option, I signed a two-year contract to play for Newport County in the English Fourth Division.

I rang Caroline to tell her she was going to be moving to Wales.

I rented a bedsit flat for us in a Georgian house on the Cardiff Road, opposite the Royal Gwent Hospital, from a man who looked like Jeffrey Archer. Along with a tiny bedroom, we had the shared use of a kitchen and bathroom. I promised that it would only be temporary, but Caroline was well used to my promises by that stage.

Things at the club weren't going well. That smell of relegation that I got at Drogheda United – I sensed it again at Newport County. They were heading for the Football Conference and there was nothing that I or anyone else could do about it. When we went on a run of six matches without a win, Lewie got the bullet.

His replacement was Brian Eastick, who didn't think much of me from day one. It didn't help that I was injured when he arrived. I'd suffered a recurrence of the groin trouble I'd had the previous season. 'Every time I see you,' he told me bitterly one day, 'you're on the treatment table.'

It was like Mansfield all over again. The longer I was injured, the more unwanted I felt. The BBC were sending a camera crew to the ground to do a report on the club's troubles. I was told that I wasn't to be on the premises when they arrived. They didn't want them showing footage of injured players hobbling around the place.

Caroline was desperately lonely in Newport, especially after Sinéad started school. I had somewhere to go every day, but Caroline was stuck in our one-room bedsit, all alone. Her only social contact was with a group of Irish Traveller women who used to use the coin laundrette across the road from us. She'd go there to wash our clothes and they'd sit on the machines and chat for hours about home. They invited us to their campsite one night for a few drinks, but I thought it wouldn't be a good look for me – Newport County's injured number nine – to be seen drinking cans around a bonfire.

One morning, Caroline was lying in bed with Sinéad when the door flew open and the landlord stormed into the room. He said he wanted to check something – I can't even remember what it was now – but the intrusiveness of it, of him having a key to our home, allowing him to come and go as he pleased, persuaded us that we needed our own front door.

So even though there were serious doubts about whether the club would be able to honour the second year of my contract, we decided to buy a house in Newport. When we moved in, we didn't own a pot, a pan or a fork. Nevy drove down from Doncaster, where he was now playing, with a cardboard box filled with cups and saucers, plates and cutlery. There was no way we could afford to pay the mortgage on what I was earning, so Caroline took a job in a hotel in Newport.

We lived the way we'd lived in Mansfield — hand to mouth. Willo sometimes arrived at the door and said, 'Come on, I'll make a wee stew for you,' then he'd fill up a pot with meat and vegetables that would provide us with dinner for two or three days.

My football career was going down the pan, but I loved Wales and the Welsh people. I stayed friends with Lewie after his sacking. He took me to his local rugby club in the valleys to watch Wales beat Scotland on TV in the Five Nations Championship. He and his friends introduced me to real ale and taught me how to sing to 'Sosban Fach', and I taught them the words to 'Molly Malone'. It was great fun until an off-duty policeman with a lot of drink on him made some off-colour remarks about the Irish. The late 1980s were some of the bitterest years of the Northern Troubles and it had only been three months since the Remembrance Day bombing in Enniskillen, which had killed eleven people. 'Your lot,' the off-duty policeman called the IRA. His friends told him to give it up, but he kept at it, then we ended up having a brawl outside, rolling around on the bonnet of a Ford Escort. A few weeks later I received a letter from the rugby club to inform me that I'd been 'indefinitely suspended' — the same phrase the Christian Brothers used when they threw me out of O'Connell's.

Newport were rooted to the bottom of the Fourth Division for most of the season. By Easter, it was a mathematical certainty that the club would lose its Football League status. Eastick wanted me off the payroll. He called me into his office and offered me £7,000 to retire. I said I'd a two-year contract with the club and no intention of giving up football. We'd just bought a house in Newport, I told him, and Sinéad had settled into the local school. And there was something else, which I didn't mention to him but which was weighing heavily on my mind: Caroline was pregnant again. By the end of the summer, there was going to be another mouth to feed.

Eastick said something to me then that I've never forgotten: 'As long as you have a hole in your arse, you will never be a professional footballer.'

Then one Thursday, totally out of the blue, Eastick got the sack. I made sure to go and commiserate with him while he was clearing out his desk. 'As long as you have a hole in your arse,' I told him, 'you'll never be a football manager.'

Two days later he was reinstated. My fate was sealed then, if it hadn't been already. As the 1987–88 season trundled to its inevitable end, I wasn't sure if I'd ever play football again. I was nearly twenty-eight years old and finally facing up to the fact that my body was failing me. We had a thirty-year mortgage on a house in Wales and no savings. I had a contract with a club that was about to drop out of the league and might even end up in administration, in which case, I'd been advised, I would become an unsecured creditor.

While I was watching my own sporting dream come to an end, my brother Stephen's career was just starting to take off. He'd won his first seven professional fights in America. At the start of 1988 he wrote me a letter, encouraging me to keep going. He'd read in a newspaper that Cyrille Regis was absolutely flying at Coventry at the age of twenty-nine and he said that being at Newport was 'way above any Mickey Mouse League of Ireland club'. He sent a photograph of himself with Marvin Hagler. 'I could have got more photos of [him] but I did not want to be a nuisance,' he wrote, 'so I just trained and acted like he was just another boxer in the club.' He finished off, 'I will be fighting in Boston Garden on St Patrick's Day so say a prayer everything goes well for me.'

It was actually the day after St Patrick's Day that he was due to fight Sam Storey, the boxer he couldn't beat as an amateur, for the Irish middleweight title. I'd forgotten all about the fight until the phone rang at three o'clock in the morning. I went downstairs to answer it. It was Stephen.

'I beat Sam Storey,' he said. 'I finally figured him out.'

I told him I was delighted for him.

'Rod,' he said, 'I'm going to be the middleweight champion of the world.'

'That's great,' I told him.

I have to admit I didn't believe it. I knew how single-minded he was, but I couldn't get my head around the fact that the little boy I used to send up the stairs to warm the bed for me back in Cabra could be a world champion like Roberto Duran or Muhammad Ali or Sugar Ray Robinson. With my own career in ruins and a second child on the way, it was also just hard to believe in dreams around that time.

Caroline found her second pregnancy very hard going. She swam every day until she developed an ear infection, which couldn't be treated with antibiotics and which caused her to lose her hearing in her left ear. There were days when she was down on her hands and knees, howling with the pain of it.

According to the newspapers, Newport County were going out of business and were unlikely to be in a position to pay me next season. Sooner or later, I was going to need a job. There was a mechanic, a lovely man from Galway named Tom, who looked after the cars for all the players at the club. He listened to Daniel O'Donnell records and had a pet mouse named Jimmy who was given the run of the house. He introduced me to his neighbour, a bricklayer known as Wobbly Bob, who said he could get me some plastering work on a building site in Tiger Bay just outside Cardiff.

I was still under contract to Newport so I had to work under an assumed name. Wally Downes was a midfielder who'd spent part of the season on loan at Newport from Wimbledon. He was a nephew of Terry Downes, the former world middleweight champion, and we clicked with each other because we both loved boxing. Occasionally, we went to the local gym, which was over a pub, to spar each other. I used the name Mick McGuire in the ring, so I decided that would be my building-site name that summer.

Wobbly introduced me to the developer, a Pakistani man with a turban named Syed, who misspelled my name as 'Mick McDwyer' on my payslip. So 'McDwyer' was what everyone called me. I loved being back on a building site. We worked hard and we laughed hard. One time, Wobbly fell into a giant ditch while pushing a wheelbarrow full of bricks, and Syed kept asking, 'Where is Wobbly Bob?' while everyone was doubled-up with laughter.

It was a glorious, hot summer. Ireland had qualified for the

European Championship for the first time and they beat England in Stuttgart thanks to a goal from Ray Houghton. I took a twenty-foot-long slating lath and used it to fly a tricolour over the roof of the building that we were working on. I was summoned to see the foreman.

'McDwyer,' he said, 'do you have any idea what this building is going to be used for?'

'Er, no,' I told him.

'It's going to be a retirement home – for former RAF personnel. So take that fucking flag down.'

Despite not knowing what the future held, Caroline and I were very happy that summer. Every night we took the TV outside and we watched the football while sitting in the back garden, me with plaster under my fingernails again, Caroline with her big bump in front of her and Sinéad, now almost six, chattering away excitedly about the arrival of her new brother or sister. When Ronnie Whelan scored his spectacular goal against the Soviet Union, I ran the length of the garden and, in my excitement, kicked a flagstone in my bare feet, flaking a bone in the process.

Not that it mattered. As expected, Newport County went bust and I was suddenly an unemployed footballer. Lewie was now playing for Swansea City, who were managed by Terry Yorath, and he managed to get me a four-week trial there. Our second baby was due any day. Caroline's ma and her sister Martina came over to be with her because I was making the hundred-mile round trip to Swansea every day, trying to impress. Caroline's due date came and went and they had to go back to Dublin. Thankfully, my cousin Jeffrey arrived to help, and he was there when Caroline went into labour that August.

Niamh was born in the Royal Gwent Hospital, across the road from the bedsit where we once lived. She was a gorgeous-looking baby. While Sinéad had fair skin and blonde hair, Niamh was dark, with deep brown eyes. Strangers in the street would gasp when they saw her coming in her pram. 'Oh my God,' they'd say to Caroline, 'what a beautiful baby.'

She wasn't a crier, which came as a blessed relief after what Sinéad put us through. She didn't need attention, just sat there and smiled, looking pretty. Her sister absolutely adored her and immediately took to mammying her. She even learned how to change her nappy, a skill that I never perfected myself – due to lack of trying, it shames me to say.

I started to fancy my chances of getting a contract at Swansea, especially after Yorath singled me out in front of the rest of squad after training one day.

'That,' he said, pointing to me, 'is what I call a professional footballer.'

And 'professional footballer' is what I wrote in proud capitals under 'father's occupation' when I filled in the form for Niamh's birth certificate. On Sinéad's, I was a plasterer. But then Yorath passed on the opportunity to sign me. At my age, and with my injury history, he decided not to take a chance on me. I was devastated.

There was one more roll of the dice. Cheltenham Town, who played in the Football Conference, were looking for a striker. Cheltenham was about an hour-and-a-half's drive away, across the Severn Bridge, and as far from the big time as it was possible to be. But it was money.

I ended up playing six times for them. And each time I asked myself, What are you doing here? We were living in the south of Wales, away from our families and our friends. Sinéad was six years old and she'd already lived in seven homes in three different countries. It couldn't go on like this. I was a twenty-eight-year-old man with two children who'd fallen through the cracks into the lower leagues. It didn't matter what it said on Niamh's birth certificate. The dream was over.

I said to Caroline, 'It's not worked out. I'm sorry.'

'Don't be sorry,' she said, 'you gave it your best shot.'

We put the house up for sale. Then we packed up everything we owned – which still wasn't much – and we drove to Holyhead to catch the ferry back to Dublin.

It was time for me to grow up.

8

Caroline's ma said there was a man called Brian Kerr at the front door. I thought she'd got the name wrong and I presumed it was Martin Kerr, a big lump of a lad I sort of knew who played centre-half for Drogheda United. But it turned out it *was* Brian. I didn't know the man, but he was the manager of St Patrick's Athletic. He asked if we could talk, so I invited him in. I sat down in one armchair and he sat on the arm of the other, so that he was looking down on me. I wondered later was it a tactic he'd learned from some business management book. He said he'd love to have me at Pat's, but what he was offering was peanuts. There was a lot more to football than money, he said, and he mentioned all the trophies that I'd end up winning under him. I was an unemployed man with a wife and two children, a mortgage and no income. I could do two things. I could plaster and I could score goals. There was no way I was going to do either for nothing. I told Brian no and I'm not sure that he ever forgave me.

Noel King had been back in touch. He was gone from Derry City and had taken over as manager of Shamrock Rovers, who were in a mess at the time. After winning the league four years in a row, they'd played the previous season at an almost empty Tolka Park. The club's owners, the Kilcoyne family, had sold Glenmalure Park in Milltown, the club's home for sixty years, to a property developer. The Rovers supporters had formed a pressure group called KRAM (Keep Rovers at Milltown) which had boycotted Tolka, forcing the club to the point of bankruptcy.

Noel King had been a favourite at Milltown, helping Rovers to two league titles before he went off to play in the French second division. Bringing him back to the club as manager was a huge step towards getting the supporters back onside. The new owners did a deal with Bohemians to share Dalymount Park on a two-year basis while looking for a permanent home. The fans had agreed to lift the boycott.

I met Kinger in the Wimpy restaurant on Dorset Street. The offer was £120 per week plus a job with a contract cleaning company that was owned by John McNamara, one of the club's new owners. I agreed and signed.

We trained three times a week in Rathfarnham on an all-weather hockey pitch belonging to Three Rock Rovers. Kinger was by far the best coach I'd ever played under. He was a million years ahead of his time. After my two miserable years at Mansfield and Newport, I rediscovered my love for football while playing under him.

I made my debut for Rovers against Bohemians at Dalymount Park on the last day of September. I scored in a 3–1 win, beating Ronnie Murphy to the ball to score with a far-post header. It didn't feel at all strange being back at Dalyer wearing the green and white hoops of Bohs' most hated rivals. Bohs hadn't tried to sign me – so I thought, That's their tough luck.

The job with the cleaning company didn't last a day. I reported for duty, as instructed, at seven o'clock in the morning outside Liberty Hall. I was collected in a van and driven with a bunch of madsers to Our Lady of Lourdes Hospital, a specialist rehabilitation unit on Rochestown Avenue in Dun Laoghaire. I thought the job would involve heavy-duty cleaning work, like sandblasting walls and stripping scaffolding, but the gaffer on the job was a strict, matronly woman, who handed me a bucket and sponge and told me to wash the walls of an operating theatre.

I was back in bed in Dunard Drive by ten o'clock. I said to Kinger at training that night: 'A fucking bucket and a sponge? Are you acting the bollocks or what?'

But I loved playing football for Rovers. We had some really good players, including Harry Kenny, Barry Murphy and Ricky McEvoy. I scored eight goals in twenty-two matches, ending the season as the club's top scorer. We finished seventh, just below mid-table. We also reached the semi-final of the FAI Cup. The mood around the club started to become positive again and it was nice to be a part of that. But we all understood that this was a stopgap team and that most of us would be moving on when the season ended. I scored in what I knew would be my last game for the club away to Cork City that April.

One evening in the summer of 1988, not long after we came home from Wales, I was sitting out the back of Walsh's pub in Stoneybatter with Caroline and a mate of mine, Tom Daly, who everyone knew as 'Donkey'. I'd known Donkey since I was a kid, playing football in O'Devaney Gardens. He was a salt-of-the-earth, call-it-as-you-see-it sort who grew up in Arbour Hill Barracks, where his father was a soldier. It was a beautiful August evening, just after I walked off the job in Dun Laoghaire, and I was thinking I might take a bit of time off to concentrate on my football. Then Donkey went and put his foot in it.

'Are you looking for work?' he asked.

'Er, I am,' I said, 'except there's nothing out there, Donkey.'

'I've a start for you in the morning.'

'Seriously?' I said, trying to sound enthusiastic while telling him to shut the fuck up with my eyes. 'Where is it? It's probably too far for me – sure, I've only the pushbike these days.'

'It's right on your doorstep,' he said. 'It's the Phoenix Park Racecourse. Sisk are putting up a big corporate stand there. I'm labouring on the job. But they're looking for people to do drywall and plastering.'

'That's great,' Caroline said. 'You've fallen on your feet again, Rod!'

The next morning I woke up with the head hanging off me and I let the air out of the tyres on my pushbike.

'Sure, it's only up the road,' Caroline said. 'You can walk.'

I arrived on the site half an hour late. The boss men were Mick and Kevin McManus, two brothers from the North.

I said sorry for being late.

'No, you're grand,' Mick, the foreman, insisted. 'Sure, you can start now.'

I spent two months on the job and did everything I could to try to get the sack.

The problem was that Mick liked me. There was one day when I was doing my usual thing, chatting about football while watching the other fellas work, and his brother said, 'Mick, what's he even doing here?'

'Well,' said Mick, 'you know the way a farmer with a herd of cattle might throw a goat in with them for good luck?'

'Aye,' said Kevin.

'Roddy's the fucking goat,' he said.

Much to my annoyance, the job lasted until Christmas. Then, in May of 1989, just as my time at Rovers was coming to an end, I started working as a trainee salesman for the Danish sportswear company Hummel.

Johnny Fallon, a mate of mine who later became the kit man for the FAI, had acquired the franchise to import and supply Hummel gear in Ireland and was working out of a basement office on Mount Street, near the Pepper Canister Church. He took me on as a salesman, although he really wanted me as an investor, because I happened to be sitting on a pile of money. We'd sold the house in Newport for a profit of £30,000 in Irish punts. I wanted to use the money to buy a piece of the Hummel franchise, but Caroline – the brains of the outfit – insisted that it was a deposit for a new house.

Johnny and I worked together for about six weeks. We drove up and down the country, visiting sports shops with a load of sample gear in a leather-look suit bag.

The only problem was that Johnny didn't have a stocking to sell. It was early days for the business and he was still waiting for the franchise documentation to come in. From Kilkenny to Galway and from Carlow to Cork, I was selling gear for fun. Then, a week later, the shops would ring the office in Mount Street wanting to know why they hadn't got it yet.

'Just a moment,' Johnny would say. 'I'm going to put you on to dispatch.'

I was sitting on the other side of his desk.

'Fuck off!' I'd tell him. 'Don't put them on to me.'

He'd hand me the phone anyway and I'd have to listen to the complaint. Then I'd say, 'I'm actually going to put you on to the managing director now,' and I'd hand the phone back across the desk to him.

The job didn't last. Before long, I was back on the sites again. One morning I was on the bike on Blackhorse Avenue, with Sinéad on the crossbar, dropping her to school on the Navan Road, when I spotted a JCB digger on a piece of waste ground. That was how you found building work in Dublin in the 1980s: you cruised around, looking for evidence of activity. Shortly after I spotted the digger, a caravan appeared. I knocked on the door. There were three fellas from Kilkenny living in it.

'Is there any chance of a bit of work?' I said.

'What can you do?' one of them asked.

'I'm a plasterer by trade,' I told him, 'but I can do anything.'

'Come back at three o'clock,' he said, 'and bring your wellington boots.'

I didn't know if he was making a laugh out of me. It was part of the culture on building sites that country fellas took the mickey out of the Dubs. But I went back in the afternoon. They were about to dig the foundations for a housing development. I ended up working with them for the whole summer. They slept in the caravan every night from Monday to Thursday, and then on Friday after work they went home to their families in Kilkenny. When the foundations had been dug, they asked me to stay on and labour for the bricklayers.

Turlough had asked me to play for Dundalk for the 1989–90 season. I got very fit on that site. I remember carrying solid blocks around, three at a time, and feeling like I was conditioning my body ahead of pre-season. Also, I started to take on more responsibility. Because I was living nearby, the Kilkenny fellas gave me a set of keys and a few extra bob to run the site for them at weekends. I'd go in on a Sunday night and stack the bricks to get ahead of the bricklayers.

One morning, a Triumph Stag pulled onto the site and a man got out of it, a big, six-foot five-inch lump of a man with a suntan who looked like a film star. It was Derry McPhillips – the man who was developing the site.

'Are you Roddy Collins?' he said. 'I've seen you play for Rovers four or five times. I saw you playing for Athlone as well back in the day. Didn't you go off to play in England?'

'I did,' I told him, 'but it didn't work out. Now I'm just trying to get a few bob together. We're living with my wife's ma. Trying to get a mortgage.'

'Can you do anything else?'

'Yeah, I'm a plasterer by trade.'

'Is that right? I'll tell you what, when the show house is built, I'm going to let you plaster it and see how you get on.'

We really hit it off. Whenever he was on the site I'd talk to him about football. He was a Manchester United fanatic and I told him about the time I was on trial at Fulham when George Best was there. I plastered the show house, and I put my heart and soul into the job. He was happy enough to give me another four houses.

'Someone like you,' he said, 'shouldn't be working for people. You should have people working for you.'

That was the start of me becoming a plastering contractor and my own boss. Derry sort of took me under his wing. He told me to apply to the tax office for a C2, a certificate of authorization to allow me to operate as a subcontractor. He helped me fill out the paperwork. Then I read the terms and conditions. To qualify, I needed to have £100,000 per year of guaranteed work.

'I've no guaranteed work,' I told him.

'Yes, you do,' he said. 'I've a hundred houses that are going to need plastering.'

He drove me out to Donabate, where there was a large estate under construction and asked me to give him a quote for the job. I said £2,500 per house. He said the job was mine. Suddenly, I was no longer the goat. I was the owner of a plastering firm with a minimum annual turnover of £250,000. Now all I had to do was find the men to do the work.

I started phoning up fellas I'd worked with over the years. I hired the Sullivan brothers, who I served my time with in Smartie Land in Ringsend. There was another group of brothers from Finglas called the Hennessys. They got work. I hired the Keenan brothers from Ardee, who I'd worked with on the Phoenix Park Racecourse. And I hired old friends and family members.

I gave up working the trowel myself and concentrated on being the boss. There were fellas who were naturally contrary and fellas who were upbeat. There were some fellas who were garglers and some fellas who resented the garglers. I was managing situations all the time – people not turning up, people walking off the job, people having fights. And I was good at it.

In May of 1989, Stephen beat a tough nut named Kevin 'Killer' Watts to win the USBA middleweight title. But I didn't properly understand what it meant. Like Stephen, my sister Audrey had moved to America and she was in the Resorts International Casino in Atlantic City to see him become the middleweight champion of America. After the fight, she rang me in a terrible state. In the eleventh round, Watts had caught Stephen with a body shot that dropped him to his hands and knees.

'He was crawling around, looking out into the audience for a familiar face,' she said, 'and there was no one there for him.'

The thought of it killed me. I promised my da in Heaven that, by hook or by crook, I'd make sure that I was in his corner whenever he fought in the future. He was due to defend his title in Boston against another world-ranked middleweight named Tony Thornton that July and I decided that I would be there.

So much had changed for Stephen since I'd seen him last. He was still only twenty-five, but he was a husband and a father now. He'd married Gemma, his childhood sweetheart, and they had a baby daughter named Caoimhe. There was no hint of the superstar athlete about him. He was still working as an electrician on building sites in Boston, living from paycheque to paycheque just like me, then training in the evenings with Pat and Goody Petronelli. He was living in a rented clapboard house that had no air-conditioning.

I got a cheap package deal to Atlantic City: fifty dollars for a return flight, a McDonald's meal voucher and a ten-dollar gaming chip for the Trump Plaza hotel and casino on the Boardwalk.

I didn't appreciate what a big deal my little brother had become until the night of the fight. Stephen was top of the bill – his face staring at me from the fight posters that seemed to be everywhere on the Boardwalk. The Broadway by the Bay Theater in Harrah's Casino was completely sold out and the fight was broadcast live, coast to coast, on HBO.

Tony Thornton – the so-called 'Punching Postman' – was a serious opponent, a hardman with a shaven head who styled himself on Marvin Hagler. I was a nervous wreck in the dressing room beforehand, in and out of the toilet cubicle every sixty seconds until Stephen reminded me that he was fighting and not me.

'You go into that toilet again,' he said, 'and I'm throwing you out.'

I couldn't believe how much he'd improved as a boxer since I'd last seen him fight. I was blown away by his footwork and his hand speed.

The fight went the full twelve-round distance and Stephen got the decision. I jumped into the ring. I'd brought a tricolour with me, the same one I flew over the RAF retirement home in Wales. I put it around his shoulders before he was interviewed on TV. Some of the American reporters asked me about it. I told them that the flag had flown above the GPO during the Easter Rising in 1916 and that the moth holes in it were actually made by British bullets in the course of suppressing the Irish rebellion.

I felt a love and admiration for Stephen that night that I couldn't adequately express. I remember Thornton and his entourage walking into the post-fight press conference wearing matching sparkly tracksuits. Stephen walked in on his own, wearing a white Aran jumper with the sleeves rolled up, looking like he'd just stepped off the set of *Ryan's Daughter*. The coolness of him. And the way he handled the press – with humour and intelligence and full eye contact. I just couldn't believe that this was the quiet, sensitive kid who we thought was destined for the priesthood.

I flew back to Boston ahead of him. I made a big banner out of paper and I wrote on it, 'Welcome Home, Champ!' then I hung it, along with some green, white and orange bunting, over the little wooden veranda at the front of his home.

We spent a few days together. He showed me all of his haunts, driving me around Boston in an enormous white open-top Lincoln that a sponsor had given to him. After a few days, the heat of the Boston summer became too much for me and I was missing Caroline, Sinéad and Niamh, so I decided to go home early. My flight to

Dublin was out of JFK Airport in New York, so Stephen drove me there. We got lost and ended up in a tough black neighbourhood – two white Irishmen and a baby sitting in a snow-white Lincoln. People started walking up to the car, demanding to know what we were doing there. A police car eventually arrived, escorted us out of there and set us on the road to the airport.

For days after I arrived home, all I could talk about was how famous Stephen was in America. Here was a boxer from Cabra, one of our own, who was in line to fight for the WBA world middleweight title, the same belt that had been worn by Sugar Ray Robinson, Jake LaMotta, Carlos Monzón and Marvin Hagler. Yet no one in Ireland seemed to know who he was.

That summer I went on a bit of a campaign to drum up some recognition for him. He and Gemma were coming back to Dublin for a holiday in August and I wanted him to return home to a hero's welcome. I put together a little package of photographs and articles about him, mostly from the *Boston Globe*, *Boxing Monthly* and *The Ring*. Then I walked into the Irish Permanent Building Society on the Cabra Road. The Irish Permanent had sponsored Barry McGuigan's fights, so I thought I was pushing an open door. I told the manager that I wanted to give Stephen the VIP treatment and I asked him could he do anything for us. He told me to wait there, then he came back a few minutes later holding five £20 notes. 'Get yourselves a drink,' he said.

'I didn't come in here scrounging for beer money,' I said. 'I'm talking about sponsorship.'

I walked straight out of there. As Caroline said, I must have been upset if I left him with the five twenties. My next stop was Louis Copeland on Capel Street. I showed everything in the portfolio to one of the older tailors and I asked him if they'd make a suit for him.

He said, 'Tell him to come in to us when he wins a world title.'

I picked up my bits and pieces and I headed for the door.

'Wait,' a voice behind me said.

I turned around. There was a bald man standing there. It was young Louis, whose father I used to see when I was mitching from school.

'Send him in to me,' he said. 'I'll make him a suit fit for a world champion.'

Then I went to Staffords Funeral Home on the Cabra Road and gave them the same story – about the local kid who'd gone to America and was on the verge of becoming the middleweight champion of the world. Would they be prepared to provide a limousine and a driver to collect him and his wife and daughter from the airport and drive them back to my ma's house in Annamoe Terrace? They said it would be their pleasure.

I went to DG Opel a few doors down. The managing director was Michael Fitzsimons, a boxing fanatic who knew all about Stephen. I asked him if he could provide Stephen and Gemma with a car while they were in Dublin. He said he'd be delighted to.

They arrived home in August. I rang big Joe Egan, the former Irish heavyweight champion, who worked in security for Delta Airways. He agreed to bring Stephen, Gemma and Caoimhe from the plane to the arrivals gate without having to queue at passport control.

When they walked through the gate, I was standing there with a sign that said, 'Welcome Home, Champ!'

Turlough wanted me back. And that was all I ever needed to hear. But he insisted on going through the motions as usual.

'There's no money in the game, Rod,' he said.

We were sitting in a little café on Capel Street and he was playing with the sugar sachets.

'Turlough,' I said, 'you asked to meet me, remember.'

'I did,' he agreed.

'Because you want me to play for Dundalk.'

'Only if we can afford you, Rod.'

'Well, Rovers are paying me £140 a week.'

'If that's what they're paying you then maybe you should stay at Rovers.'

I didn't want to play for Rovers. I wanted to play for him. And he knew it.

'Well, what about £120 then?' I asked.

I couldn't believe it. I wasn't on great money to start with and now I was negotiating downwards.

'We couldn't afford to pay that,' he said, 'to a man of – what are you now, Rod?'

'I'm twenty-eight,' I told him.

'Twenty-nine – no?'

'In another few weeks, yeah.'

'Twenty-nine, Rod – and with your injury history.'

'Well, what about £100 then?'

More silence. More fiddling with the sugar packets.

'Look, leave it with me,' he said. 'I'll see what I can do.'

Turlough had worked his magic with Dundalk just as he did with Athlone Town, leading them to the Premier League and FAI Cup double in 1988. He did it without bankrupting the club – and he wasn't going to start splashing the cash for me. He got me my £100 and he made me feel grateful for it.

The season started that August. Stephen was home from America. It might have been our first home game of the season when I arranged for him to walk out onto the pitch at half-time in Oriel Park to show off his USBA belt. I could hear the roar from the dressing room.

Turlough had built a really good squad at Dundalk, and it was one of the best dressing rooms that I was ever in.

I set myself three goals that season. I was going to be the top scorer in the League of Ireland. I was going to win the Player of the Year award. And I was going to win the Premier League. It hadn't occurred to me that I might not be a regular starter. The competition for the front two positions was intense and Paul Newe was banging the goals in that season.

For Turlough, dropping a player was easy, because it was never personal for him. He was able to separate the way he felt about you as a person from the way he felt about you as a player.

But I was young and stupid and I took it to heart. He used to tell people that I was 'impossible to drop', and it wasn't intended as a compliment.

One time, he put me in the reserve team and I didn't bother

showing up. The following Tuesday night I turned up at training and attempted to brazen it out.

'What are you doing here?' Turlough asked.

'I'm training,' I said, 'amn't I?'

'No, you're not,' he told me. 'You're suspended for two weeks and you're fined two weeks' wages.'

'You can fuck off,' I told him.

I went home and I didn't come back for two weeks. When I did, nothing was said. We shook hands and that was the end of it. Typical Turlough. He didn't hold grudges.

He didn't give the money from my fine to the club. It was Barry Kehoe's testimonial year and he bought a bunch of tickets for the big raffle that followed the black-tie dinner and he gave them to me. I thought my luck was suddenly changing, because I won £1,000.

I had other things going on in my life other than football. I was running my own plastering company, employing more than thirty men, working on two or three different jobs. Caroline and I were also in the process of trying to buy a house in Castleknock. We had a lump of money in the bank from selling the Newport house, then Turlough sent me to see his bank manager in Phibsboro, who agreed to lend us the balance we needed on the strength of my contract with Dundalk. We were sure we could cobble together the rest of the money. But then we found ourselves in an auction situation with another buyer, and the price kept going up every week. Suddenly the best offer was £64,500 and there were no more money trees left to shake. I rang Turlough in desperation.

'Who's the estate agent?' he asked.

I told him the name.

'Leave it with me,' he said.

Turlough rang me back and asked me to meet him in the Phoenix Park. He handed me £500 in cash – a loan – and said, 'Pay the deposit tomorrow and the house is yours.'

I don't know who Turlough spoke to, or what he said, but we got the house. We moved in before Christmas and set about turning it into a home.

One day that Christmas there was a knock at the door. I answered it and there was a stout man standing there in slacks and old plimsolls who said his name was Gerry.

'So?' I said – not especially friendly to him.

'I just wanted to tell you,' he said, 'that your brother is going to be fighting for the world title in Boston on the first weekend in February. If you see him, tell him.'

Then he walked down the path, got into his little Fiat and drove off.

Stephen was home for Christmas. He was training in Arbour Hill and I drove up there to see him. When I told him what had happened, he started laughing.

'That was Gerry Callan,' he said.

Gerry wrote about boxing for the *Irish Daily Star* and was the best boxing writer in the business. He usually knew that a fight was going to happen before the boxers themselves were told. But in this case, Stephen had known about it since that morning. Mike McCallum, the WBA world middleweight champion, was due to defend his title against Michael Watson in the New Year. But Watson was injured and Stephen was being drafted in as a replacement. The fight would take place in the Hynes Convention Center in Boston on 3 February 1990.

Christmas came and went. Stephen went back to America to train. I promised him that I'd be there, but Dundalk had a match against Galway United the next day. I didn't want to let Turlough down. There was a flight out of Boston the morning after the fight that arrived in Dublin around midday on Sunday. I rang a helicopter hire company and discovered that for a few hundred quid I could charter a chopper to take me from Dublin to Galway to arrive at Terryland Park an hour before kick-off. I laid out my itinerary to Turlough after training one night.

I realized just how far down the pecking order I'd fallen when he looked me in the eye and said, 'You're not going to need that helicopter, Rod.'

There were so many familiar faces on the flight to Boston. Fellas from Cabra. Fellas from St Saviour's. Fellas from O'Connell's. Fellas from

Walsh's. There was a crew from Stoneybatter, led by an old friend of ours named Paddy Bolton. And a father and son named Jackie and Ski Wade, who never missed one of Stephen's fights.

Most of the Collins family had never been on a transatlantic flight before. A member of the cabin crew offered my uncle Terry a drink and he said he'd like a beer. He asked how much it was and he was told that there was no charge.

'In that case,' he said, 'could I have a little Jameson with that?'

'Yes, of course,' she told him.

By the time we landed at Logan Airport, everyone was banjoed.

Stephen had a secret that week that he kept from almost everyone. He'd badly bruised a rib in training and was in a lot of pain. But he didn't want anyone to know. It wasn't for nothing that McCallum was nicknamed 'The Bodysnatcher'. He was one of the most fearsome body punchers in boxing.

On the night of the fight the atmosphere was electric. Everyone kept saying how proud my da would have been if he'd lived to see this day. But I always said that if my da hadn't died, Stephen would never have become a professional boxer, because he wouldn't have let him leave a good job in Guinness.

Caroline and I had ringside seats, right next to Stephen's corner. Someone pointed out the famous Boston mobster Whitey Bulger to me – he was sitting with his crew a few feet away.

Stephen fought a completely different fight to the one he'd fought against Thornton. He started cautiously and it was clear that he was worried about his rib. At the end of the fifth I could hear him tell Pat and Goody that he was throwing the game plan out the window and he was going after McCallum. And for the rest of the fight, that's what he did. It turned into an all-out slugfest. The crowd loved it. Stephen kept coming forward, throwing punches, but unfortunately it wasn't enough. For years afterwards, McCallum said that Stephen was the toughest opponent he ever fought.

When the scores of the judges were announced, no one had any complaints, least of all Stephen. He had lost fair and square to one of the best pound-for-pound boxers in the world. But I was heartbroken for him. In the dressing room afterwards, he was sitting there, hunched over, with a towel over his head, just sobbing. I was standing there with Caroline, my ma and Gemma, none of us knowing what to say to comfort him. He kept apologizing, saying, 'I'm sorry, Ma. I'm sorry, Gemma. I let you all down,' and it was too much for me to see my little brother in that kind of distress. I went into the toilet cubicle, sat down on the jacks and cried my eyes out.

The next day we all went shopping together – me and Caroline, Stephen and Gemma, and my ma. Stephen had been to the hospital to have his face stitched. He was holding little Caoimhe in his arms. She was kissing him and hugging him to try to make him better and I could see that he was sore from the punches he'd taken. It was the morning after his world had been torn asunder and there he was, doing the simple, human things that I'd never done as a father – changing his daughter's nappy and giving her a bottle. And all I could do was watch him, feeling like a fraud, thinking that I wasn't half the man that he'd turned out to be.

'Are you OK?' I asked him.

'Fine,' he said, just like that. 'It's one fight.'

'So what happens now?'

'Nothing's changed, Rod. I'm going to be a world champion one day.'

9

It was the summer of 1990 – the summer of Italia '90. Ireland had qualified for their first World Cup. Business was good. For the first time in my life I had real money in my pocket. A builder I was working for at the time named Martin Dunne introduced me to a crew of fellas he was going to Italy with. Some of them were former Dublin football legends, like Paddy Cullen, Jimmy Keaveney, Ray Moran, Bobby Doyle and Seán Doherty. Then there was Finbarr Crowley, the solicitor, John Drumgoole from St Vincent's GAA club and John Holmes, a trade-union man who worked for B&I ferries. I tagged along with them. They were a brilliant bunch of blokes.

Ireland played the Netherlands in their final group game in Palermo on the island of Sicily. The day before the match, I was walking along this stunning beach in Mondello with all the former Dublin boys and we were spotted by an Irish photographer, who wanted to take our picture. He got a few bikini-clad Italian women to stand with us and shout 'Ireland!' at the count of three.

We went on the lash that night. The next day I got up with a hangover I'll never forget. I rang Caroline. At that time she was working in Guinness, in the main office.

'Ah, Caroline,' I said, 'I'm in a heap, I am. I'm after been vomiting and everything. I was thinking I might need an injection or something.'

'Is that right, Rod?' she said. 'Well, you looked all right to me on the front page of the *Irish Press* this morning.'

Just after I came home from the World Cup I got a message that Mick Leech was looking to talk to me. He'd just taken over as the manager of Athlone Town. I rang him from a phone box on Dawson Street and he asked me would I be interested in coming back to St Mel's

Park. I told him I'd a two-year contract with Dundalk and I didn't want to let Turlough down.

'You're grand,' he said. 'It was Turlough who gave me your number.'

I rang Turlough. I was raging with him.

'What the fuck are you doing,' I said, 'trying to offload me to Athlone?'

'I was thinking of you,' he said. 'Rod, I can't guarantee you first-team football.'

I didn't care. I wanted to stay. Because it was Turlough. Because I thought I could play my way into his plans. And also because there was something building at Dundalk. You could sense it. Then Turlough made a decision that nobody could quite believe. He sold Paul Newe, our leading goal-scorer, to Shelbourne. The fans were furious – even more so after our first match of the season. Shels beat us 5–1 at Oriel Park and Newey scored four of the goals. I remember Turlough being pushed and jostled as we were leaving the ground. Then someone spat on his shoulder. It was horrendous. It was like watching someone spit at my da.

It turned out that Turlough knew what he was doing. He'd signed Peter Hanrahan, who would finish the season as top scorer in the league and Player of the Year. After Newey left, I thought I might get more games, but Turlough moved Terry Eviston up front to part-ner Peter and they scored thirty goals between them. I only played nine games that season, most of them coming on as a second-half substitute.

At the start of October we played Sligo Rovers at The Show-grounds. We travelled to the match by train, as we always did. I ran into my brother Mick at Connolly Station. Mick was the most charming, big-hearted, happy-go-lucky man in the world. The kind of fella who, if you met him in the morning, you'd have a smile on your face for the rest of the day.

'Where are you heading?' I asked him.

'Where do you think I'm heading?' he said. 'I'm going to Sligo to support you.'

We lost the match and Turlough was fuming with us. We had our own carriage on the train back to Dublin and no one was talking. It was like someone had died. I was eating a mixed grill and staring out the window, when all of a sudden I heard someone say, 'Cheer up, lads – it's only a game!'

I looked up. It was Mick. He was locked. I was thinking, Fuck's sake, Mick, this is all I need. With my Cabra eye I could see Turlough staring at me with a face like thunder. Everyone just looked out the window and pretended they couldn't hear him.

'Do you know what this team's problem is?' Mick said. 'Yous have to be better at heddying the ball.'

After losing to Sligo we went on an unbeaten run that lasted until after Christmas. Peter and Terry were banging in the goals, but the success of that Dundalk team was down to the meanness of our goal-keeper and our back four. Alan O'Neill was one of the best keepers I ever saw. Ronnie Murphy and James Coll were the centre-halves. Ronnie was an absolute Rolls-Royce of a player, brilliant on the ball, whereas James couldn't trap a bag of cement. But I played against him at various times and he let nothing past him – in the air or on the ground. The full-backs were Dave Mackey, who was hard as nails, and Martin Lawlor, a club stalwart and an absolute leader of men. A goal against us was treated like a personal affront to them. After letting in five in the first game of the season, they conceded only twelve over the course of the next thirty-two league games. During the run-in, Alan kept ten clean sheets in eleven matches.

There was a togetherness about that group of players that you might experience once or twice in your career if you're lucky. Everyone worked hard. Then Sunday night was party night. After a game, most of us went to Rumours to let off steam.

Sometimes Turlough would offer me a lift home after a match. He had no idea that I drank – I'd made out to him that I lived like a monk. He'd drop me back to Castleknock and we'd sit in his car in the driveway, talking about the match we'd just played. Things we did well. Things we could have done better. I'd be thinking about the boys, having the time of their lives in town. Turlough could sit there all night talking about football, so I'd yawn and tell him I needed to get some sleep, then as soon as he turned the corner, I'd run into the house, throw on a splash of aftershave and get a taxi into town.

After Christmas, we only lost once. That was in the first round of the FAI Cup against non-league Ashtown Villa, who were managed by Tony O'Connell, Turlough's boss at Jodi. I played that day and missed two absolute sitters. We just couldn't get the ball in the net.

But we were on an incredible run of form in the league. So too were Cork City. We were neck and neck for the whole year. It all came down to the last game of the season – which was against Cork in Turner's Cross. We had to avoid defeat to win the league.

We travelled to Cork on the train. There was a problem on the line and we got delayed. Turlough told us to change into our gear, then he gave us our team talk while we were sitting on the train. The bus met us at the station and took us straight to Turner's Cross, where the Cork players looked fully rested, having spent the night in a hotel.

I watched the match, as I watched most of that 1990–91 season, from the bench. The pitch was bone-hard. It was 0–0 after an hour. I was walking up and down the line, begging Turlough to throw me on, but he wouldn't. Then, in the seventy-third minute, Tom McNulty scored for us. It was one of the scruffiest goals I've ever seen. It bobbled over the line like it was on a bumpy beach.

The final whistle blew. But I experienced no joy. I'd played no real part in it and I felt like a fraud collecting my winner's medal along with the rest of the team. As soon as Martin Lawlor lifted the trophy, I went back to the dressing room. I couldn't face the lap of honour. I was taking a shower when Turlough walked in. He said, 'Get out there and celebrate with the boys.'

I said, 'Fuck you, Turlough,' like the pup that I was, 'you wouldn't give me a fucking game.'

We got the train home that night. All the fellas were still in their full kit. When we arrived at Heuston, I went with Terry Eviston and a few of the others to a pub on Parkgate Street, where we had an unforgettable night of drinking and singing and telling stories. I'd a medal in my pocket, but it meant absolutely nothing to me. Years later I met a fella whose kid was a fanatical Dundalk supporter. He asked me if he could borrow the medal to show it to the young lad. I gave it to him and never bothered asking for it back. But the memory of being around that group of footballers – winners, every single one of them – is something I will cherish for ever.

I had more work than I knew what to do with in those years. The economy was emerging from nearly a decade of recession and suddenly there was building going on everywhere. I was pricing two or three new jobs every week and I'd dozens of men on the payroll. I hired everyone and anyone. Fellas who went to school with me. Fellas who played football with me. Fellas who drank with me. Brothers, cousins and long-lost friends. One or two fellas I used to know who were just out of Portlaoise Prison – they got jobs.

It was easy – maybe too easy – to find labourers. The biggest difficulty was in finding skilled men. I got the contract to do a job in Temple Street Hospital. I was short a plasterer and I knew I was going to struggle to bring the job in on schedule. I was driving past Hanlon's Corner one morning when I spotted a fella standing at a bus stop with a plastering bag and a mixing wheel. I pulled over the van and I wound down the window.

'You Tommy's mate?' he asked.

'Yeah, that's right,' I told him. 'Hop in there.'

He got into the van. His name was Mick. He was a giant of a lad from Achill Island.

'So where are we going?' he asked.

'Temple Street Hospital,' I told him. 'Did, er, Tommy tell you the rate? It's a oner.'

A oner was £100 per day.

'A oner?' he said. 'I wouldn't take my tools out of my bag for that. It's £120 a day. Tommy knows that.'

'Fair enough,' I said, '£120 a day, then.'

The lad was worth twice that. He turned out to be the Leonardo da Vinci of plasterers. And he was a fast worker as well. Every morning after that I picked him up at the bus stop at Hanlon's Corner. He kept asking me, 'Where's Tommy, by the way?'

'I'm going to be honest with you,' I eventually told him, 'I haven't a fucking clue who Tommy is. All I know is that whoever was supposed to pick you up that morning didn't get there quick enough. But you've a job with me for as long as you want one.'

He broke his bollocks laughing. He stayed with me for about two years after that.

We plastered walls all over Dublin in those years. We did Liberty Hall. We did IBM in Ballycoolin. We did a home for asylum seekers in Mountjoy Square. We did the Rock Garden in Temple Bar for Paddy Oman, a well-known businessman who'd transferred his overseas removal and storage business to East Wall and was having the premises converted into a pub and music venue. The builder was Tom Wallace of TP Wallace Construction and I was a subcontractor working for him. I was under pressure to get the job finished by the end of the weekend, but I couldn't get anyone to work on the Sunday. So I went in on my own at eight o'clock in the morning and I worked all day, then right the way through the night, plastering in the dark, with a giant searchlight trained on the wall. It was eerily quiet, but then I started to become aware of this low but persistent murmuring sound coming from the basement. By four o'clock in the morning I'd convinced myself that the building was haunted. Then I heard a voice say, 'Are you all right?' and I let out a scream like I was in a horror movie. It was Paddy Oman himself. He was out late and he was showing a few people around the building.

I got the job finished on time. Tom Wallace must have been impressed because he started to throw more and more jobs my way, all prestigious work in and around the Grafton Street area. I wasn't on rainy, rat-infested building sites any more. This was Switzer's and The Westbury Hotel. Unfortunately, not all of the fellas who worked for me were onboard with my efforts to take the business upmarket. I had three or four jobs on the go at the same time and my working day was like a plate-spinning act. I'd splashed out on a pager in case anyone needed to contact me in a hurry. Tom messaged me early one morning and told me to ring him.

'One of your men,' he said, 'is walking around Switzer's in his underpants.'

Before I even got there I knew who it was going to be: Donkey Daly, my childhood friend, was my loyal lieutenant throughout that time. He was part of a crew who were fitting a fireproof ceiling in a sectioned-off area of the department store, but they were working in full view of the shop's customers. It was a hot summer's day. I walked in and there was Donkey, the sweat beating out of him, strolling around in his boxer shorts with his big belly hanging over the waistband like an untrimmed pie crust.

'The fuck are you at?' I said, pulling him to one side. 'It's fucking Grafton Street, Donkey. You can't wander around a shop like this in your jocks.'

'It's roasting, Rod. I'm sweating here.'

'So are the customers looking at you. Put your fucking clothes on.'

That was Donkey. He was one of the smartest people I've ever known – but there were no frills to him. In football terms, he was route one. But he also had a twenty-four-carat heart. I remember one Friday afternoon, when times were tight, I was paying everyone and a labourer named Johnny started complaining to me that his wage packet was light. I had to remind him that he owed me money because I'd subbed him twice that week.

'Yeah,' he said, showing me the inside of the envelope, 'but you're only after leaving me with two hundred quid. I'm going home with a man's flute and a boy's wages.'

'You think that's bad?' I said to him. 'I'm going home to Caroline and my two children with a fucking oner, Johnny – that's after a week's work.'

It was a point of principle for me to make sure that everyone on the job got paid before I did, even if it meant that I didn't get paid at all. I dropped Donkey home that evening. As he was getting out of the van, he pressed something into my hand.

'What's this?' I asked.

'It's half my wages,' he said.

I said no to him, but I never, ever forgot it.

Stephen had grown unhappy in America. Just before Christmas in 1990 he had moved back to Ireland and signed a new management deal with Barney Eastwood, who'd guided the careers of world champions like Barry McGuigan and Dave McAuley. He spent his weekdays living in digs in a guesthouse in Bangor, Co. Down, while training in Barney's famous gym above the bookmakers on Castle Street in Belfast.

Barney was trying to bring about a rematch with Mike McCallum, but that autumn the news broke that McCallum was planning to fight the IBF world middleweight champion, James Toney, instead. The WBA stripped him of its belt. Stephen was the number two contender. The number one was Reggie Johnson, from Houston, Texas. Behind the scenes, a deal was being done to put them in a ring together in New Jersey in the spring of 1992.

In the meantime, Stephen wanted a tune-up fight and he wanted it to happen at the National Stadium in Dublin, where he had loved fighting as an amateur. Barney flew over Danny Morgan, a Minnesotan journeyman of Irish heritage who'd been around for the same length of time as Stephen but who'd had twice as many fights. Danny was a decent boxer, but he wasn't in Stephen's class.

As a natural super-middleweight, it was no surprise when he weighed in two pounds over the middleweight limit. He was told to go away and shed the excess timber or the fight was off. Someone took him in a taxi to the Olympus Gym on Capel Street, where the owner, Tommy Donnelly, looked after him, sending him into the steam room to skip rope until he lost the weight. From what I heard, it was a miracle that poor Danny wasn't washed down the plughole.

Stephen gave him an unmerciful beating. The fight lasted three rounds before the referee stepped between them.

When the stadium had emptied out and we were standing around, still celebrating Stephen's success, Danny emerged from his dressing room, all on his own, his face absolutely battered. He walked down the corridor towards an exit that I knew was locked. I ran after him.

'You won't get out that way,' I said.

I led him to the proper exit, then watched him step out onto the South Circular Road, his breath fogging in front of him in the cold December air.

I remember thinking how horribly cruel sport can be for the loser. It really upset me. Because, looking at Danny Morgan, I saw a little bit of me.

I did a stupid thing that year. I signed for Sligo Rovers. I knew it was a mistake before I'd even done it. Dermot Keely was the manager. I liked him a lot. A hardman and a man of the road like me. I met him in the Swiss Cottage pub on the Santry Road and he told me what I could do for him.

'I need someone who'll put himself about,' he said. 'Break a few noses and score a few goals.'

Inside, I was thinking, Is that all you think I'm good for?

'How much are you looking for?' he asked.

'I'm worth a oner,' I said, a little bit of me hoping that he'd say no chance.

'I'll do better than that,' he said. 'I'll give you £120 per week and a £1,500 signing-on fee.'

No one else was banging on the door looking for me, so I said yes.

'Will you have a pint?' Dermot asked.

'I'll have a Britvic orange,' I told him.

'No, you won't,' he insisted, 'you'll have a fucking pint.'

'Dermot,' I said, 'the only time I ever drink is the night of a match.'

Even at thirty-one, I still had ambitions in the game.

Most of the players were from Dublin. We trained on a football pitch next to the Central Mental Hospital in Dundrum, in the shadow of its twenty-foot-high perimeter wall. Sligo finished fifth in the league the previous season, but I didn't sense any great desire in them to push on from that. I liked the fellas, but very early on I could see there were a few garglers in the team.

We went to Belfast to play a pre-season friendly against Clifton-ville and I got a hairline fracture at the bottom of my shin. I was brought to the Mater Hospital on the Crumlin Road. I was three or four hours in casualty and I got talking to two fellas in their forties who'd been in a fight and were getting their faces stitched.

When I was leaving the hospital, I called a black cab and the two boys asked if they could share it. I told them I was going to the

Lansdowne Hotel on the Antrim Road and they said that was good for them. But when they got in, they changed their minds and gave the driver an address. They were chatting away to me like they were my pals. I was looking out the window, noticing the loyalist murals and the kerbstones painted red, white and blue. They told the driver to pull up next to a piece of waste ground, where a hundred or so people were sitting around a bonfire, drinking cans of beer and wine straight from the bottle. It was 10 August 1991 and they were having a party to mark the twentieth anniversary of internment.

'Come and have a wee drink with us,' one of them said. They spent a couple of minutes trying to coax me out of the car.

'Lads, I'm grand,' I told them, because I suddenly felt very, very far away from Cabra.

They got out of the taxi. As the driver pulled away he caught my eye in the rear-view mirror. He said, 'Do you know where you are, son? You're in Tiger's Bay. And if you'd got out of this car, you'd have been filled in.'

I didn't need him to explain what that meant.

My leg healed and I played a handful of games for Sligo. I knew I didn't want to be there. There was no one in the dressing I didn't like, but they had a 'win, draw or lose – straight on the booze' mentality that I hated. The goalkeeper was an American lad called Nick Brujos. Nick wasn't a drinker, but he played the guitar and it came out on the train whether we'd had a good or bad result. Then the sing-song would start.

I rang Dermot and offered to repay the £1,500 signing-on fee. He agreed to let me go.

The next thing, I had a call out of the blue from Turlough.

'Tony O'Connell wants to talk to you,' he said.

I didn't know Tony, except as a Bohemians legend and Turlough's boss at Jodi. He was good friends with Harry Corry, the Belfast businessman who owned a home-decor empire. It was through him that Tony had become involved in Crusaders FC, an Irish League team who were based in North Belfast. I rang him up.

'Howiya, son?' he said – he always called me 'son'. 'How would you fancy playing up the North?'

I said I didn't know. I had a wife and two children, it was one of the bitterest periods of the Troubles, and my brush with death that night in Tiger's Bay wasn't far from my mind.

'Just come up and watch a game,' he said.

He drove me up to Belfast in his S-Class Merc. Crusaders played in Seaview, a small ground on the Shore Road, a predominantly Protestant area one mile north of Belfast city centre and not far from the scene of the bonfire where I might have lost my life. They were playing a match that day in front of a crowd of a few hundred. The football wasn't great. Martin Murray, who'd played for Ashtown Villa when they dumped Dundalk out of the FAI Cup, was in midfield for Crusaders. He was thirty-three years of age and running the show.

The team was managed by former Luton Town player Roy Walker, but it was really Tony who called the shots, signing players from the Republic and picking the team.

'It's Saturday football,' Tony said. 'A hundred pound a week in your hand. And I'll give you a signing-on fee.'

He took me into the dressing room. I met Kirk Hunter, the legendary Crusaders midfield hardman, a proud loyalist who was born, bred and buttered on the Shankill Road. He'd never been across the Irish border and rarely been outside Belfast except to play football. He was covered in tattoos and his leg was in a cast. He picked his way over to me on crutches.

'What about you, big man?' he said. 'Will you have a cup of tea?'

He brought me around and introduced me to the rest of the players. They made me feel so welcome. I knew in that moment that this was where I was meant to be.

Soon I was banging in the goals and enjoying football like I used to when I was a kid. The club had a hard rump of loyalist supporters who took a shine to me straight away. It had been a long time since I'd heard a football crowd sing my name. They sang: 'Rod the Prod! Rod the Prod! Rod the Prod!'

I was playing football with a smile on my face again. All I could think was that I should have come here years ago.

10

There were four teams in Belfast. Linfield and Cliftonville were famous for the bitter political and religious differences between their supporters. Then there was Glentoran, with their proud history of glory nights in Europe. And then there was Crusaders – very much the badly dressed, snot-nosed kid brother of the four, who happened to be second from bottom when I arrived.

The Shore Road, where we played our home matches, was the scene of many Troubles-related murders. The UVF were active in the area. No one needed to sit me down to explain the rules. When you came 'down the Dublin Road', as they insisted on calling it, you played your football and you kept your mouth firmly shut.

At the start, the only Dublin accents in the dressing room belonged to me and Martin Murray. Then Derek Carroll arrived from Galway United, followed by Robbie Lawlor from Bohs. During the week the Dublin players trained with Ashtown Villa in the Belvedere Sports Ground on the Navan Road. On Saturday mornings, Tony drove us to Belfast for the match and back home again after the final whistle.

The Crusaders supporters appreciated us for coming across the border to play, especially given the sectarian abuse we faced in a lot of grounds. As the focal point of the Crusaders attack, I took the worst of it. Surprisingly, Windsor Park was never a problem. Linfield was cosmopolitan compared with Portadown, where the supporters would spit at you if you dared to take a throw-in. I remember one Portadown player giving me dog's abuse, calling me a 'Fenian fucking scumbag' for about an hour until I said to him, 'Do you even know what a Fenian is, you fucking dope?' and I gave him a slap in the head.

Our nickname was 'The Hatchetmen', because the club crest once had an axe on it before it was replaced by a Crusader with a sword.

We started playing up to the name during my three years at the club, introducing a bit of physicality into our game, which – along with my goals – helped to lift us out of the bottom three and into the top half of the table during that 1991–92 season.

We had some decent players, but the standard of football in the Irish League was lower than it was in the League of Ireland. From the day I arrived, I couldn't stop scoring goals. I'd be doing my warm-up, looking at the opposition, and I'd be thinking, I'm definitely going to score today.

Kirk Hunter played in the centre of midfield for us and he was the hardest man I ever saw on a football pitch. But he could also play with both feet and no one ever beat him in the air. We hit it off from the moment we met. The only thing we never discussed was politics. He didn't talk to me about growing up on the Shankill Road as a proud Orangeman and I didn't talk to him about marching in support of the IRA hunger strikers back in Cabra. Everything else was on the table.

We finished sixth in the league that season, which was great considering where we were when I arrived. We also beat Glenavon 2–1 in the final of the County Antrim Shield, a knockout competition for Irish League and non-league teams from East Ulster. I probably didn't enjoy the moment as much as I should have. Football in the North had a load of competitions – 'a trophy for everyone in the audience', I used to call it. What I didn't appreciate was that it was the only medal I ever felt I truly won as a player.

But what was more important about that first season was the bond that developed between us as a group of men. When someone was going through a hard time in their lives, everyone rallied around. Everyone knew the name of everyone else's wife, girlfriend or children. If someone in your family was sick, they asked after them by name. Flowers would be sent to the house. I'd always been a selfish bastard in the past. If we lost 2–1, but I scored a goal, I didn't give a fiddler's, because I'd done my job. It was me, me, me. With Crusaders, it was us.

After one home match, early in the 1992–93 season, I got into the big communal bath with a bottle of Budweiser and I started singing

'The Wonder of You'. I think I was listening to a lot of Elvis Presley around that time. The rest of the team joined in. It became the song we sang in the bath after every match and the fans adopted it as an anthem.

We went twenty-six matches unbeaten that season – from push-overs to title contenders in the space of a year. I loved pulling on that jersey, so much so that Tony discovered something that Turlough may have warned him about. I was undroppable.

One morning, we were in Tony's car, heading north for a match. He'd only driven as far as the Bottom of the Hill pub in Finglas when he broke the news that he was giving me a rest that day.

'A rest?' I said. 'I don't need a rest. I slept great last night.'

'I thought you looked tired in training the other night,' he said. 'You're on the bench today.'

I told him to pull over. I threw open the door, got out, then slammed it shut.

'You're a fucking lunatic,' he shouted at me.

I kicked his Mercedes S-Class, putting a dent in the door. Fuck! I thought. That's going to be about two grand's worth of panel work. A day or two later Tony and I shook hands and agreed to put it behind us. He never mentioned the door.

The next time he dropped me, for a match against Carrick Rangers, he waited until we were across the border to tell me. We were sitting in the Road Chef Diner just outside Newry. I was eating a plate of scrambled eggs and beans when he said, 'I'm playing big Johnner up front.'

Big Johnner was John Cleary, who was sitting across the table from me, eating his breakfast. He was another Dublin lad that Tony had brought in that year. He'd played for Turlough as a centre-forward for Dundalk, but he was thirty-five now and Tony had signed him as a centre-half.

'I just want to see how he does up front,' he tried to explain, 'in case you ever get injured.'

'Fuck that,' I said, throwing down my knife and fork.

I stormed out. It was lashing rain. I'd no coat on me and no money. I was walking on the hard shoulder of the A1 in the direction of the border, thinking, 'Please come after me, Tony!'

Thankfully, he did. I came on with fifteen minutes to go. I scored the winner and I ran straight to Tony to celebrate.

Linfield were the best team in the country but we were right on their tails. We beat them 1–0 at home just as the title race was heating up. I'd annoyed a section of their supporters before some cup final or other by bending down to tie my lace during 'God Save the Queen'. Kirk and the others understood. I said to them, 'Would you sing along to "Amhrán na bhFiann" in Dublin?' But the Linfield fans hadn't forgiven me when we met in the league. I was suspended for the match but they abused me from the first whistle to the last. When the match was nearly over, I walked around the pitch to get to the dressing room ahead of the other players. It meant passing the railway end, where the diehard Linfield fans were standing. There was one who had his face pressed against the wire fence: it reminded me of round steak going through the mincer when I worked in the butchers back in Cabra. He was frothing at the mouth, screaming, 'You fucking Free State fucking scumbag fucking Taig fucking fucker. You're going to fucking get it.'

'Yeah, fuck you,' I told him, which aggravated him even more.

Our goalkeeper, Kevin McKeown, pulled off an incredible save right at the end. I was distracted. The next thing, I got a punch in the side of the head, an absolute cracker. I turned around. The lad whose face was pressed against the wire was now standing in front of me, with no fence between us. He wasn't what I imagined a loyalist would look like. He was a big, red-headed fella who looked like he'd just stepped off a fishing boat in Killybegs.

I made a run at him and shoved him back in the crowd. He grabbed a hold of me and took me with him. The RUC weighed in there and dragged me out – the only reason I'm still here today.

We beat Linfield at our place but we lost 1–0 to them at theirs, and they pipped us to the title on goal difference.

People in football talk about the narrow margins. You couldn't have got a cigarette paper between us. To lose out like that at the end of a long, hard season was as cruel a blow as football ever dealt me.

★

The venue for Stephen's second crack at the WBA world middle-weight title was the Brendan Byrne Arena, in the shadow of Giants Stadium, five miles across the Hudson River from Manhattan. His opponent, Reggie Johnson, was a tough southpaw with a fast, trombone-action jab. Stephen had watched tapes of him and wasn't worried about his power. The question was, could he outbox him?

Again, the extended Collins family decamped to America, along with old friends, workmates and neighbours from Cabra and Stoney-batter, filling fifty or sixty rooms in the Meadowlands Hilton. The fight was promoted by Murad Muhammad, who had once served as Muhammad Ali's personal minder and had close ties to Don King. We were sitting around the hotel the night before the fight when Ali shuffled into the lobby. My da's all-time hero was in town to watch my little brother fight. It didn't feel real. Parkinson's syndrome had silenced the voice that my da loved hearing, the voice that screamed, 'I shook up the world!' but the man still radiated charisma and a sort of quiet dignity. I walked up to him and I blurted out that Stephen Collins was my brother and that my da loved him and that we used to listen to his fights together on the radio in the middle of the night in our tiny house in Cabra. He looked at me and stuck his top teeth out over his bottom lip. Then he produced a handkerchief. He screwed it up into his fist, then showed me his hands and it was gone.

It's a well-known saying in boxing that styles make fights, in which case it was never going to be a classic. Stephen just couldn't get to grips with Johnson's 'lefty' style. They tripped over each other's feet. They banged heads. There was very little by way of boxing. Johnson kept Stephen on the end of his long left jab. Stephen got through it a few times and landed some hard punches, but not enough of them to persuade you that he was comfortably racking up rounds. Then Stephen was deducted a point for hitting below the belt and I knew that in a close fight that might be the only thing that separated them.

After twelve rounds, it was announced that there was a split decision. I hoped for the best but feared the worst. One judge gave the fight to Stephen, but two gave the fight to Johnson.

Stephen thought he was robbed, but he put on a smile when he walked into the post-fight press conference. Don King was sitting next to Johnson at the top table, holding court, making it all about him. As Stephen walked behind him to take his seat, he said, 'All right, Don?' and he mussed King's famous troll-like hair with his hand. Everyone gasped. No one touched Don King's hair. My brother had more nerve than anyone I knew.

He took the loss on the chin, but I was worried about him. Where did he go now? He was about to turn twenty-eight. He'd fought for the world title twice in two years and come up short both times. Then a new opportunity presented itself. Barney Eastwood managed to get him a crack at the European middleweight title. The holder was Sumbu Kalambay, a Congolese-born Italian and a former world champion who'd beaten a lot of big names in his career. The good news was that he was now thirty-six and considered by many to be on his last legs. The bad news was that the fight was going to be in Italy, where – as they say in the business – you have to knock the hometown fighter out twice just to get a draw.

The fight took place in Verbania, a small but stunning town in the north of Italy, on the shore of Lake Maggiore. It was 22 October 1992, six months to the day since Stephen lost to Reggie Johnson, but this represented a chance – quite possibly his last chance – to become a contender again.

I was in the corner that night with Barney, John Breen, who was Stephen's trainer in Belfast, and Paddy Byrne, whose job it was to look after any cuts. My job was to keep an eye on the time and let Stephen know how long was left in each round.

There was a series of disasters in the corner that night. Somehow, between us, we forgot to bring water for Stephen to drink between rounds. So Paddy Byrne asked a journalist to run to the little tuckshop at the top of the steeply banked arena to buy some. When I opened the bottle, I realized that the water was fizzy. In all the confusion, I forgot to set the stopwatch and I had to guess how long was gone in one round.

'Minute to go, Stephen!' I shouted, urging him to up the pace – even though there was at least two minutes left.

Stephen came back to the corner, saying, 'That was a long round.'

The fight went the full twelve rounds. To this day, I still believe that Stephen did enough to win it. The scores were read out in Italian, so none of us knew who'd won until we heard the cheering of the home crowd. Even allowing for everything I knew about boxing, I couldn't believe it when the referee lifted Kalambay's hand.

Stephen was furious with Barney. He wanted him to lodge an official protest that might at least lead to a rematch in Dublin.

'Go out and earn your fucking money,' he roared at him.

Stephen's face was busted up. I went with him and Gemma in a taxi to a hospital just outside Milan to get his cuts stitched. Then we went back to the hotel in Verbania and we drowned our sorrows in the hotel bar until the following morning. I remember, at one point, me and Stephen were sitting on two low stools, performing that scene from *On the Waterfront* where Marlon Brando as Terry Malloy blames his older brother Charlie for destroying his boxing career: 'You don't understand. I coulda had class. I coulda been a contendah.'

I honestly couldn't see a way back for Stephen – not after losing three major title fights in less than three years. I thought he might come home and work on the building sites with me. I knew he hadn't made the kind of money he deserved from boxing, but he was a qualified electrician and I figured that me, him and Paschal might even set up a building company together.

We all flew back to Ireland the day after the fight. Stephen and Gemma were on an earlier flight than me. I remember sitting on my own in this little rinky-dink fast-food restaurant in the airport, eating a hamburger, then suddenly bursting into tears in front of strangers.

Our reward for finishing as runners-up in the league was a place in the first round of the 1993–94 UEFA Cup. We were drawn to play Servette FC from Switzerland. The first leg was in Belfast in the middle of September – and I wasn't in the squad.

UEFA had brought in a rule to limit to three the number of foreign players that any team could field in a European club competition. The club now had a brilliant young striker named Glenn Hunter, so I was one of the foreigners sacrificed. I was disappointed. But I was thirty-three. I knew the score. I left Tony's bodywork undisturbed.

We drew the first leg 0–0 and headed to Geneva full of hope for the return at the end of September. Roy Walker was the player-manager but Tony was still the man in charge. Roy looked after the training for the Belfast players, and he gave a team talk before every match, but Tony always had the last word before the players went out onto the pitch, issuing instructions with a big Cuban cigar burning in the V of his fingers. Tony asked me to fill in as the manager on the bench that night. 'Run things from the touchline,' he said.

I didn't know it then, but he had a hunch that I had leadership potential. I remember watching the match from the bench and seeing different things because I was looking at football from a completely different vantage point. We were holding our own against Servette until about ten minutes into the second half. Then we conceded four goals in six minutes and that was that.

Roy was playing as a sweeper and I figured it was pointless playing with an extra man in defence now that the tie was over. So I decided to take him off and throw on an attacking player in the hope of getting a goal back. When he saw his number being held up, Roy just stared at me, as if to say, The balls on this lad, trying to sub off the manager. I changed my mind and subbed off Jimmy Gardiner, one of our two strikers, instead.

I realized something during my time at Crusaders. I'd wasted my career. I wanted to be Joe Jordan. I should have aimed to be Duncan McKenzie. The Irish League wasn't a blood and guts league like the League of Ireland. It allowed me to work on my touch, my concentration and my awareness. In my three seasons at Crusaders, I scored forty-eight goals in ninety-nine matches. The pity was that I was well into my thirties then and I was really starting to feel it.

That season, the club signed another Dubliner, Harry Kenny, who was a full-back and one of the stars of the Shamrock Rovers four-in-a-row team. He squeezed into the back of Tony's Merc along with the rest of us. I loved those journeys up and down the motorway — especially returning home after we'd won. We'd be drinking bottles of beer from the moment we left Belfast, then as soon as we were across the border we'd start pestering Tony to let us out for a slash. Our usual stop was outside the GAA club in Castlebellingham,

Co. Louth. We'd have our Jimmy Riddle, then we'd throw the bottles over the wall. Tony would drop us off at the Hole in the Wall pub on Blackhorse Avenue, where Caroline and the other wives would meet us at 7.30 p.m. and we'd head into town for a night out.

Usually, we travelled back and forth across the border without any fear, except occasionally when we were stopped at a British Army checkpoint and ordered out of the car. We'd stand there looking at these soldiers, who were often just terrified kids with sheet-white faces, holding these high-powered rifles in their trembling hands.

In the autumn of 1993, in my last season at the club, a few things happened to make the Troubles feel uncomfortably close. One Saturday towards the end of October we were playing Bangor at home. We were in the ground, about an hour and a half before kick-off, when we heard a loud boom in the distance. Everyone just stopped and looked at each other. It was impossible to tell which direction it had come from but it was obviously a huge explosion.

The match was played in a strangely subdued atmosphere. After the final whistle, I went back to the dressing room. I was about to get into the shower when someone raced into the room and said, 'Fucking quick – get the boys on that Dublin Road. They're baying for Catholics.'

I didn't stop to ask what happened. We all piled into Tony's car, still wearing our kit. Tony switched on the radio and we listened to the news. An IRA bomb had destroyed a fish-and-chip shop on the Shankill Road and there were believed to be multiple casualties. None of us said a word in the car until we reached the border. We pulled into a hotel, where we had a wash in the toilets and changed out of our football kit before continuing on to Dublin. Tony dropped me and Martin Murray off at the Hole in the Wall. The other fellas went home. I ordered two pints and I said to the barman, 'Rough day, what?'

'Why, what happened?' he said.

Belfast was only a hundred miles up the road – and it might as well have been in Timbuktu. I picked up my pint and I saw that my hand was shaking. Caroline arrived, looking forward to her night out, and I said, 'Let's just go home.'

The IRA had planned the bombing because they were looking to kill the leaders of the local UDA, including Johnny Adair, who were supposedly meeting in a room above the chipper. The blast killed ten people, eight of whom were civilians, after the device went off prematurely. More than fifty others were injured.

In the week that followed there was a wave of revenge attacks by loyalists, targeting mostly Catholic civilians. The following Saturday loyalist paramilitaries opened fire in a crowded pub during a Halloween party in Greysteel, Co. Derry, killing eight people and wounding nineteen.

It was a horrible time in the North. Suddenly, when we were on the team bus on the way to matches, I started to notice the army patrols and the burned-out cars and the graffiti that talked about 'nutting' Fenians. Although we had an unspoken agreement with Kirk and the others not to discuss these things, it suddenly felt like that wasn't good enough, because not saying something seemed like you were saying something.

A couple of weeks later, in the middle of November, Ireland were due to play Northern Ireland in a World Cup qualifier. With sectarian tensions so high, there was talk of moving the match to a neutral venue. In the end, it went ahead in Belfast. A mate of mine from Dublin, Roger O'Connor, asked me if I could get him tickets. Through the club, I managed to get a hold of two. What I didn't realize was that they were for the home section of the ground. He spent the match surrounded by Northern Ireland fans, who put the fear of God into him by repeatedly asking each other, 'Can anyone else smell a fucking Taig?'

On the pitch, Crusaders couldn't keep up the intensity we'd shown the previous season and we finished fourth. I knew my time with the club was up. I was nearly thirty-four with a lot of miles in my legs. Jimmy Gardiner and Glenn Hunter had established a great scoring partnership that year. They were the future and their goals would help Crusaders to win the league the following season.

All I could do was thank Tony, Roy, Kirk and the rest of the fellas for what had been the best three years of my career. I only wished it had been ten.

★

Stephen and Barney parted ways after what happened in Italy. They both agreed that they'd done everything they could for one another and it was time to move on. Stephen signed to fight for Barry Hearn, the snooker and boxing impresario, who promoted Chris Eubank, the WBO world super-middleweight champion and the biggest name in British sport.

Stephen reminded me so much of my younger self in those years. He left his wife and kids behind in Dublin and moved into digs in Romford in Essex, just around the corner from the Matchroom gym, where he set about putting his career back together just like I'd tried to do at Newport. He spent the next year and a half beating up a succession of British journeyman middleweights.

There was to be no rematch with Kalambay. He'd finally been toppled by Chris Pyatt, a tough English fighter, when they fought for the vacant WBO world middleweight title in the spring of 1993.

The WBO was the newest and least well known of boxing's four major sanctioning bodies, but as far as Stephen was concerned, Pyatt was a world champion and he had his sights set on him at the start of 1994. Barry Hearn put the fight together for 11 May in the Ponds Forge Arena in Sheffield.

It was a bittersweet time for me. The football season was nearly over and I was saying goodbye to Crusaders. But at the same time, Caroline was pregnant again and we were looking forward to the arrival of our third child that summer.

There was a big crowd planning to travel over to England for the fight. Stephen was a bit overwhelmed by the number of people ringing him to ask about tickets, so I offered to take the job off him. He concentrated on preparing for the fight while I got a block of tickets from Barry Hearn's office, then went around Cabra and Stoneybatter collecting money from fellas.

There wasn't a doubt in Stephen's mind that he was going to beat Pyatt, who was really a blown-up light-middleweight. I remember looking at Stephen's shoulders as I walked behind him to the ring: they were broad and defined like the withers of a racehorse. I looked across the ring at Pyatt and he was like a pony compared with him.

Stephen blew him away that night. A lot of people felt the referee stepped between them too early, but all the fight went out of Pyatt after Stephen floored him with a right in the fifth. After that, he retreated to the ropes and had stopped throwing punches by the time the referee decided he'd seen enough.

I was the first through the middle rope afterwards. I grabbed Stephen around the waist and I picked him up. Mick and Paschal were next into the ring. The three of us lifted him onto our shoulders as they handed him the title belt. He'd finally done it. He was a world champion. When he was interviewed afterwards, he dedicated the fight to our da. I could see my ma and my uncle Terry crying their eyes out at ringside.

It was as if a physical weight had been lifted from Stephen's shoulders that night. This goal that he'd been working towards for eight years – this ambition that he set himself after our da died – he'd achieved it. It was the happiest I'd seen him since he was a kid.

The baby arrived on 6 August – the day before my thirty-fourth birthday – and it was a boy. I was thrilled to finally have a son. It had been the subject of dressing-room and building-site banter for years.

'Hey, Rod,' the fellas would say to me – this was in front of Caroline – 'if you want a son and heir, maybe you should ask a real man to do the job for you.'

The reason I wanted a boy so much was because my relationship with my da was so special and so fundamental to the man I was, and I wanted to recreate that. And now I finally had a son. 'The Messiah', as his sisters still call him to this day. When it came to naming him, there wasn't even a debate. He was going to be Roderick – or Roddy for short. If I had to go through life with that awful name, then my first-born son should have to do it too. It would be character-building.

Like his father, he demanded attention – and he knew he had a captive audience. His sisters adored him as much as I did. There was six years between Sinéad and Niamh and six years between Niamh and Roddy. Our kids never really had to be competitive with each other, because they all got years and years of attention from me and Caroline before the next sibling came along.

We had a big party in the house to celebrate his christening. We rented a marquee and invited a crowd of more than a hundred to the house, including all my old Crusaders teammates. It was the first time Kirk had ever been across the border and it was nice to see him mixing with my friends from Cabra. I had this mad idea that I was going to introduce Roddy to everyone by carrying him into the room, like the last emperor of China, on a sort of ceremonial chair that I was going to make myself. But wiser heads prevailed.

We decorated the house for the occasion. Caroline had seen this wallpaper she loved in Laura Ashley that had a fuchsia pattern on it. It cost about a hundred quid per roll – but I said, 'Yeah, let's really push the boat out for the christening.' My brother Mick offered to decorate for us, but he hung the paper the wrong way up. There was a typical Collins family row then – loud, with an accompaniment of banging doors – as me and Mick argued about whether the fuchsia was a hanging or non-hanging flower. Everyone who walked into the house admired the wallpaper and then, after a moment's pause, said, 'Is it upside-down, though?'

I stood up and made a speech. I babbled away for a few minutes about love and parenthood and friendship and then I said I wanted to sing a song that was very dear to my heart. Caroline, standing a few feet away, was looking at me all teary eyed, thinking I was about to launch into Neil Diamond's 'Sweet Caroline', which I had been known to sing at parties. Instead, I sang 'The Wonder of You'. All the Crusaders boys joined in like we were all in the bath back in Seaview. Caroline told me afterwards that she felt like going upstairs and packing her bags.

My heart was broken after Crusaders came to an end. I still felt the pull of the club. Every Saturday I had this urge to drive up to Belfast to watch them play. Or even train with them, just to feel like I still belonged. But the sad truth about football is that once you're gone, you're gone. Crusaders would go on to win the league that season and sadly I wasn't part of their story any more. As a matter of fact, I wasn't sure if I'd ever kick a ball again.

Then, out of the blue that summer, I had a phone call from Nigel Best, who was the coach of Bangor. He said he was looking for a big striker who knew his way around and he wondered would I be interested in playing for him. I drove up to meet him and his assistant, Colin McCurdy, who played for Fulham while I was there on trial as a teenager. The three of us hit it off.

It wasn't Crusaders – it wasn't even close. But it was football, and I thought I'd give it one more season before I folded my hand.

While I was finding my feet with a new bunch of teammates, Stephen was dealing with his own career uncertainty. He was supposed to fight an American middleweight named Lonny Beasley in Hong Kong that October, but the fight was cancelled at the last minute when the promoter failed to come up with the money to pay the fighters on the card. It was rescheduled for Boston in December, but again it was cancelled, this time because Stephen was suffering from a virus.

I saw him that Christmas. He looked absolutely wretched. I think he was burned out. He'd been on the road for going on nine years, he had a world title belt that he hadn't yet defended, and he was still living in a rented house with two kids and a third on the way. Everything had caught up with him. You couldn't have known by looking at him that his life was about to change in all the ways he dreamt it would.

And, in a more modest way, mine was about to change as well.

II

Bangor was a rugby town, not a football town. It was predominantly Protestant, with a large population of older people who'd made a few bob and retired to the seaside, but also a core of loyalist hard chaws who were hiding out in plain view.

The dynamic in the dressing room was brilliant. But there was a quiet sectarianism bubbling just below the surface.

In August of 1994 we went to Slovakia to play Tatran Prešov in the qualifying round of the European Cup Winners' Cup. As a 'foreigner', I was again left out of the match-day squad but travelled anyway. When we arrived, the hotel management had put on a bit of a spread to welcome us. Unfortunately, they didn't understand the nature of a divided Ireland and laid out tricolours on all the little tables. I watched one of our players, with his face set hard, walk from table to table, removing every single one.

Nigel Best was a brilliant manager. He'd never played football, but he was an absolute genius when it came to tactics. I was enjoying my football, even if our results in the first few months of the season weren't good. We were dumped out of Europe. We lost the first leg in Bangor 1–0 and the second leg in Prešov 4–0. By the end of November we were near the bottom of the table. The league was about to undergo a major restructuring. Its sixteen teams were going to be divided into two divisions for the following season. At the end of the 1994–95 season, the top eight teams, based on the previous two seasons' overall results, would join the new Premier League and the bottom eight would be relegated to the new First Division. It was brutal. And there seemed no doubt that Bangor were destined to be in the second tier.

One Saturday at the end of November, I was walking off the pitch when Wilson Matthews, a member of the board, asked if he could have a word. He took me into the boardroom and told me that Nigel had resigned. I was still processing this when he asked me if I would take over as manager on an interim basis.

I had no great ambition to be a football manager. I didn't think I knew enough about tactics. But I was confident that I could motivate a dressing room, which was the job of a caretaker boss. So I said yes.

I took my first training session the following Tuesday night. I was working on a new housing estate in Swords that day. I finished work early and drove to Bangor. I put the traffic cones out and told the lads to go for a run. I noticed that a few of them were cutting corners, being lazy. After the warm-up, I called them together and said, 'One or two of you decided to run inside the cones and the rest of you followed like a herd of sheep.'

'It's a flock of sheep,' one of the players said with a challenging stare. 'Not a herd of sheep.'

That's when I first sensed that there might be a bit of resistance to the idea of me as the manager.

'A flock of sheep or a herd of sheep,' I said, giving him full eye contact, 'run around the fucking things in future.'

My first match in charge was away to Larne. I'd never made a speech before in my life. All week I was composing in my head what I was going to say. I barely slept. I practised it in the mirror. Then I got lost on my way to Inver Park. I made it to the ground about fifteen minutes before kick-off and walked into the dressing room to find the players already in their kit and twenty pairs of eyes staring at me. My mind went blank. I walked into a toilet cubicle and closed the door behind me. I've blown it, I thought. It was one of those fight-or-flight moments – and I would have definitely flown if the window had been big enough for me to squeeze through it. Instead, I opened the door again, picked the team on the spot, then I started bawling out the players, fired by pure adrenaline, pointing at each one in turn and telling him what I expected of him.

I played that day and we won 1–0. Then we went on a bit of a run. In my first four matches as caretaker manager, we won two and we drew two. It was a positive start and there was talk of me being given the job on a permanent basis.

I was fortunate at Bangor to have one of the three most naturally gifted footballers who ever played for me. Marc Kenny was a midfielder who was part of the famous Home Farm schoolboy team from the 1980s that went unbeaten for six seasons. A younger brother of Harry Kenny, he'd spent two years at Liverpool but didn't make the breakthrough and had somehow ended up playing in the Irish League. He could do anything with a football. Marc used to travel up for matches in a car with Ricky McEvoy, another Dub, who I'd played with at Shamrock Rovers and Dundalk. They were allies of mine in the dressing room, but I knew that changes were necessary.

Stephen Brown was an absolute rock at the heart of our defence and a brilliant bloke, but he was very close to Nigel, who'd consulted him on everything. I wasn't going to do that. If I was to put my own mark on the dressing room, I knew that he had to go. As it happened, Nigel wanted him at his new club, Glenavon. We also had a central midfielder named Jonathan Magee, who'd played for the Northern Ireland under-21 team under Bryan Hamilton. He didn't think much of me and he didn't make any secret of it, so I put him in the reserves and he eventually went out on loan.

The club offered me a two-year contract to take the job on a permanent basis. I signed it. And no sooner was the ink dry than the campaign began to have me sacked. I was invited to a meeting of the supporters in the local Orange Hall to listen to their concerns. Bangor was a small town, and ignoring them was not an option, so I went to face them. When I walked into the hall that night, the first thing I saw was a massive statue of a man on a horse. I remember thinking, 'I bet that's not Pat Eddery.'

The fans had their say. They had a lot of good football reasons for thinking I wasn't the right fit for the club – two fan favourites were gone from the first team overnight – but the fact that I was from 'the Free State' never seemed far from the conversation. I explained that the club was heading for relegation; they should hold off on judging me until the end of the season, when – I made them a solemn promise – we would secure a place in the Premier League. Clearly, I was improving as a public speaker because at the end I got a round of applause.

I started looking around for new players. On Christmas Day, our reserves were playing against the Linfield Swifts in the final of the Steel & Sons Cup, an intermediate cup competition run by the County Antrim and District Football Association. I watched this young kid who was playing for us glide onto the pitch, smash someone in a tackle, drag the ball back and then ping it forty yards. I turned to Wilson Matthews and I said, 'Who's that?'

'His name is Stuart MacPherson,' he said. 'He's a nephew of George Best – except he doesn't want anyone to know.'

'Well, if he insists on playing football like that,' I said, 'people are *going* to know.'

I hung around for him after the match and I introduced myself. The following week, I met him in the train station in Belfast, along with his grandfather, Dick Best, who was George's dad. He signed a two-year contract to play for us and I gave him his debut against Glentoran. We played up front together. There was a definite hint of genius off him. But what I didn't realize was that he was cripplingly shy. I had inquiries about him from Middlesbrough, Bolton and Raith Rovers, but he just didn't have the confidence to make it in the game. He finished playing football at twenty-one.

Our results started to improve. We put a string of victories together and we began to climb up the table until finishing in the top eight started to look like a very real possibility.

Over the course of the season I started to think that maybe I had what it took to be a manager. I began to really enjoy engaging with the media and built up a great rapport with Jackie Fullerton of the BBC. He interviewed me regularly and I used it as an opportunity to try to wind up other managers.

I started to remember things I'd learned from Turlough. I discovered that I could be ruthless like him. I signed a lad named John Swift. I saw him playing in a seven-a-side tournament in Ballyfermot. He was thirty-two but he moved like he was ten years younger. Someone told me that he'd played for Pete Mahon at St Francis. I rang Pete. 'Swifty will do a job for you all day long,' he said. 'He's a fitness fanatic. Not a drinker. He won't let you down.'

So I signed him. I gave him his debut against Portadown on the right side of midfield and he was the man of the match. We had a cup game coming up against my old club, Crusaders. The best player in the league by a mile was Sid Burrows, who played on the left wing for them. On the night of the match I decided to leave Swifty out to protect him. I broke the news to him an hour before kick-off.

'Are you serious?' he asked. He was devastated, standing there in his brand-new suit.

'Dead serious,' I told him.

'My entire family's after driving up,' he said. 'Three carloads, Rod.'

And I felt no remorse at all. I didn't even send him on as a substitute. We lost the match. He might have made a difference or he might not have. The point was that I put my personal feelings to one side. I think Turlough would have been proud.

We were climbing the table. I wasn't picking myself every week, but I was still our top scorer. Not everyone was persuaded by our results, though. There was a hard rump of loyalists who wanted to run me out of town. The phone beside the bed rang one night and when I answered it a man said, 'Don't come down that Dublin Road again because if you do you'll get a bullet.'

'If you're going to shoot me,' I said to him, 'do it fucking properly, because I don't want to be left in a wheelchair. I'll see you Saturday.'

The only time I felt truly frightened was one Saturday when I was driving home to Dublin with an uncle of mine named Tony Lambert, who was home from Dallas, Texas, and wanted to watch a match. We were on the motorway, just south of Belfast, booting it home, when the car wobbled on the road. It felt like we had a flat tyre, so I pulled into the hard shoulder. That's when I discovered that all of the nuts on the front passenger-side wheel had been loosened until they were on the second-last thread.

The vast majority of people I met in Bangor were brilliant, but I never felt like I could fully relax there – too many sinister political or religious undercurrents. One day I was in the bar in the ground, having the craic with a man who was close to one of the players. By accident, I tried to pay for a round of drinks with an Irish £20 note. We had a good laugh about it.

'Ah, well,' I said jokingly, 'you'll all be getting paid in punts when Ireland is reunified.'

'Not as long as I have this,' he said, then he pulled back his jacket to reveal a gun in a shoulder holster.

On the last day of the season we played Ards. To be absolutely sure of staying in the Premier Division we needed to win. But Coleraine were playing Ballymena at the same time. A draw there and they would both be relegated and we would stay up. We lost 2–0, then we waited for news to come through from Coleraine. It was scoreless and there were still five minutes to play. Eventually, the news came through that it was over. We finished eleventh – but when the results of the two seasons were taken into account we were eighth. We'd secured our Premier League status for the following season. The sense of relief was unreal. Then it turned into jubilation.

And like a gobshite, I thought that would be enough to keep me in the job.

Just after I was made the permanent manager of Bangor I was working on an apartment block on Ellis Quay on a freezing cold January day when the foreman came to me and said that my wife was on the phone. I headed for the site office.

'Roddy,' she said, 'Barney Eastwood is looking for you. He said it's urgent.'

I rang him back. He sounded agitated.

'I need to talk to Stephen,' he told me, 'but I can't get him.'

'I haven't seen him,' I said, 'but I know he hasn't been well.'

'Roddy,' he said, 'I have something to tell you in the strictest confidence. Ray Close has failed a medical.'

Ray Close was a boxer from Belfast – nicknamed 'The Stormin' Mormon' – who put the first blemish on Chris Eubank's unbeaten record when he fought him to a stalemate in Glasgow in the summer of 1993. A year later, they fought again in the King's Hall in Belfast. This time, Eubank was awarded the victory by a controversial split decision. They were due to fight again in Belfast in February 1995. But a routine MRI scan had revealed two lesions on Close's brain and the British Boxing Board of Control had revoked his licence to box.

I was wondering what this had to do with Stephen when Barney said, 'I want to put Stephen's name forward for it. Can you find him?'

By the time I tracked him down, Barney had already found him. Stephen had no fear of Eubank. He always felt he could beat him. It was clear that he was in no fit state to fight – he was still pale and he'd lost a lot of weight – but he was never going to say no. Then he got a lucky break. Sky Sports, who had a broadcasting deal with Eubank, realized that they were missing a trick. They had a far bigger fight on their hands than Eubank v. Close III. This was a world middleweight champion squaring up against a world super-middleweight champion. By putting the fight on in Belfast on a Saturday night in February, they were sort of throwing it away. So it was decided to abandon the original date and promote Eubank v. Collins as a contest in its own right.

A new date was set: the day after St Patrick's Day – Saturday, 18 March 1995 – in the Green Glens Arena in Millstreet, Co. Cork. The previous year it had hosted the Eurovision Song Contest, when the cast of *Riverdance* made a spectacular debut as the interval act. I couldn't believe it when Barry Hearn agreed to let the fight go ahead in Ireland on a Paddy's weekend. While he managed both fighters, Eubank had a million-pound-per-fight deal with Sky and was his most bankable asset.

A press conference was arranged for the Burlington Hotel in Dublin. The atmosphere around it was dark and strange. Stephen showed up wearing a tweed jacket and a flat cap, with a shillelagh and an Irish wolfhound on a leash. I've no idea where he got any of it. I never saw the dog before and I never saw it again. During the press conference he started talking about how proud he was to come from Ireland and accused Eubank of denying his African heritage. This wasn't Stephen. I knew he was in acting mode. He had a fight to sell. But I just found the whole thing uncomfortable. After that, I didn't see or hear from Stephen until the night of the fight. He went off to Tenerife with his trainer, Freddie King, to prepare. I knew he'd started working with Tony Quinn, the nutrition expert and mind coach, who had a chain of vitamin and supplement shops. I'd never met the man, but when I heard that Stephen was taking him to Tenerife I felt very uneasy. Perhaps it was just the lack of contact with him, the distance that seemed to open up between him and the rest of the family while Quinn was on the scene, but I remember having an anxiety attack one day at the junction of Kinvara Avenue and the Navan Road and I had to pull over the car.

As the date of the fight came nearer, I had a dilemma. I wanted to be in Stephen's corner in Millstreet, but I was in the middle of a relegation dogfight. We had a match against Newry on the afternoon of the bout. There was no way I could miss it, but at the same time I couldn't imagine not being in my brother's corner for what might be the biggest night of his career.

Graham Henry, a local businessman and sponsor of the club, had a friend with a private plane, which he kept at a private airfield in Ards, half an hour's drive from Belfast. I spoke to the owner and pilot, who said he could fly to Farranfore in Co. Kerry, which was the nearest airport to Millstreet. He said the flight would take about two hours and he quoted me a price of £1,500 for the round trip. In my head, I started to put a timetable together. If our match finished at 4.50 p.m., I could be in Newtownards by 5.30 and in the air by 6. We'd land in Farranfore around 8 o'clock. It was a forty-five minute drive from there to Millstreet. Stephen was due to make his entrance to the ring around 9.30, which meant I would make it in time – provided nothing went wrong along the way.

The big day dawned. I was more nervous than I'd ever been in my life. The first part of the day couldn't have gone better. We drew 2–2 with Newry and took another step towards safety. But at half-time a man from the BBC asked me if I'd heard that the fight might be off. Apparently, Stephen was claiming that Tony Quinn was going to hypnotize him so that he wouldn't feel any pain. And now Eubank was refusing to fight. I can't even remember what I said to the reporter. I had no doubt that the fight would go ahead. But I also remember thinking, Jesus! I hope he isn't hypnotized.

After the match I left the ground and Graham was waiting in a car to drive me to Newtownards. It was lashing rain when we left

Belfast. I'd invited Kirk Hunter to come to the fight with me, along with his wife, Denise, and Pete Batey, a big boxing fan who played in midfield for Bangor.

We arrived at the Ards airfield. The departures lounge was a little prefab building. There was a man inside putting up a partition wall. None of us knew him from Adam. He asked us where we were going and we told him we were off to Cork to see the Collins v. Eubank fight. He decided to come with us. He grabbed a bottle of red wine and a bottle of vodka and he followed us out onto the tarmac.

When I saw the plane, I couldn't believe my eyes. I was expecting a private jet, with a leather interior and a bottle of champagne on ice. Instead, it was a little three-wheeler propeller plane, that looked like Del Boy's van except with wings. The pilot insisted on weighing us before deciding where each of us should sit.

'Are you absolutely sure about this?' Kirk asked me.

'Of course,' I said, with more confidence than I felt.

We took off. The rain was thundering down and I noticed that the plane had windscreen wipers like my van. I'll never forget the screaming sound that the engine made – like a car with a busted fan belt. I kept staring out the window at the propellers, thinking, Are they the only things that are keeping us up here? The stranger we picked up at the airport was milling the vodka and I didn't blame him.

It was pitch-dark when we landed in Farranfore after two of the most nerve-racking hours of my life. A friend of mine named Christy Gogan was waiting for us in a people carrier and he drove us to the venue in Millstreet through the lashing rain. I made it to the dressing room at 9.15, with just fifteen minutes to spare before Stephen made his entrance.

I don't know what I expected to see when I got there – maybe Tony Quinn swinging a watch backwards and forwards in front of Stephen's face. But everything was normal. Stephen was his usual highly focussed self. Freddie King was giving him his instructions. Quinn was standing off to the side with the big bouffant of curls and the Jesus beard on him.

There was a knock on the door and it was time to go. I said good luck to Stephen and I gave him a hug. Then Quinn snapped a pair of cheap Walkman headphones over his ears. It was apparently part of the ruse to make Eubank think Stephen was listening to one of his hypnosis cassettes.

We did the slow walk to the ring. The noise of the crowd was like nothing I'd ever experienced before. While Eubank made his traditional entrance to Tina Turner's 'Simply the Best', Stephen sat on his stool, with his earphones on, his eyes closed and the hood of his robe pulled over his head. I thought the whole thing was ridiculous. Stephen never needed gimmicks to win fights and I was sure he could beat Eubank without any of this stupid carry-on.

I wasn't one of his seconds that night, but I was in the corner. When the bell rang, Stephen went straight for Eubank. He grazed his chin with a punch and the roof nearly lifted off the place. But I was so worried that I couldn't enjoy the fight, even as Stephen overwhelmed him with his work rate and put him on his arse in the eighth round. Every time Stephen got hit, I kept saying under my breath, 'Please, Da, let him be OK.'

When Eubank put him on the deck in the tenth round, I nearly vomited. People still talk about the aftermath of the knockdown as being the moment that decided the fight. Eubank never moved in to finish him off. The popular theory at the time was that he no longer had the stomach for fighting. Two weeks earlier, Nigel Benn had stopped Gerald McClellan after ten brutal rounds at the London Arena, at the end of which McClellan had slipped into a coma and still hadn't woken up. A lot of people thought it had triggered Eubank's memory of his own 1991 fight with Michael Watson, which left Watson with devastating brain injuries. It was suggested that this was why he couldn't bring himself to close the fight against Stephen. I'm not convinced. Eubank realized he couldn't hurt him. He'd landed his best punch and Stephen had got to his feet, smiled, and winked at his corner.

After twelve rounds, we all flooded into the ring to wait for the scores of the judges. Eubank had benefited from some very questionable decisions in the past so we couldn't take anything for granted. But when the referee announced that Stephen was the winner, the crowd went absolutely wild.

In all the pandemonium, I missed Stephen leaving the ring. When I made my way back to the dressing room, I was shocked to see him laid out on the floor with bags of ice piled on top of him. He was overheating and they were trying to bring his body temperature down. I saw Caroline, my ma, Gemma, Freddie King and Tony Quinn: all of them looking worried. It took about half an hour for him to recover. Then we kicked off a hooley that lasted for three days.

It was around that time that we had a knock on the door one week-day morning and there was a man there who said he was from the Revenue.

'I'm looking for twenty grand,' he told me.

'Come on in,' I said to him, opening the door wider, 'and we can look for it together.'

I can't say that the knock on the door came as a surprise. It had been coming since the day I agreed to become the manager of Bangor. All day, every day, I was thinking about players, about tactics, about upcoming matches. When it came to the plastering business, I'd taken my eye off the ball.

The toughest part of being a contractor is managing cash flow. Usually, at any given time you have several jobs on the go, all at different stages of completion and all paying out at different times. So when the money comes through for finishing one job, you use it to pay the wages of the fellas starting a new one. And if there's anything left over, you pay something off your account with whoever supplies your materials. You're constantly taking from one pocket to put it into another. To operate like that, you have to have a good head for numbers, which I did. But in the year I spent managing Bangor, I lost my focus completely and the business started to unravel.

When it came to paying people, I prioritized my workers. It was a principle for me that you paid a man what he was worth. I was proud to say that no one who worked for me ever went home on a Friday without his wages, and everyone's PRSI got paid. With everything else, though, I was spinning plates. By the summer of 1995 I owed money to the Revenue and I owed money to Chadwicks, the builders suppliers. I asked an accountant to look at the books for me.

'Who are all of these people?' he asked.

He was talking about all the names on my payroll.

'Just lads who work for me,' I told him. 'Lads I know from school. Lads I know from Cabra. Lads I know from football.'

'The problem is this, Rod,' he said. 'You're running a dole office for your mates.'

Contracting, I'd discovered a long time ago, was a thankless business. Even when there was work to be had, there were people out there who would watch you do it and then refuse to pay you. You could be working as a subcontractor for a builder who wanted to maximize his profit – or maybe he was juggling money and using what he owed you to pay someone else. Sometimes they came up with a pretext not to pay you. Other times they didn't bother. They'd tell you they didn't have it, or they only had half of it, or come back some other time. Sometimes it was just a simple 'Fuck off!'

Occasionally, I went to desperate lengths to send the fellas home with their wages. I doorstepped developers and contractors in their offices, in their homes, in their local pubs. One time I confronted a contractor on the football pitch where he was coaching a local team. Another time I tipped a bucket of lime mortar down the crisp white shirt of a developer who refused point-blank to pay me.

Turning over desks was my speciality – once, I found a developer hiding underneath after his secretary told me he was out of the country. I did everything and anything to get the wages for my workers. I threw things across rooms. I put my foot through a wall and went home missing a shoe. I arm-wrestled a fisherman, with a big, woolly head on him, in O'Brien's pub on Sussex Terrace and all the skin was torn from my elbow.

Years earlier, when I was in my early twenties, I was working on a small development of houses in Finglas with Caroline's brother Liam and another lad. When the job was finished, the developer started acting the maggot. He put a level up against the wall and said, 'Sorry, that's off. You're not getting paid for that.'

If it was off, it was off in a way that was not visible to the human eye.

'You better have what you owe me on Friday,' I told him.

I was completely broke. We had nothing.

'You won't be getting a penny,' he said.

I was walking past a newsagent's shop in Finglas and I saw a little police set for kids in the window. It had a pair of plastic handcuffs, a police badge and a toy gun that shot plastic darts with little rubber suckers on the end of them. I bought the set and threw everything away except the gun, which I stuck into the inside pocket of my tan leather box jacket. I returned to the building site on Friday and asked the foreman where the developer was.

'He's not here,' he said. 'But he'll be here at half-three with the wages.'

I told him I was one of the plasterers on the job. I asked him to pass on the message that I'd be back at four o'clock to collect what we were owed. Then I opened my jacket and showed him the handle of the toy gun. I returned in the afternoon and the developer paid us in full, counting off the money from a wad of notes that was four inches thick and even throwing in twenty quid for a drink. The story would develop a life of its own. A few months later I was in the waiting room in the tax office when I got chatting to a lad who was working in construction. We started talking about different jobs we'd been on recently and I mentioned the one in Finglas. 'Were you there,' he asked, 'the day the lad turned up with a shooter and starting firing into the air?'

I should add that I'm not especially proud of any of this. But everyone who works in construction will have come up against someone who just refused to pay. I couldn't tell my workers, 'I've no money for you this week, I'm afraid, but don't worry, that fella will soon be seeing his name in *Stubbs Gazette*.'

My men always got paid. By hook or by crook, I got the money. And I managed my business very well – until I took the job at Bangor. And that was when I stopped paying attention to it – and the whole house of cards came down. One day, in the summer of 1995, I was having dinner with Barney Eastwood in the Europa Hotel in Belfast when Caroline rang me in tears.

'The sheriff is at the door,' she said. 'He's threatening to take everything.'

This was over unpaid VAT. I told her I was on my way, made my excuses to Barney and pointed the car in the direction of Dublin. I was passing the exit for Ardee when a thought struck me – we didn't actually own anything. There was nothing for the sheriff to take except for the roof over our heads.

Eventually, everything got sorted. The accountant sat me down and I did my Bill of Quantities. I figured out what I was owed and what I had to pay out. I called in as much money as I could and I reached settlements with my creditors. My account with Chadwicks was £15,000 in the red. They took me to court. My solicitor met their solicitor. He asked me how much could I give them. I told him I had £1,500 in my stocking. That was how you always carried large sums of cash in Cabra. They agreed to take it in full settlement of what I owed then.

Then, with no fanfare but with a huge sense of relief, my plastering company went into voluntary liquidation.

Like me, Bangor were broke. I tried to get Barney Eastwood involved as a sponsor. He lived in Holywood, Co. Down, on the road between Belfast and Bangor, and he'd ring me from time to time and ask me to drop in for a 'wee cup of tea' if I was passing.

'How are things going up there?' he asked me one day.

'We've a lad there and he's busted ligaments in his leg,' I told him. 'And we can't afford to pay for him to have an operation.'

Barney agreed to put up the money. He was interested in opening a bookmaker's in Bangor and he saw the value of making friends in the local community. He started coming to matches. Soon he was in the boardroom, hobnobbing with the bigwigs, who loved having him around and obviously didn't understand the extent of his connection to me.

'I don't know how you're still in that job,' he told me one day.

'What do you mean?' I asked.

'Roddy,' he said, 'they hate you.'

It turned out he was right. And no one in the boardroom disliked me more than Gifford McConkey, the Bangor chairman. Two of my least favourite kinds of people in life have been schoolteachers and blazers – and McConkey just happened to be both. During the season I'd taken part in a discussion programme on BBC Northern Ireland about the move to split the league in two. McConkey was furious and he confronted me about it.

'How dare you presume to speak for this club,' he said. 'I've been a member of Bangor FC for more than fifty years.'

The message came through loud and clear. I was an outsider and I would only be here for as long as he was prepared to suffer me.

Gifford was a brother-in-law of Wilson Matthews, the board member who first asked me to take over the dressing room after Nigel Best left. He and Gifford fell out over me and Wilson left the club because of it. It was Gifford who would eventually get his way. When our Premier League status was secured, I immediately started making plans for the next season. I drew up a shortlist of new players that I was confident we could get, including Tom McNulty and James Coll from Dundalk, Liam Coyle from Derry City and Jonathan Speak from Finn Harps. With those signings, I was sure that we could win the league the following season.

What I didn't know was that my future was being debated in the boardroom. I was due to present my plans for the new season to the board in early May. But then Noel Brotherston, the former Northern Ireland international, died very suddenly and at the tragically young age of thirty-eight. The meeting was put off as a mark of respect. The next time I heard from Gifford, he phoned me to say that they'd had an emergency meeting.

He said, 'I've been tasked with the unenviable job of telling you that we do not require your services any more.'

I was sick to my stomach, so much so that I didn't want to see another football ground, or another football person, for the rest of my life. Between that and the business collapsing around my ears, it was a miserable summer.

But there was at least something to look forward to at the end of it. Stephen was going to fight Eubank in a rematch, this time outdoors, in front of 50,000 people, in Cork's Páirc Uí Chaoimh.

Tony Quinn was still on the scene, still talking up the part he played in Stephen beating Eubank the first time. A few days after the

Millstreet fight, Stephen had been given an open-top bus ride around the city of Dublin and there was Quinn, front and centre on the upper deck. You would have sworn that he beat Eubank himself, listening to some of the rubbish that was reported. Not just that he'd hypnotized Stephen to make him impervious to pain, but that he'd speeded up his synaptic responses so that Eubank's punches appeared to move through the air more slowly and that he'd made Eubank's head appear like it was twice its regular size. This stuff was off the wall and it started to really get to me, especially when I heard people repeating it.

In all the time Quinn worked with Stephen, I never had a conversation with the man. Once or twice members of his circle came to me and said, 'Tony would love to talk to you,' like I was to be granted an audience with him. I gave him a wide berth and he must have picked up on the fact that I was a non-believer. One day, one of his people handed me a brown envelope and said, 'Tony wants you to have this.'

I opened it up and it was one of his meditation cassettes – *Relaxation with a Purpose*. I listened to the first couple of minutes out of curiosity. It was him saying, 'You're in an elevator and you're going down, down, down, into the deepest levels of your unconscious.'

I pulled it out of the tape machine and threw it at the wall.

I never asked Stephen his business, but I just hoped the man was being paid in free publicity and not in hard currency. One day I lost it with him and I said, 'Stephen, you'll be going around in a loincloth with nothing and he'll be telling people that he beat Chris Eubank.'

As the date of the rematch approached, I was once again the first port of call for people looking for tickets and accommodation in Cork. Since my plastering company was gone, my cousin Jim and I saw a great opportunity so we started putting together packages, arranging discounted rates with various hotels for block-booking rooms. It was the beginning of a joint business venture.

Stephen beat Eubank for the second time. I wasn't worried and I actually allowed myself to enjoy the fight. This time there was no knockdown to survive when the fight entered the championship rounds. He didn't need tricks or gimmicks. He didn't need shaggy dogs or shaggy dog stories. He fought with his heart and his hands. And that was all he ever needed.

12

Stephen was my little brother. That was how I thought of him from the day he was born. But that all changed when he beat Chris Eubank. Suddenly, I was *his* brother. For about two years afterwards my relationship to Stephen was what defined me more than anything else. I embraced it. I grew a goatee like his and people started to mistake me for him. It was great craic.

Caroline and I went to London to see a show in the West End. We had a few beers with John Swift, who I'd signed for Bangor, and his wife, Lorna.

'Here,' I said, 'what's the best nightclub in London?'

Swifty told me about a place in Covent Garden where the celebrity crowd hung out.

'But we won't get in,' he said.

'We'll see about that,' I told him.

The four of us jumped into a taxi. When we pulled up outside the club, I slipped the driver an extra twenty quid and said, 'Do me a favour – will you go up to the bouncer and say that Steve Collins is in the car?'

The driver was happy to do it. The next thing, the bouncer walked up to my door, saying, 'Facking Steve! Come on in! Who's wiv you, champ?'

'Er, Dean Holdsworth,' I said.

Swifty was a ringer for Holdsworth, who played up front for Wimbledon.

'And this is Caroline and Lorna,' I added.

A couple of minutes later, he was leading us up a spiral staircase to the VIP lounge. The place was filled with famous faces. Caroline spotted Naomi Campbell. Swifty recognized Tony Hadley from Spandau Ballet. We spent about an hour there, knocking back champagne and chatting to boxing fans.

'You gonna beat Nigel Benn?' I was asked.

'I'm gonna knock him out,' I said. 'Have you met Dean Holdsworth?'

Next of all, I got a tap on the shoulder. It was the bouncer.

'Champ, you'll never guess who's on his way down here,' he said. 'Gary Stretch.'

Gary Stretch was a former British light-middleweight champion. He knew Stephen well – they'd shared digs together in Romford.

'I told him you were here,' the man said, 'and he's very excited to see you.'

I turned to Caroline.

'The game's up,' I said. 'We'd better get out of here.'

I thought I'd had my fill of football when Bangor sacked me. I was thirty-five and it was time to retire. But when Marty Quinn, the manager of Cliftonville, phoned and asked if I wanted to finish out my career in Belfast, I was flattered that he thought I had something left to give.

We shook hands on a twelve-month contract and he gave me a £1,000 signing-on fee. The relationship didn't last long. Once you've been in charge of a dressing room, I discovered, it's very difficult to go back to being just a player again. At half-time, in a match against Ards, I started bollocking one of the senior players out of it like I was the boss. After the match, Marty asked if we could have a chat outside.

'Rod,' he said, 'I don't think this is going to work out.'

I understood. If a player had undermined me like that, I'd have slung him out too. I saved him the embarrassment of having to sack me.

'Yeah, I know,' I said, 'my legs are gone,' and Marty – a decent man – let me pretend that that was why I had to go.

Two weeks later I drove up to Belfast and I gave the £1,000 signing-on fee back to Jim Boyce, the chairman of the club.

'It's your money,' he insisted. 'We gave you a contract and the manager decided that he didn't want you any more.'

'No, Jim,' I said, 'I don't want nothing for nothing.'

Then Turlough turned up – as Turlough had a tendency to do. He was now managing Bohemians and he asked would I be interested in coming back to Dalymount. The idea of finishing my career back where it started really appealed to me. So, for the third time in my career, I said yes to Turlough. But then he signed Padraig Dully from Shamrock Rovers. Not only was he a centre-forward, he was five years younger than me.

'Turlough,' I said, 'what are you doing to me?'

If I wanted regular, first-team football, he said, Martin Bayly and Austin Brady, my old Bohs team-mate, were interested in having me back at Home Farm, who were in the First Division and were now called Home Farm Everton. The season was turning out to be a bit of a farewell tour of my old clubs. I left Bohs without getting a game and spent the 1995–96 season as a Farm Boy again. I played about twelve matches, but it was an exciting season because we were going for promotion and we secured a two-legged play-off against Athlone Town, another one of my old clubs, for a place in the Premier Division. The tie was eventually decided by a penalty shoot-out, which we won 4–3. Athlone were relegated to the First Division, where they would remain until seventeen years later, when I took them back up in my first season as manager.

Playing just up the road in Whitehall meant I could give more time to Dublin Party Planners, a business that I set up with my cousin Jim Collins arranging stag parties and hen nights in Dublin as well as corporate packages to Stephen's fights. We got to know the managers of various pubs, restaurants and hotels around the city, who would offer us generous discounts to bring business to them.

We were operating out of Tommy Donnelly's Olympus Gym on Capel Street. Before Stephen returned to Millstreet in March 1996 to defend his title against Neville Brown, I went to various hotels and negotiated discounts for block bookings, then I sold the rooms as part of a package, along with a ticket to the fight and a minibus transfer to the Green Glens Arena.

I enjoyed it – the wheeling-and-dealing aspect of it. It became a regular thing then. Stephen would tell me in advance where and when he was fighting. I'd get onto Aer Lingus and start booking seats on flights. The first ones were always cheap. Sometimes I got them for as little as a tenner. I'd get a stack of fight tickets from Frank Warren, Stephen's promoter, on sale or return. I'd negotiate a group rate with a hotel. Then I'd bundle them up into a corporate package.

I got to know Joey the Ticket, as he was known, the best ticket agent in the business. Later, Joey and I went into business, putting together concert packages under the company name of Corporate Tickets, Tours and Events. When Oasis played the Point Depot in Dublin, the gig was sold out within minutes. But Joey could get tickets for anything. We put together packages that included entry to the concert, four free drinks and a bit of finger food while they watched an Oasis tribute act in Slattery's on Capel Street, then a fifty-two seater bus to the Point. We made a fortune on that one.

They were happy, carefree years. I was freed from the stresses of managing a football team while trying to run a plastering business.

Being around Stephen at that time was exciting. He changed quite a few things after he beat Eubank the second time. He split with his manager, Barry Hearn, and his trainer, Freddie King. Tony Quinn was also gone after Stephen beat Cornelius Carr at the Point in November 1995. It was one of his worst-ever performances. I remember being in the Gresham Hotel afterwards and Stephen's face was in bits. Quinn was sitting there, surrounded by sycophants, and I remember thinking, Are you not going to use your faith-healing powers to close up those cuts?

His new trainer was an American named Freddie Roach, who even at the age of thirty-six was regarded as one of the most knowledgeable men in the business. Stephen and Gemma had built a mansion in Castleknock that included a boxing gym, where he worked out between fights. Freddie would come and stay with them in the house. I loved watching them work together.

In the summer of 1996 Stephen was getting ready to defend his title against Nigel Benn. The atmosphere around the house was electric. Stephen sparred with Paschal and they absolutely milled each other. I would have paid money to watch those rounds. Then Jim Rock, a middleweight from Castleknock, would come in and they'd go to war on each other. Then it was my turn to do my four rounds with him. One day Freddie came to me and said, 'I'm going to throw you in with Steve tomorrow, but I want to show you something first.'

He taught me a move that he said would expose a weakness in Stephen's defence. It was jab, dip underneath, body shot, right hook, left hook, right hook. That night, Caroline was in bed and I was still practising the move in front of the mirror. She said, 'Get into bed, you gobshite.'

The next day I stood with Uncle Terry and watched Stephen box four rounds with Paschal and four with Jim. Then Freddie told me to get greased up.

While Terry greased me up, Freddie told me out of the corner of his mouth to just box normally for the first three rounds, so Stephen didn't suspect anything. In the last minute of the fourth round, Freddie gave me the signal to unleash the move. I jabbed him, then dipped to go underneath. What I didn't know was that Freddie had told Stephen what I was going to do. He caught me with a punch as I ducked, then he followed up with about twenty more until he left me dazed on the ropes.

'You bastard!' I said to Freddie as Stephen – nearly doubled over with laughter – returned to his corner.

It was his last spar before he went to Jersey to prepare for the Benn fight. Afterwards we had a barbecue and a big session that ended with a sing-song around the piano. I sat there with a big black eye forming, looking like a chastised puppy. They were the happiest times of our lives.

Stephen gave Caroline an envelope and told her to give it to me later. That night, we went to Fitzsimons Hotel in Temple Bar, where my second cousin Jeffrey worked on the door, to watch Michelle Smith swimming in her first Olympic final. I opened the envelope and there was a cheque for ten grand inside. I rang Stephen from a payphone.

'What are you doing?' I said. 'What's this cheque for?'

And he said, 'Rod, if I can't give it to my brother, who am I going to give it to?'

★

Around that time – it might have even been the day that Stephen left for Jersey – the IRA detonated a 1,500-kilo lorry bomb on Corporation Street in Manchester, injuring two hundred people and causing mass destruction to the centre of the city. They were still sweeping up broken glass three weeks later when we arrived in town for Stephen's fight with Benn at the NYNEX Arena.

There was a rabid anti-Irish atmosphere at the fight that night – worse than anything I experienced playing football in the North. You could feel the charge in the air even through the door of the dressing room. Stephen was serenity itself. He managed to shut out the noise. But the bombing overshadowed the whole fight.

I popped out of the dressing room for five minutes. I wanted to make sure that Caroline and my ma got to their seats safely. I was wearing a jacket made from the same tartan as Stephen's shorts. People started spitting at me – strangers with pure hatred in their eyes. I ran into my cousin Christy. He said there'd been a problem. Someone in the crowd had pulled up Caroline's dress and she and my ma were upset. He brought me to them. I called over a security guard and he took them to a part of the arena where they'd be safe.

I walked back to the dressing room, where Freddie was reminding Stephen of the game plan.

'Don't get drawn into a war,' he warned him.

Benn was still a puncher – and, as the old boxing cliché said, a champion's punch is the last thing to go.

There were three loud bangs on the door and someone shouted, 'Collins – one minute!' and I suddenly felt like I was the one who was going out to fight.

I picked up Stephen's belt and we were led downstairs to an underground car park, where the Sky cameras were going to capture our walk to the ring. They were still on an ad break and we had to stand there shivering in the freezing cold until they were ready.

We walked down the tunnel and into the arena to the loudest chorus of boos I'd ever heard in my life. I was walking behind Stephen, holding the belt over my head, when something hit me on the shoulder. It was a pound coin. Then they started raining down on us. I tried to cover Stephen's head.

'They're throwing pound coins,' I told him.

'Fucking pick them up,' he said.

He was completely calm, even when someone in the crowd reached out and punched him in the side of the head.

We got into the ring. I could see Liam Gallagher from Oasis sitting with Patsy Kensit at ringside. The boos were still echoing around the arena. There was a section of the crowd singing, 'No surrender to the IRA.'

'This is great,' Stephen said to me.

I could see that he was drawing energy from it. I started walking around the ring, holding up the belt. Fired up on adrenaline, I started shouting at Benn: 'You're fucking getting it tonight, pal.'

The fight was a brawl. Stephen went to the body to try to weaken Benn, who kept swinging wildly and missing. It turned on a moment in the third round, when he caught Stephen with a left hook. It was the hardest punch I ever saw my brother take. Stephen stopped in his tracks, then, a second later, stepped forward again. I could see the surprise in Benn's eyes. I think he knew that the fight was over. He didn't have the stamina for twelve rounds, and now he knew he couldn't knock Stephen out. In the fourth round, Benn fell over. When he got up, he was limping. A few seconds after that, he turned his back on Stephen and the referee waved the fight over. I've no idea how injured he was, but I thought he was happy to get out of there. We were too. It was a horrible night.

Back in the dressing room, Stephen said to me, 'What's the story with you? What were you doing shouting at Benn before the fight?'

'I was winding him up,' I said.

'You weren't winding him up,' he said. 'You were motivating him. Then you got out of the ring and you left me in there to do the fighting.'

We bought a party bus. It seemed like a good idea at the time. I bought it with Jim Collins for £3,000 and we dickied it up, fitting it with strobe lights and a state-of-the-art sound system.

We thought it was the absolute business. We drove it around Phibsboro, trying to drum up a bit of attention. You couldn't miss us. It had lights on the roof that flashed so that if you saw it in your rear-view mirror you'd think it was a fire engine.

It wasn't long before we got our first booking – a group of posh ladies from a yacht club somewhere out Sutton direction. We picked them up from a pub on the Howth Road and drove them into town. I was behind the wheel while Jim – an old smoothie – was the DJ. We had a whole itinerary planned, starting with a bite to eat in the Thunder Road Café in Temple Bar. Whenever we stopped at traffic lights, people were banging on the doors, asking to get in. I told them it was a private party, but the phone number was on the side if they wanted to book it.

We crossed O'Connell Bridge with the bus rocking to ABBA's 'Dancing Queen' and the ladies knocking back cheap Liebfraumilch that I'd bought from a lad on Capel Street. People stopped and stared at us open-mouthed as we passed. I drove around College Street onto Westmoreland Street, then swung the wheel left onto Fleet Street. And that was when the music stopped, the lights went off and the engine died.

'Fuck!' I said. I turned the key a few times, but it wouldn't start. 'Jim, I think the battery's after going flat.'

My guess was it was the fault of the electrician who'd wired the lights.

'What are we going to do?' he asked.

We had a problem on our hands because we were blocking Fleet Street and there was suddenly a line of cars and buses behind us, their drivers leaning on their horns.

'You get them off the bus and into Thunder Road,' I said. 'We'll throw in a starter and dessert and buy ourselves some time.'

I started ringing around fellas I knew who might own a set of jump leads, but it was a Saturday night and I couldn't get anyone.

Jim arrived back.

'What's the story?' he asked.

'The story is that I'm resigning from the party bus hire company,' I said. 'You can have my shares.'

By then the traffic was backed up all the way around College Green and halfway up Dame Street and the gardaí were on the scene. Jim managed to get a mate of his to come into town to get the engine started. Then we brought the ladies back onto the bus and we drove them to Joys, a late-night wine bar on Baggot Street.

'Jim,' I said, 'I'm getting locked. Will you drive them home?'

'No, I'm getting locked as well,' he said.

So we persuaded a fella we knew to come into town and drive the ladies home for a few bob while me and Jim milled into the Liebfraumilch. When Joys was over, we sat in the front, well-oiled, while our new driver took everyone to the drop-off point in Howth, where the ladies disappeared off into the night.

I was looking forward to my holidays. Caroline and I were bringing the kids to Florida the next day and we had an early flight out of Dublin. By now, it was about three o'clock in the morning.

'Right,' I said, 'I've to be up in four hours to catch a flight. Get me on the M50 and home.'

And that was when the engine died again. Our friend kept turning the key, but he got no response.

'Heap of junk!' I said, the happy buzz I had from the Liebfraumilch quickly wearing off.

There was a knock on the door of the bus then. It was a woman in a dressing-gown. She said we were obstructing her gate. I told her we'd broken down.

'You, er, couldn't ring us a taxi, could you?' I asked.

'When will this be removed?' she asked.

'Don't worry, madam,' Jim said, exuding his usual charm, 'you'll wake up tomorrow and it'll be gone.'

I was thinking, I don't know about the bus, but I certainly will be.

It was five o'clock in the morning when I arrived home, absolutely banjoed. Caroline had a face like thunder.

'I only had two drinks,' I told her.

'Yeah,' she said, 'a bucket and a basin, by the looks of you. Get up to bed. You've two hours to sleep that off.'

Jim got the bus jump-started the following morning. By the time I got back from Florida he'd sold it for scrap. And that was the end of the party bus.

★

My ma and da – the best-looking couple in Cabra.

The luckiest break of my life was when I met Caroline, and our wedding day was the best day of our lives.

I was registered as an apprentice plasterer in 1978, and I often returned to the trade during my career as a player and manager.

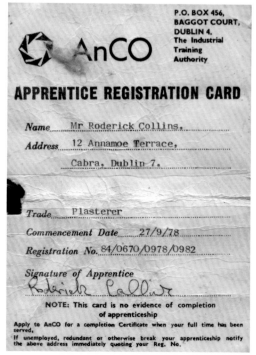

P.O. BOX 456,
BAGGOT COURT,
DUBLIN 4.
The Industrial
Training
Authority

AnCO

APPRENTICE REGISTRATION CARD

Name Mr Roderick Collins.

Address 12 Annamoe Terrace,

Cabra. Dublin 7.

Trade Plasterer

Commencement Date 27/9/78

Registration No. 84/0670/0978/0982

Signature of Apprentice

Roderick Collins

NOTE: This card is no evidence of completion
of apprenticeship

Apply to AnCO for a completion Certificate when your full time has been
served.

If unemployed, redundant or otherwise break your apprenticeship notify
the above address immediately quoting your Reg. No.

With Mansfield Town teammates including Neville Chamberlain (*second from left*). Nevy was very kind to me when I arrived at the club and we became great friends. To the extreme left is defender David Logan and to the right of me, with the moustache, midfielder Tony Lowery, two equally brilliant blokes.

With members of the Bohemians team before a European Cup match against Sporting Lisbon at the Estádio José Alvalade in September 1979. I'm the one in the white vest, sitting next to Bohs manager Billy Young.

One of the many strange twists in my career was the great experience I had at Protestant clubs in the North. Kirk Hunter, a loyalist from the Shankill Road, became a great friend at Crusaders. We never discussed politics, but everything else was on the table.

When my brother Stephen was little, we thought he would become a priest. Instead he became super middleweight champion of the world – and I was proud to lift him on my shoulders after he defended his title against Nigel Benn in Manchester in 1996. (Alamy)

I ended my playing career at St Francis FC, a formerly non-league team that had made it up to the First Division under Pete Mahon. By then I'd had a taste of management, and I knew that's where my future lay.

I first met Vinnie Jones in Las Vegas, at the time of the second Tyson–Holyfield fight in 1997, and we've been great friends ever since.

In the same year I first met Vinnie Jones, I also met another sportsman who became a great friend: Shaun Edwards, the rugby league star turned rugby union coach. Here I am serving as godfather at the christening of his daughter Kitty. (Photo: Michelle Charnock)

My first big coup as a manager of Bohemians was beating Aberdeen over two legs in the UEFA Cup in 2000. (© INPHO/Andrew Paton)

With Steve and the League of Ireland trophy we won in 2001. We went on to win the cup that year too – and yet I got sacked. (© INPHO/Andrew Paton)

My kids Niamh, Sinéad and Roddy Jr in the Millennium Stadium in Cardiff for the final of the LDV Vans Trophy, which was the high point of my dramatic tenure as manager of Carlisle United.

During a period in the wilderness as a manager, I opened a gym, staged unlicensed boxing shows and trained Travellers for bare-knuckle fights. While football was my first sporting love, I was never shy about climbing into a ring. Here, I'm doing pads with the Cuban trainer Nicolás Cruz Hernandez. (© INPHO/Lorraine O'Sullivan)

While managing Monaghan United, I was banned for badmouthing the FAI. I watched from the terrace as we beat Waterford United, and celebrated by screaming 'Fuck you, Delaney, and your fucking ban!'

With Caroline's brother Liam, his partner, Rose, and their daughter, Lauren, whom Caroline and I fostered, on the day of her First Communion.

One of my favourite family photographs, taken at my Hawaiian-themed 50th birthday bash. (*Back row, from left to right*) Sinéad, Donnacha, me, Caroline, Niamh and Roddy. (*Front row*) Lauren and Padraig.

With the grandkids: Fiadh, Grace, Donnacha and Sonny.

It turned out that my football career wasn't over. Around the time of my thirty-sixth birthday I had a call from Larne, who'd just finished second from bottom in the First Division of the Irish League. They thought I could do a job for them.

'No problem,' I said – famous last words.

I played only one match for them. It was against Ballymena United. I drove up with Sinéad, who was now fourteen, and Roddy, who was two. I was named man of the match, but I knew that I didn't have it in my legs any more.

That didn't stop me saying yes to everyone who asked. Next it was Pete Mahon. He was someone I'd always admired. In 1990 he took St Francis, a team from the Liberties, on a fairytale journey all the way to the FAI Cup final, the first non-league team to make it that far. Pete was a football man to his core. I used to drive past his house in Castleknock and see the green-and-white hooped jerseys hanging on his washing line. I'd been telling him for years that he should have been managing a League of Ireland club. And now he was making the leap along with St Francis. In 1996 they joined the First Division. Pete wanted a few older heads who knew their way around the league.

I played the first match of the season against Longford Town. The night before, I had a sharp exchange of views with a lad over a business matter and he nutted me. My head was busted and I was stitched just above the hairline. At some point in the game, a ball was dropping out of the sky and I took it on my chest.

'Head the fucking thing!' Pete shouted.

'Fuck off,' I shouted back.

It was the same problem I had at Cliftonville. I couldn't go back to taking orders again. The following Tuesday we trained in Dolphin Park and Pete said, 'Rod, I'm sorry.'

'Pete, we won't fall out,' I told him.

I never played in the League of Ireland again.

Stephen beat Benn a second time that November – again, at the NYNEX in Manchester. The atmosphere this time was less hostile, and the ending was more decisive. Stephen battered him around the ring and Benn quit on his stool at the end of the sixth round.

After that, he made just two more defences. In February 1997 he beat Frederic Seillier in five rounds at the London Arena. Then, in July 1997, he stopped Craig Cummings in the third in the Kelvin Hall in Glasgow. Jim and I brought a couple of hundred fans over for both fights. For the first, we block-booked a load of rooms in Jurys in Kensington. They'd given us a favourable rate and a function room downstairs to host an after-fight party. I was checking passes at the door along with my bouncer, Decky Weldon. I let Jason McAteer and Phil Babb in, Bonehead from Oasis and his crew, then Martin Offiah, who was with a man I thought was the welterweight boxer Steve 'The Viking' Foster. 'In you go, Martin,' I said. 'Have a good night, Steve.'

The man looked at me strangely. Decky laughed.

'Who did you think that was?' he asked.

'Was it not Steve "The Viking" Foster?' I said.

'No, it was Shaun Edwards – the rugby league player.'

I felt like a right dope. I used to watch matches on TV on a Sunday afternoon, when he was a star for Wigan, and I thought he was brilliant. I went over to apologize.

'OK, pal,' he said.

We got talking. It's happened to me only a handful of times that I've met someone and within five minutes felt like I've known them all my life, and this was one of them.

A few weeks later Shaun rang me to say he was coming to Dublin with a few mates. I had a great night out with them. Shaun loved a pint and a sing-song. But there was real substance to him as well. He was dedicated to his job. He wanted to become a coach when he finished playing and he was interested in learning anything he could from other sports. I also admired him for his faith. He was a practising Catholic and he took it very seriously. It was five o'clock in the morning when our night out ended and he was at Mass in the Liberties at nine o'clock.

We became great mates. Caroline and I started going to England a few times a year to watch him play for the London Broncos and we had some great nights out with him and his partner, Heather Small from M People.

★

After beating Eubank and Benn twice each, Stephen knew that there were no more big paydays for him on this side of the Atlantic. What he needed at that point in his career was to go back to America to fight one of the big names in the division. And they didn't come any bigger than Roy Jones Jr, who was thought by many to be the best pound-for-pound boxer in the world. The problem was that Jones didn't need him, not when he could go on making tens of millions of dollars for knocking over bums and has-beens.

In June 1997, I took it upon myself to try to make the fight happen. Through Dublin Party Planners I had met Miles Saward, who was the CEO of a travel company called Sports Events Worldwide Limited. He introduced me to John Hyland, the Liverpudlian boxing promoter who managed welterweight Shea Neary. They were interested in putting together a purse that might entice Jones into fighting Stephen. They arranged for me to meet Jon Robinson, who was the head of the World Boxing Union, the newest of the governing bodies. The four of us met in the Waldorf Hotel in London. My job was to deliver Stephen. They asked me how much I thought he might want for the fight. I told them to put an offer together and I would bring it to Stephen. A couple of days later, Miles rang me.

'What are you doing for the weekend?' he asked.

'Nothing,' I said.

'Good,' he said. 'You're coming to Las Vegas with me to see the Tyson v. Holyfield fight. It's all paid for – flights, tickets, the lot.'

Caroline couldn't come, so I brought Barry 'Rambo' Smith, my right-hand man in my new plastering company.

It was the second Tyson v. Holyfield fight – the one where Tyson bit off a chunk of Holyfield's ear. I was sitting in my seat in the MGM Grand, waiting for it to start, when who swaggered past with his entourage? Only Roy Jones Jr himself. Rambo and I jumped up and started roaring at him: 'You're a fucking coward! You won't fight Stephen Collins! You're a fucking windbag!'

It was on that trip that I became friends with Vinnie Jones. One night I overheard someone say, 'There's a famous British footballer down in Circus Circus,' so out of curiosity I headed down there to see who it might be. I walked into the bar and there he was – big

Vinnie Jones, holding court. I loved him as a player, especially for his aggression and his refusal to be intimidated by players' reputations. He reminded me of Big Kirk. I'd a few drinks on me, so I tipped over and said, 'How are you, Vinnie?'

He looked at me. He was half-steamed as well.

'You the facking boxer?' he asked.

'No,' I said, 'I'm his big brother.'

'Here, have a drink.'

We ended up in a nightclub that night. Vinnie and I were still going when the sun came up, singing songs and telling football stories like two old war veterans.

The following weekend, Stephen fought Cummings. Shaun Edwards came to Glasgow to see the show. As a professional athlete, he was obsessed with how Stephen prepared, and he was in the dressing room with me before the fight. Vinnie came to Glasgow too, along with his wife, Tanya. It was the start of a beautiful friendship that has endured for more than twenty-five years.

The talk about a Collins v. Jones fight petered out. I told Stephen to go to Jones's house in Pensacola, Florida, and cause murder outside, the way Muhammad Ali turned up on Sonny Liston's doorstep and acted the maggot. I would have gone with him, but Stephen wasn't up for it. He agreed to fight Calzaghe, then changed his mind and announced his retirement from boxing.

A few weeks before that, I'd announced my retirement from football, which didn't generate nearly as many headlines. I had thought I was going to play for one more season. Brian Arkins, my good friend, was the manager of Leinster Senior League side Whitehall Rangers and Fran 'Alf' Hitchcock, who scored the goal for Athlone Town the night we lost 8–2 to Standard Liège, was his assistant. They asked me to play. They had Brendan Toner in the squad – the man who shouted, 'Let's knock the bollocks out of these English fuckers!' before my first match for the Mansfield Town reserves.

I said I'd give it a go. They had a very professional set-up. We went to Liverpool for pre-season training. That was at the start of August 1997. We played a friendly against Tranmere Rovers. I was playing as a centre-half. I went to clear a ball, but wasn't quick enough. A young lad nicked it off me and scored. I signalled to Fran on the bench.

'Hamstring's gone, Alf!'

But it was me who was gone. We went to the pub afterwards. All the Whitehall players were young fellas and I suddenly felt my age. So I decided that was it. And this time, I meant it.

Life went on. Over time, I lost interest in Dublin Party Planners. The logistics of moving large numbers of people around the place became a headache. Jim took over the company and turned it into a highly successful travel company called Best4Travel with his son Jeffrey. I started drifting back into contracting again. The Dublin skyline was full of cranes and there was no end of work for tradesmen.

One Monday in the summer of 1998, Stephen asked me to come with him to meet the sponsor of a boxer he was considering training. 'You'll know who it is when you see him,' he said.

We walked into O'Donoghue's on Merrion Row. The man was sitting at the bar with his back to us, wearing a polo shirt which was on backwards. He turned around on his stool. It was Oliver Reed.

Stephen was never a drinker. I think that's why he wanted me along. I wasn't a drinker either, but I had some chance of keeping up with Oliver. Or so I thought. I ordered a Guinness. Oliver was drinking pints of Guinness with gin and tonics to chase them down. I'd seen a lot of big drinkers in football and in construction, but I'd never seen anyone with a tolerance for alcohol like him. After two hours of trying to match him drink for drink, I was locked.

We went back to the Clarence, the hotel where he was staying. His wife, Josephine, was with him, although she wasn't drinking. I rang Caroline. I said, 'Get dolled up quickly and come out. I'm on the lash with Oliver Reed.'

Caroline arrived and so did Stephen's wife, Gemma, and a couple of friends of theirs. And that's where my memory becomes hazy. All I can remember are little snapshots from the evening. Oliver challenged each of us to arm-wrestle him on the floor. He threw his boot across the room. A round of drinks arrived on a tray and he picked up each and every one of them and knocked them back. He threw a champagne glass over his shoulder and it smashed on the floor. He stood on the glass in his stockinged foot and it started pouring with blood.

At the end of the night we walked Oliver up the stairs to his room and said goodnight. I woke up the next morning with a hangover that stuck around for about four days.

A few weeks later, I had a call from Vinnie Jones, who was in Dublin to promote *Lock, Stock and Two Smoking Barrels* with the director, Guy Ritchie, and his co-star, Jason Statham. We all headed to Café en Seine for a few drinks.

I told Vinnie, Guy and Jason that I had to go because we had a family do back in the house. They said they'd come with me.

We arrived back in Castleknock. There was drinking, singing and laughter. I kept the Veuve Clicquot flowing for hours. Guy pointed out that our Waterford Crystal champagne saucers were in fact Waterford Crystal dessert bowls. The three of them were doubled over with laughter at that one.

I was driving through Phibsboro one day that same summer when I decided to stick my head into Dalymount Park to have a look at the old place. Tony O'Connell was the main sponsor of Bohs now through his soft-furnishings company, Jodi. He'd invested a lot of money in the club. There was talk of the ground getting a new €2-million stand and I thought I might tender for the building contract when the time came.

One Monday night towards the end of September I was asleep in bed when the phone rang. It was Turlough.

'How are you, Roddy?' he said.

'Jaysus, Turlough, it's after midnight,' I told him.

'Would you be interested in a job at Dalymount?'

'Is it the new stand?' I asked, sitting up in the bed.

'The stand?' he laughed. 'Roddy, I'm asking would you be interested in being the manager?'

13

The morning after Turlough had phoned, I met him in the coffee shop in Brown Thomas and he brought me up to speed. Joe McGrath, who'd replaced him as manager of Bohemians, was out the door after only a few months in the job. The team was in trouble. They were down near the bottom of the table and it looked like they were going to be fighting a relegation battle. Turlough had been asked to come in to steady the ship. He asked if I'd be interested in being his assistant with a view to eventually taking over the job.

'Turlough,' I said, 'I haven't watched a game in years. I don't know any of the Bohs players.'

'You know Peter Hanrahan,' he said. 'You won the league with him at Dundalk.'

I didn't win the league with Dundalk. But I never could say no to Turlough. Our first training session together was on Monday, 5 October 1998. I wasn't comfortable taking the warm-up. I was too nervous, so I asked Brendan Place, an assistant coach, to do it. As I stood there with Turlough, I noticed quite a few of the players sniggering behind their hands. I don't think Peter took me terribly seriously. He'd scored a load of goals for Dundalk while I was on the bench and here I was giving him instructions.

Our first match in charge was against Shamrock Rovers at Tolka Park on a Friday night. We lost 3–0. An angry crowd waited for us outside the ground. They roared at me: 'Collins, you muppet!' and, 'You're only Turlough's boy!'

A lad spat at Turlough, so I gave him a punch in the head. The gardaí arrived, put us in the back of a Garda van and drove us down Richmond Road. We'd gone about fifty yards when I said, 'Let me out of this van.'

I walked back to the ground, where the supporters were still gathered. There was a trailer there. I climbed up on it, thinking I was Michael Collins. I said we'd have a meeting in Dalymount Park on Monday night if they wanted to talk about things in a civilized manner. I was remembering the Orange Order hall in Bangor.

The meeting was set for seven o'clock in the bottom bar in Dalymount. I had a fear that it could turn ugly, so I asked my brother Paschal to come with me, and a great friend of mine, Stevie Spicer – 'The Driver', we called him, because he drove a taxi. I arrived early and the place was already jammed. A deathly silence fell on the room when I walked in. I stepped up onto the little stage and I said my few words. I understood their concerns. I said it hurt me deeply, as a Bohs fan from childhood, to see the team humiliated by Rovers like that. Someone shouted that we were going to be relegated. I said, 'I promise you, we won't be relegated.'

Tony O'Connell was at the meeting. I appreciated him showing up. 'I want you to know,' he said, waving a piece of paper in the air, 'that I'm fully behind you, son. And here's some money towards a few players.'

It was a cheque for ten grand.

'I'm asking you to be patient,' I said. 'And I promise, in three years, we'll win the league.'

Paschal started clapping, prompting about half the room to join in. I took it as my cue to leave. Not everyone was won over. As I looked over my shoulder, I saw that Paschal had a fella up against the wall by the throat.

'Did you hear what he called you?' he asked me afterwards.

'I'm sure I'll be called worse,' I said.

Shaun Edwards came over to Dublin to stay with us. He was coming to the end of his rugby career and he was planning to move into coaching. He arrived with a stack of books about football, boxing, rugby, and all sorts of other sports, which he studied for hours in our spare room while drinking endless amounts of tea from a soup mug. He used to demonstrate tactical ideas sitting at the table using the salt and pepper shakers and whatever else was to hand. 'Doesn't matter what sport you're on about,' he said to me one day, 'defence is the bedrock of every great team. Defence is what wins you leagues.'

That stuck with me. Shortly after that, we played Derry City. I noticed that Liam Coyle kept dropping deep and I said to Turlough that someone needed to pick him up. Turlough didn't listen to me and Coyle scored. A day or two later I was having a cup of coffee with Louis Copeland in the little room above his shop on Capel Street. In the nine years since I'd asked him to make a suit for Stephen, Louis had become a friend and confidant. He knew something was bothering me.

'It's not going to work out at Bohs,' I told him. 'I can see ways to make the team better, but I've too much respect for Turlough to question him.'

He picked up the phone without saying a word. He rang Tony. He'd known him for years, just as he knew Turlough.

'I've Roddy here,' he said, then he handed the phone to me. 'Tell him what you just told me.'

So I did.

'Leave it with me, son,' Tony said.

The next day Turlough rang and asked me to meet him in FXB in Blanchardstown. Turlough let me do all the talking as usual. I told him I couldn't be his number two. I had to be the manager or nothing.

'You've no experience,' he said, fiddling with the salt cellar. 'You're going to be in a relegation battle. And the supporters don't like you.'

He wasn't doing a lot for my confidence.

'So who would you have with you,' he asked, 'as your number two?'

'Terry Eviston,' I said. 'Matter of fact, he's outside.'

'Bring him in,' said Turlough.

Terry had won the league twice with Turlough at Dundalk and he loved the man as much as I did.

'I don't think you have enough experience,' Turlough said, 'but sure you might as well have a go at it. And if you need any help, just ask and I'll be there beside you.'

He stood up and gave us both a big hug. And that was it. At thirty-eight years of age, I was the manager of Bohs, the club I supported as a boy.

My first match in charge was against UCD at Dalymount. I threw a tracksuit on before I went out for the warm-up. The next thing, Tony was screaming at me from the sideline to go back to the dressing room to take it off. He was right. He'd hired Roddy Collins, the man with the bespoke suits and the swagger and the big statements, not a man who looked like a PE teacher.

We won the match, but I knew that a lot of things had to change. The atmosphere was more like a social club than a football club. There was a pool table and a dartboard in the dressing room. In my first week, I was having a meeting with a player when one of the fellas walked in with a tray of drinks and a set of darts. I went home and came back with a screwdriver and a ratchet set. I took the pool table apart and threw the pieces out into the hallway. I hoped the message was clear – I'm the king of this castle now.

I rang an old friend of mine from Cabra, Thomas Sinnott, a painter and decorator and a Bohs supporter. I asked him to paint the walls of the home dressing room in red and black stripes and the away dressing room the most insipid shade of white he could find. He did it for free. I asked Brian Arkins, my old manager from Whitehall Rangers who ran BA Engineering, to make some aluminium benches for the away team to sit on. I wanted them to feel like they were in a South American jail.

The next thing I had to tackle was our playing personnel. When we lost at home to Sligo Rovers, I knew we were going down unless I had a clear-out. I told the lads we were going to train on Sunday morning. I put on my pinstriped suit, a crisp white shirt and a red tie. I'd read somewhere that an American president – might have been John F. Kennedy – used to wear a red tie if he wanted to give off an air of authority. I walked into the dressing room.

'Nobody strips,' I told the players. 'We're going to have a meeting.'

First, I picked out Joe McGrath's son, Derek – a great midfielder and a brilliant bloke.

'Derek, I want you to leave,' I said. 'Your father's been sacked and I don't want you to hear anything that upsets you.'

'No problem, Rod,' he said.

'Lads,' I said. 'We're going to get relegated this season and I'll tell you why.'

I went around the room and told each player what he was doing wrong and what I expected him to do to put it right. I was in mid-flow when in walked Donal Broughan, kit bag slung over his shoulder. Donal was a decent defender, but I didn't like his attitude. 'Donal,' I said, 'get your bag and fuck off. You're finished.'

'I'm what?' he said.

'You're never going to play for us again,' I told him.

Now I definitely had the full attention of the room. Before he took the Bohs job, Joe McGrath had managed New Zealand and he'd brought three Kiwi players over with him. I didn't think much of them. 'Lads,' I said, 'you're not going to be good enough for this level. It'd be best if you went back to your families.'

The next day, I called in Fergal Harkin, a right-sided midfielder, another signing of Joe's. 'Fergal, if we were winning the league, you'd be my kind of a player,' I said. 'But not for a relegation dogfight.'

He stood up, shook my hand and left.

That was six players gone. The others now knew I was serious.

We trained in Santry on Tuesday night and we didn't have enough players for a seven-a-side. Terry was seriously worried.

'It's grand,' I told him. 'I've a plan.'

I'd no plan. By Friday morning, I was the one who was worried. In desperation, I rang John Still, who was manager of Barnet and had an encyclopaedic knowledge of English non-league football. According to Stilly, there were 1,500 professional footballers on the dole in England. I told him what I needed. A midfielder and a forward. They didn't have to be the most skilful players in the world, as long as they were men of the road who knew how to play the game and had the guts for a relegation battle.

'Your luck's in,' he said. 'I know two lads who've just come back from Hong Kong Rangers and they're training here with me.'

I'd never seen these fellas play. He hadn't even told me their names.

'I'll take them,' I said. 'I need them to be in Cork for Sunday.'

It was Friday. To play that weekend, they had to be registered by five o'clock that day. I asked Stilly to get them to put their signatures on a sheet of A4 paper, then fax it to me, so that we could then cut them out, glue them to the registration forms and fax a photocopy to the FAI. Then, when they came in the following morning, they could sign the originals and we'd post them.

'Hang on,' I said, 'I haven't even asked you their names.'

'Kevin Hunt,' he said, 'and Dean Martin.'

'Dean Martin?' I said. 'Stilly, are you winding me up?'

I got the players registered. On Saturday morning my friend Stevie drove to the airport to collect them and bring them to training in Santry. When they got out of the back of Stevie's taxi, I couldn't believe what I was looking at. They were tiny. And Kevin had a haircut like a young Pam Ayres. I put them up for the night in the Arlington Hotel on Bachelors Walk. I rang Stilly again.

'Trust me, mate,' he said.

The next morning, we travelled to Cork on the bus. I spent the entire journey picking the team, then unpicking it, then picking it again. In Newbridge, the two new fellas were playing. By Portlaoise, they were on the bench. By Thurles, they were back in the team. When we reached Cork, I decided that I was going to start them.

'Number eleven,' the stadium announcer said through the loudspeakers, 'he's not a singer, he's a winger – it's Dean Martin.'

The whole crowd laughed. I was having palpitations in the dugout, thinking about the headlines if this went wrong, Rat Pack song titles that could be used against me. I was looking at Hunty in midfield, trying to convince myself that he was tough enough. After about five minutes he went in for a fifty–fifty with Mark Herrick and Herrick went about four feet in the air. I thought, 'You'll do for me, son!'

We drew with Cork. Deano did well, but he did his hamstring. Then we went on a bit of a run – and you could see the belief growing in the players. But the pressure of managing a team like Bohs was all-consuming. I could be out with Caroline for a meal and afterwards I couldn't tell you a single thing she said. After a bad result, I was like a bear. I'd go home, put Roddy into the bed with Caroline and I'd lie awake all night in his room, staring at the Power Rangers wallpaper, feeling like I'd a steamroller parked on my chest, worried I was going to let Tony down. There was a feeling of joy that came in the closing minutes of a match when you were winning handily and you knew it was down to something tactical that you did. But it never lasted beyond that night. The next day, I'd be back in a trance again, thinking about the next match.

Deano came back against Shamrock Rovers and he did great. But I'd been told that we could only afford to keep one of the two players and it was always going to be Hunty. Deano was a brilliant bloke. A clean liver. A fitness fanatic. He also had his girlfriend living with him in the hotel and she was pregnant. He was devastated. Him and Hunty had been mates since they were kids and they'd been in Hong Kong together. I was devastated too, but I couldn't afford to be sentimental.

Our form was up and down over the season. Graham Lawlor was banging in the goals for us and then they suddenly dried up. And so the pressure on me increased. From the start, I knew I wasn't liked at the club. Someone told me that one of the old Bohs stalwarts said, 'Can he not tone down the accent? He talks like a docker.'

'What's wrong with dockers?' I asked. 'My wife comes from a family of dockers. And if I *was* a docker, I'd be getting paid a lot more money than I am for managing this team.'

It would have cost me nothing to walk away. For my first ten weeks at Bohs I wasn't paid at all; then I agreed to a basic wage of £200 per week. I didn't need the money. I was back running a plastering company again and it was flying. I just didn't want to be the manager who got Bohs relegated for the first time in their history.

The committee that ran the club weren't convinced by me. I was Tony's man, not theirs, anointed by the club's biggest benefactor and appointed without any interview process. When we hit a bad patch that season, I remember Gerry Cuffe, one of the committee men, standing in the dressing room one day with a big Amen face on him. I said, 'Get the fuck out of my dressing room,' and I ran him out.

Politically, it wasn't the wisest thing I ever did. But we were in relegation trouble. The last thing I needed was men sucking the energy out of the dressing room.

One Saturday morning I went with Turlough to watch our reserves play against Shelbourne in Harold's Cross – and there, in the centre of the pitch, was Paul Byrne. I'd admired Byrnesy for years. When I was at Crusaders, he played against us for Bangor. I was on the bench. He'd brought his little boy to the match and the kid sat beside me in the dugout as we watched his da put on this absolute masterclass. Since then, he'd gone to Celtic and scored a famous volley in the Old Firm derby. But then he left Parkhead and there were questions about his attitude and his fitness. He'd spent the last few years drifting, from Brighton to Southend, to Glenavon, and now to Shels, where he was on trial, getting no money. I barely recognized him. He was about two stone overweight, but you could see that the magic was still there. He could make a football do anything.

I told the club that I wanted to sign him, but they said no. I persuaded Shels to let us have him on trial and I put him on the payroll of my plastering company for two months while he got fit. Every morning, he got up at six o'clock and ran with my brother Paschal, who was now training boxers. I played him against Waterford United in the FAI Cup. He was still carrying a bit of weight. I asked Caroline's sister Martina to sew an extra inch onto either side of his shorts to make him look thinner. He was goggle-eyed looking at the things. 'If there's a big wind,' he said, 'I'll be found in Tipperary.'

We won 4–0 and he was the man of the match. By Monday morning he was my player. His weight was never an issue for me after that. There was no flab on Byrnesy. He was big, but he was solid, like Paul Gascoigne. And whether it was a fifty-yard sprint or a five-mile run we did in training, he never finished outside the top five.

I mentioned that Marc Kenny was one of the three most talented players who ever played for me. Byrnesy was another. He drove me absolutely mad, of course. But he was a brilliant fella. An absolute one-off. His awareness was such that he could tell you who was at the match and where they were sitting. He used to chat to his mates in the crowd while the game was going on. Someone threw a can of beer at him once. Byrnesy picked it up, had a mouthful, then set off down the wing with it in his hand. He was a great character to have in the dressing room.

As we came nearer the end of the season, we were still in relegation trouble. The abuse from the crowd was horrendous. Sometimes the only thing you could do was laugh. In one match, one of our players limped off the pitch, cupping his groin. A man shouted, 'I know how you feel. I've a pain in me bollicks looking at yous.'

The worst of it was aimed my way: 'You're a fucking dummy, Collins!' and, 'You don't know what you're at.'

I had two allies in the boardroom. One was Tony, the other was Jim Fitzpatrick, a member of the committee, who let me know what way the wind was blowing. He'd say to me, 'Lose this one, Roddy, and you're going to be sacked.'

From March onwards, the pressure was intense and unrelenting. If we won, Caroline needed a lasso to get me out of Lillie's Bordello. If we lost, I'd creep up the stairs and sleep in the Power Rangers room. And it was around that time that I saw the ghost.

Caroline and I had been hearing strange noises in the house for a while. We'd be watching the telly and we'd hear footsteps coming down the stairs. I'd check and find Sinéad, Niamh and Roddy asleep in their beds.

One night in bed, I opened my eyes and I saw a little girl poking her head around the bedroom door. She walked into the room and she stood next to the bed. She had a little angelic face on her. She stared at me, then disappeared out of the room. I jumped out of the bed, threw on my trousers and checked on the kids. They were all conked out. I went downstairs and sat at the kitchen table, thinking I was cracking up. I went back to bed. Caroline was awake.

'I saw her,' she said.

'Did you?' I asked.

'It was a little girl.'

We asked a priest to come around to say some prayers. Not long after that, I woke up to see the same little girl with a tall man and then a smaller lad, standing against the wall at the end of our bed. They walked towards the window and disappeared behind the curtains. And I never saw them again.

I couldn't tell anyone outside of our families, because they'd have thought I was losing the plot. And with good cause, because I was under severe pressure. We lost at home to Waterford. I went into the boardroom afterwards and it was like someone had died. Tony was

smoking one of his big Havanas, looking worried. The most important thing when you're a manager fighting relegation is never to show
whatever turmoil is going on inside you.

'Cheer up, Tony,' I said. 'Have you seen what's happening in
Kosovo?'

He took a big drag on his Havana.

'If you get us relegated,' he said, 'you'll be fucking going to live
there, son. And I'll pay for your flight.'

Our last match of the season was against UCD in Belfield. Their
season was over. They had nothing to play for. We needed a draw to
be safe. The pressure got to us. We lost 2–0. We now faced a two-
legged play-off against Cobh Ramblers to remain in the Premier
Division. As I was heading back to the dressing room, one of the
Bohs supporters handed me a giant card. I thought it was a good luck
card until I opened the envelope. It said, 'Congratulations on Your
Retirement.' It had been signed by thirty or forty supporters.

The next day was Monday. I called everyone in for a team meeting
in Dalymount. I tried to fire the fellas up. I told them we were in a
cup final. Two cup finals. 'I wish the match was tomorrow,' I said.
'We're going to tear them apart.'

We trained that week at King's Hospital and we trained well. But
as a manager, things happen that are outside of your control. Ray
Kelly was a player I'd brought over on loan from Manchester City.
He was a lovely kid and a brilliant goal-scorer. Five days before the
first leg, he came to me, upset. His fiancée had called off their wedding. He was heartbroken and I wondered if he would be emotionally
strong enough to face Cobh. I asked him not to tell the rest of the
team. I didn't want it to bring down the mood of the dressing room.
Two days later another player came to me and said he'd been in a car
accident and hurt his back. I asked him could he even sit on the bench,
but he was worried it might affect his insurance claim.

On Sunday morning we got the bus to Cobh. We stopped at a petrol station in Horse and Jockey so the players could stretch their legs
and buy a bottle of water and a newspaper. I went in to have a slash
and I spotted Byrnesy at the deli counter, ordering a full Irish breakfast roll. I stood behind him and I had a listen. 'Yeah, throw a few

more sausages on that,' he was saying. 'A few more rashers there, love – yeah, why not.'

I couldn't believe it. Along with Hunty, Byrnesy was my star man.

'Bit of black pudding as well,' he said.

'All right, Byrnesy?' I said.

'Yeah, boss, super-duper.'

'Getting a bit of a roll there, are ye?'

I was looking at the woman wrapping the thing. It was about a foot-and-a-half long.

'Are you having a fucking laugh?' I said.

'What's wrong?' he said. 'We're not playing until eight o'clock tonight.'

'That thing'll be in your stomach for three fucking days,' I told him.

In the end, the bus driver got Byrnesy's breakfast roll. He was still eating it when we pulled into Cobh.

When I looked at the boys in the dressing room before the match, it was the most uptight group of players I'd ever seen. They'd all heard about Ray's broken engagement and I could see that they were down in the dumps for him. So at the end of the team talk I said, 'And by the way, lads, if anyone's looking for a wedding dress, Ray's bird is selling one.'

Ray laughed. And then there was this huge dam-burst of emotion from everyone. We were ready. We went out to play. We got a lucky break when the Cobh keeper gave Ray a punch in the mouth and got himself sent off. We battered them 5–0.

The second leg was three days later. I couldn't sleep the night before. To be a football manager is to never relax. All the worst-case scenarios played out in my head. But we won 2–0. It felt like a physical weight had been lifted from my back. I'd kept my promise to Tony. I'd stopped Bohemians from being relegated for the first time in their history. I looked around at all the players who'd given their heart and soul to the team. And I knew that most of them would have to go.

That summer I was summoned to Dalymount for a meeting. After saving Bohs from relegation, I presumed the committee wanted to thank me for my service and give me a two-year contract. But when

I walked into the boardroom I sensed the coolness right away. Gerry Cuffe, Felim O'Reilly, Oliver Ward and Stephen Burke – all the usual suspects were there. And they weren't exactly falling over themselves to be the first to shake my hand.

'Is everything all right?' I said, taking a seat.

Everything wasn't all right. They gave me a laundry list of all the things that were wrong. The supporters hated me. Half the players were fighting with me. They didn't like the way I conducted myself in my dealings with the media.

'I kept us in the Premier Division,' I said. 'That was my brief.'

With the players I had at my disposal, I was told, we should never have been in the play-offs in the first place. I felt a cold rush. I wanted to turn over the table – I thought, Fuck you! – but I managed to resist the urge. When I got home that day, I rang Tony. He was on holiday in Italy. I told him there was a heave on against me.

He said, 'Leave it with me, son.'

He rang me back later on and said the board wanted me out. He'd managed to buy me some time, but I'd have to sign a document. The next day I was presented with it – a typed statement on a single page. It said that if the officer board were unhappy with me after eleven matches of the 1999–2000 season, I would resign with no remuneration and without speaking to the media or any third party. It was Tony who suggested the terms of the agreement because he believed that eleven matches was all I needed to prove the board wrong. The alternative was that I was out. So I signed it and went home to Caroline in a terrible state.

I had a vision for Bohemians. I wanted to turn them into a full-time professional club and that was my plan for my second season at Dalymount. People asked me at the time was I copying the Scandinavian model, which had helped small, unfashionable clubs like IFK Göteborg and Rosenborg BK to punch above their weight in the European Champions League. The truth was I didn't know the first thing about the Scandinavian model. To me it just stood to reason that the players would be better off if they weren't going to training exhausted after being on a building site all day like I was.

We had no budget to pay players a full-time wage, so I started looking at ways to make it work. I went to FAS, the training and employment body, who gave us £140,000 to employ players as apprentices. I brought in new sponsors to try to beef up our payroll. I was friendly with Des Kelly, the carpet man. I asked him to give us £25,000 a year for pitchside advertising and the naming rights to one of the club bars and he agreed. I promised him that I'd tell the players to celebrate all of their goals in front of the hoarding bearing his company's name.

We needed a change of scenery as well. I arranged for us to move our training ground to the ALSAA Sports Centre on the Old Airport Road. Then I started putting together a proper backroom team. I wanted Terry Eviston to become my full-time assistant manager, but he already had a job as a schoolteacher, which he loved. So I brought over John Lewis, my old pal from the Welsh valleys who'd been my manager, briefly, at Newport. Lewie was the head of youth development for the Football Association of Wales but wanted to get back into management. I brought in Stefano Manassero, a masseur and champion powerlifter who'd worked with Paschal. Stefano was an expert in soft-tissue injuries and using massage and stretching techniques to avoid them.

We lost a few players during the summer. Some of them we needed to lose, but some of them broke my heart when they went. Paul Byrne drove me mad at times, but it was a huge blow when he told me he was moving to St Patrick's Athletic.

Then I got a lucky break. Rob Kelly was a cousin of mine from Birmingham who worked as the Youth Development Officer with Wolverhampton Wanderers. He rang me and said, 'There's a kid from Dublin here who's after getting released. He's an absolute goal machine.'

'What's his name?' I asked.

'Glen Crowe,' he said. 'Livingston are interested in him, but I think he'd prefer to go home to Ireland. Roddy, trust me, this lad is the real deal.'

I met Crowey in The Bell in Blanchardstown with Bernie and Tommy, his ma and da. They were lovely people. Crowey sat there and didn't say two words. But I told him my plans. Within two years, I told him, we were going to win the league. We agreed a deal. That night I woke up in a cold sweat. I realized that I didn't have his signature, which meant – as Turlough had taught me – I didn't have the player. I checked the clock. It was five in the morning. I got out of bed. Crowey had mentioned that he was going on holidays the next day with his mot, Alison. I drove to Dublin Airport and I waited for them in the departures hall, staring at the door like a bear at a fox-hole. An hour later, they walked in with their suitcases. Crowey was shocked to see me there.

'Glen,' I said, 'can I have a word? Were you happy with what we discussed last night?'

'Yeah,' he said, 'very happy.'

'I'm sorry to do this to you. I know you're off on your holliers. But could I get your name on a bit of paper?'

It was one of the most important signings I ever made as a manager. Crowey was what every club with ambitions of winning the league needed – a striker who was guaranteed to get you more than twenty goals a season.

I brought other players in. Mick Riordan, a lifelong friend who I played with at Home Farm, was now coaching in America with the Boston Bulldogs. They had a centre-half named Avery John, who'd played international football for Trinidad and Tobago and wanted to come to Europe. I collected him at Dublin Airport and took him straight to the dole office on the Navan Road to sign on. Three days later I brought him to FAS on Jervis Street to register him as an apprentice, making up the rest of his wages in expenses.

If players couldn't commit to full-time football, I moved them on. I tried to change the mindset of the players by doing things the Arsène Wenger way, which meant constantly reinforcing the message that they were athletes. The League of Ireland had always been a league for garglers and the idea of abstaining from alcohol and eating healthily was revolutionary in the late 1990s.

I met Jason Cowman, who's now the strength and conditioning coach for the Ireland rugby team. Back then, he was a young Sports Science graduate bursting with ideas. He gave me a training plan and diet sheets for the players, outlining the kind of foods they should be eating and avoiding. Half of them ended up on the floor. I picked them up and made the players take them home. I brought in Brendan

'Foxy' O'Connor, a chef who was married to Rose Dunne, an aunt of boxer Bernard Dunne and an old friend of Caroline's from O'Devaney Gardens. He cooked for us.

As the second season wore on I became more and more concerned with what players were doing to recover after matches. In my time, we went to Rumours and sank seven or eight pints of stout, and it set our fitness back two or three days. That couldn't go on any more. Before every away match, Caroline put together twenty-two recovery packs, each one containing a chicken sandwich, a protein bar and a litre of water. They were waiting for the players when they returned to the dressing room.

Suddenly, the players were doing things they'd never done before, like rehydrating, cutting down their alcohol consumption, eating carbs at the right times, avoiding red sauces, stretching and having their muscles massaged. I also had them doing intense boxing training in Tommy Donnelly's gym on Capel Street. But even full-time players couldn't train all day. Professional footballers have a lot of downtime. During my years in England I'd seen a lot of young players drawn into pubs and betting shops to kill time in the afternoons. I visited the Blanchardstown Institute of Technology and they agreed to offer courses to some of our younger fellas. I wanted a dressing room full of players who were intellectually curious and socially confident and could hold their own in any kind of company.

Everyone could sense that I was building something at Bohs, and that second season was all about laying the foundations for it. We trained five times a week, three mornings and two evenings, working together as a unit. And we were on fire. We started putting together back-to-back wins, which was impressive, given that we were forced to play our home matches at Tolka Park while a new stand was being built at Dalymount.

And that whole time I was on trial, the threat of being sacked hanging over me. Our eleventh match of the season – the last covered by the agreement – was against Sligo Rovers on 31 October, the day the new stand opened. We won 3–2 to go top of the table. I knew I was unsackable – for now, anyway. After the match, I lost the plot. I tore into the boardroom where the committee men were having their post-match drink and I roared, 'Fuck you – and fuck your fucking legal papers!' Tony grabbed a hold of me and hustled me into the corner to try to calm me down. I thought, Top of the table. I fucking showed them – these fucking eejits.

We were never going to win the league. Shelbourne were the best team in the country by a mile. I knew what was required to match them and we didn't have that yet, but I thought we could finish inside the top three and maybe go on a cup run. The axe had been lifted from over my neck for now. But a lot of my time and energy was wasted on petty rows with the committee and other figures within the club. I found myself involved in almost daily battles for things big and small: a set of training balls that actually matched; aluminium skips for the kit; Jelly Babies and bananas for the players at half-time, which everyone thought was a hilarious request, even though professional athletes had been using them for years for short-term energy gains.

'Are you going on a fucking picnic?' one committee man asked.

It seemed to me that everything I suggested was either questioned, sneered at or shot down in flames. Ireland was in the middle of a building boom and I had loads of mates in the construction industry who were suddenly millionaires. I came up with the idea of roping off one of the bars and selling a VIP experience to them. I was told that the members wouldn't like it.

It was exhausting. But as long as I was winning matches, I was untouchable. Things were going great. I was tearing up trees with Bohs and my plastering business was thriving thanks to my increased media profile. For the first time in a long time, everything seemed to be coming together. One afternoon I was driving along the quays, heading towards Parkgate Street, when Caroline rang.

'Pull over,' she said, 'I have to tell you something.'

I thought someone had died. I pulled up onto the footpath.

'What's wrong?' I asked.

'I'm pregnant,' she said.

This wave of pure and utter joy swept over me. Of course she was pregnant. There were six years in age between all of our children. With Roddy about to turn six that summer, we were going to have another baby – at forty years of age.

'Are you happy?' Caroline asked.

'I couldn't be happier,' I told her.

It was a great age to be parents again. Life wasn't a struggle any more. All of the uncertainties and fears that had hung over us when Sinéad, Niamh and Roddy were born were gone now.

In May, Shelbourne won the league. We finished third, only a point behind Cork City in second, and we qualified for the UEFA Cup. By any measure, it was a very successful second season and I'd managed to win over a lot of the Bohs fans.

We also reached the FAI Cup final. As well as a chance of winning a first major trophy in nine years, we had an opportunity to stop Shelbourne from doing the double. The final, at Tolka Park, finished 0–0. The replay was fixed for Dalymount the following weekend.

That week, I trained with the fellas on the pitch. I spotted Gerry Cuffe standing on the sideline with a face on him.

'Oi, what are you doing?' he shouted.

I said, 'I'm training,' and then under my breath I said, 'You fucking dope.'

'On the pitch?' he said. 'Did you clear it with Noel Farrell?'

Noel was the committee member in charge of the pitch. Like patron saints, there was a committee member for everything.

'Fuck off, Gerry,' I said.

'We'll see about this,' he said, then off he went in a huff.

I spent the days leading up to the replay winding up Ollie Byrne, the chief executive of Shels, who was famously quick to anger. In Steve Williams he had a brilliant goalkeeper, but he only had him on loan from Dundalk and he hadn't tied him down for the next season. I told the papers that we were going to offer Dundalk £25,000 for him and we'd be discussing personal terms with him before the replay. Ollie went mad. On the way to the dugout he hit me a thump on the stomach and said, 'You won't be getting our fucking goalkeeper!'

The mind games didn't work. We lost the reply 1–0 and Shelbourne claimed the double. We were all desperately disappointed, but I told the players that next year would be our year.

And I wasn't wrong.

14

There was a big do at the end of the season in the Ierne Social and Sports Club in Drumcondra. I could feel a certain coolness in the air. Awards were given out. Speeches were made. And my name wasn't uttered once. I was Roddy the Unmentionable, while everyone went to great lengths to praise Gerry Reddy, the head of youth development. Tony O'Connell pulled me to one side and said, 'Don't open your mouth, son. Leave it.'

I had a little black book in my pocket. In it, I'd written three page headings: 'Allies', 'Enemies' and 'Don't Knows'. After that night, there were no 'Don't Knows'.

I had to face the committee for another performance review. We spent an unnecessarily long time discussing a youth-team player I'd let go who Gerry was convinced was a future Ireland international. But the young lad was a gargler and a bad influence on others. John Lewis, my assistant manager, said something in support of Gerry. I'd already formed doubts about Lewie. During the season I'd seen him pulling players into little huddles to give them instructions after I'd done my final team talk. Now I noticed that he was sitting next to the chairman and not next to me. And suddenly I could see it clearly. Lewie's ambition. When the meeting was over we had an angry exchange of words outside, then I told him to go back to Wales and never set foot in Dublin again.

As a manager, I knew I was on borrowed time. Tony's money wasn't going to keep me there for ever. There was only one way I was going to keep my job and that was by winning the league the next season.

But first I needed a new assistant manager. I was driving through Castleknock one day when I saw Pete Mahon out cutting his grass. I pulled in and I asked him would he come to work with me at Bohs.

'Sure none of them lads will know me,' he said, leaning over his lawnmower.

'Are you having a laugh?' I said. 'You played in the League of Ireland. You managed St Francis.'

He asked me to leave it with him. Later that night he knocked on my door and said he'd do it.

Then I brought in Liam O'Brien as a player-coach. Liam had had a great football career in England with Manchester United, Newcastle United and Ireland and I thought it'd be useful to have someone of his experience on the staff. Liam was brilliant. He called everyone 'Egghead' because it saved him having to remember names, but I liked his abrasiveness.

I had another clear-out that summer. I let six players go, including Robbie Brunton, Eoin Mullen and Derek Swan, because they couldn't commit to full-time football. As well as that, if we were going to push on, we needed fresh blood. The player I wanted more than any other was Trevor Molloy. He was a brilliant striker who I knew would be the perfect partner for Crowey up front. Trevor was a St Patrick's Athletic player. His manager, Pat Dolan, was happy to sell him if the price was right, but it took weeks for us to agree what that price might be. We were meeting for dinner twice a week to discuss it. I put on half a stone trying to sign Trevor.

Eventually, I said, 'Pat, I'm fed up eating. Let's just go for a walk in the Phoenix Park.'

Pat wanted £50,000 for Trevor. I told him the best I could do was £25,000. I asked was there anything I had that he wanted. He said he liked big Jamie Harris, a centre-forward who wasn't part of my plans for next season. So I said I'd give him £25,000 plus Jamie and we shook on the deal. I was pushing my luck because I knew that the Bohs board didn't want Trevor.

'Here, Roddy,' Pat said after we'd concluded business, 'will you show me how to box?' and he put his two fists up.

'Give over, Pat,' I told him.

We were standing on Chesterfield Avenue, near the gates of the Áras.

'Come on, Roddy,' he said, bouncing up and down on the balls of his feet, 'I want to learn how to throw a punch properly, how to jab and duck, all that.'

So I demonstrated for him the basic boxer's stance, then we started snapping jabs at each other. People driving past in their cars started honking their horns at us. Then two or three days later, the story made it into one of the papers – the manager of Bohs and the manager of Pat's had had a straightener in the Phoenix Park.

But I got Trevor. And then I bought Dave Hill from Cork City to be the rock at the heart of my defence. I'd played against Dave in an FAI Cup match in my last days at Home Farm Everton. He was small for a centre-half. I thought, I fancy myself to score against this lad. I didn't win a single header against him. He was a hard-as-nails Englishman who read the game like Paolo Maldini. He stuck in my mind. When we played Cork the previous season, I said to him, 'I'm going to fucking sign you – whatever it takes,' and he laughed.

He was my Roy Keane figure. He wasn't afraid to offer me his opinion – for instance, if he thought I was overtraining the players. He was a model pro. His boots were immaculate. I think he ironed his laces. And it wasn't long before you could see the younger players in the dressing room copying the things he did.

I also brought in Simon Webb, a left-back from Mayo who'd spent a few years in the reserves at Tottenham, and Dave Morrison, a midfielder who played for Leyton Orient when Simon was on loan there. Then I got Tony Hopper, a midfielder who played for Carlisle United. Derek Mountfield, the manager of Cork, was taking him on loan until Christmas. Tony was friends with one of our players, Rob Bowman, who asked me if Tony could train with us for the morning before he headed for Cork. I liked the look of him, and I said to him, 'Don't go to Cork. Play for us.'

So I stole him off Derek. And in more ways than one, it was one of the most important decisions I made in all my years in football.

The players trained every weekday morning. The only exception was Tony O'Connor, or Toccy, our right-back, who worked as a jeweller and came in three days a week. Everyone else worked together at the same time every day. I finally had what I wanted. And

I knew at the start of August 2000 that I had the squad to win the league.

We didn't have time to find our feet as a team. Our first competitive match was in the second week of August, away to Aberdeen in the qualifying round for the UEFA Cup. I picked a starting eleven that had never played together before.

From my own experience of playing in Europe, I knew that our only hope of winning was to get Aberdeen to underestimate us. Whenever a Scottish reporter rang me, I made us out to be a bunch of butcher-baker-and-candlestick-maker part-timers, and we were so short of players we'd be lucky to fill the bench. A letter arrived from a junior player in Scotland offering to play for us if we were short a man and I made sure to give it to the press.

I continued to play the eejit in Scotland. The Aberdeen officials said we could train at Pittodrie the next day. But I said we needed to train that night, since most of our players were working over the weekend and hadn't kicked a ball for nearly a week. There was a massive roundabout in front of our hotel. I said, 'What about that? Could we train on that?'

They looked at me, wondering, Is this yahoo for real?

The next morning we trained in Pittodrie. It was a big, 20,000-seater stadium. I made sure the players went out in mismatched training gear and I told them to warm up with a game of Gaelic football. The Scottish reporters were laughing their heads off. They asked if I thought we had a chance and I said it would be a win for us if we didn't get beaten 10–0.

The night before the match I decided we were going to set a new standard in defensive football. I was going to drop Crowey and put ten men behind the ball, with Trevor Molloy on his own up front. No one was to go up for corners. If we happened to win one, we'd kick it straight out for a throw-in, then invite Aberdeen to try to play through us. I explained the idea to Dave Hill.

'That's mad,' he laughed.

But it was what we did. We frustrated the life out of Aberdeen, with five players strung across the middle of the field. They were running out of ideas when a defensive mistake allowed them to take the lead. But we hit back with just eight minutes left. We won a corner and this time I told everyone to go up for it. Aberdeen were thrown to see so many men in the box. No one knew who was supposed to be picking up who and big Shaun Maher equalized with a bullet header. Then, in the last minute, Darren O'Keefe got hacked down in their box and the ref blew for a penalty. Trevor buried it.

Afterwards, Ebbe Skovdahl, Aberdeen's Danish manager, was asked if he was embarrassed to lose to a team like us. He said no, just disappointed.

'If I was him,' I said, trying to mess with his head, 'I'd be embarrassed. He's on about eight grand a week. I'm on two hundred quid. Maybe I should have his job.'

Afterwards, Pete and I were having a pint in the stadium with Jim McInally, the former Dundee United player who I'd known for years. When I was at Mansfield, he was at Nottingham Forest and we drank in the same pub. I went to look for a toilet. I was having a slash when a drunken Bohs fan at the next urinal looked at me sideways and said, 'Are you fucking having a drink with the supporters or what?'

'I'm having a drink with my friend,' I told him. 'I'll have a drink with the supporters when I'm ready.'

When I turned around I noticed that one of the committee members was listening to the conversation.

'Don't you start getting big-headed,' he said.

I thought, Imagine that's all you can think to say to a manager on a special night like this.

The second leg was played at Tolka Park, because Dalymount didn't meet UEFA's minimum seating requirements. We had a full house and the match was shown live on RTE. Jim Beglin interviewed me sitting in the stand before the match. He said, 'Are you worried?'

'No,' I told him, 'we're going through here,' and I think Jim was taken aback by my confidence.

I put Trevor up front on his own again. He was one of the most streetwise footballers I ever saw. He could win us free-kicks whenever and wherever he wanted. I flooded the midfield with players — five against their three — to stop them creating anything. The plan was to frustrate them into panic.

It was going well until just before half-time when Darren O'Keefe clocked one of their fellas and got sent off. In the second half, Dave Morrison scored an own goal to level the tie. We had the advantage of the extra away goal, but they were throwing their full weight at our ten men, looking for a winner. Trevor played out of his skin, holding up the ball and running down the clock. It was the best performance I've ever seen from a League of Ireland player. The referee indicated five minutes of injury time. Wayne Russell tipped a rocket of a shot over the bar. I turned to Pete and I said, 'We're through.'

And he said, 'Shut up, Rod.'

'Pete,' I said, 'we're through.'

The final whistle blew. All hell broke loose. We were the first Irish team ever to knock a Scottish team out of Europe and our name would go into the draw along with Inter Milan, Liverpool and Loko-motiv Moscow. I went to shake Ebbe Skovdahl's hand and he gave me a good dig in the ribs.

I can't say he wasn't entitled.

We were top of the league at the start of September. Crowey was banging in the goals and we had seven points from three matches. One lunchtime I was on a building site when I had a call from Garry Doyle from the *Irish Daily Star*. He said we'd drawn Kaiserslautern in the next round of the UEFA Cup.

I said, 'Really? Where are they from?'

If I had to guess, I'd have said Norway or Sweden.

'Are you joking me?' he said. 'They're in the Bundesliga, Rod.'

'And are they any use?' I asked.

Garry laughed.

'They've got Mario Basler and Youri Djorkaeff,' he said.

I honestly didn't know who those blokes were. It turned out that Djorkaeff had won the World Cup and the European Championship with France and Basler had won two Bundesligas with Bayern Munich and the European Championship with Germany.

Two weeks later I stood and watched them get off the bus when they came to train at Tolka Park. All the Kaiserslautern players looked like film stars. They didn't think much of the ground. I saw them looking around and laughing. Otto Rehhagel, their manager, told the press that it was smaller than his living room. Then Basler said something about the Irish being famous for fighting and drinking whiskey and I thought, Fuck you, pal. I never wanted to beat a team more than I wanted to beat Kaiserslautern.

About ten minutes into the match, a ball dropped in front of the dugout and Basler came running for it. I shouted, 'Fucking break him in two, lads!'

The man looked at me and he didn't need a translation. Shortly after that I saw him signalling to the bench. His hamstring. Off he came. We were doing well. Coming up to half-time, it was still 0–0 and Wayne hadn't had a save to make. I thought if we could keep it like this for the next forty-five minutes, what a result that would be. But then, a minute before half-time, one of the Kaiserslautern players spat at Trevor Molloy and Trevor gave him a slap. Red card. Suddenly, it was a different game.

Even with ten men we managed to hold out until halfway through the second half. Then we took a split-second longer to clear the ball than you're allowed at that level. The next thing it was in the back of the net. The Germans switched up a gear then and scored two more in the next eight minutes. In injury time, we won a penalty and Crowey buried it. I thought getting beaten 3–1 after losing a man wasn't a bad result.

I brought Billy Bagster, the former Monaghan United manager, to Kaiserslautern with us for the second leg. Bohs didn't want him there, but I said he was coming with us even if I had to pay for his flights and accommodation myself. When it came to football, Billy had a mind like a computer hard drive. He followed the Bundesliga and knew all the players, right down to who was weak on their left side and who went to sleep for corner kicks.

The night before the match I was invited to the Fritz-Walter-Stadion for a tour of the arena. It would have been an insult to refuse. When I arrived I was handed a goody bag containing a stick of rock, a pen, a pendant and a signed photograph of Mario Basler. I thought, What the fuck am I supposed to do with this? Then I was shown around.

'This will be your dressing room,' I was told, and they all stared at me like they were waiting for me to say thank you for letting us in to dirty their floor. There was condescension in everything they said.

'I want to go back to the hotel,' I told them.

'No,' someone said, 'you are Irish – you must stay for a drink!'

I turned my back on them, threw the goody bag in a bin, then spent the next twenty minutes trying to find my way out of the stadium. I ended up having to climb over a ten-foot-high gate in my Louis Copeland suit. When I got back to the hotel, the players were finishing their dinner. They weren't expecting me back so soon and they all hid their bowls of jelly and ice cream on their laps.

'Lads,' I said, 'they fucking think we're here for a holiday. We cannot – fucking *cannot* – let them beat us tomorrow night.'

I thumped the table and nearly broke my fist.

I woke up with one of my moments of 5 a.m. inspiration. I opened the drawer in the bedside table. There was a pencil in there and some hotel stationery. I wrote on an envelope, 'Back four don't cross the halfway line. Midfield four don't cross the halfway line. One striker and one player hugging the sideline, staying just onside.'

Kaiserslautern played with three central defenders. I noticed that the left-sided one would wander forward but was slow in coming back, leaving a big, gaping hole. My plan was to try to exploit it by getting the ball wide to Davy Williamson, who would then look for Crowey. At breakfast, I showed the plan to Bob Breen, our English-born marketing manager, who I'd poached from Waterford United.

'What's Davy doing out there?' he asked.

'He's doing nothing,' I said. 'Just waiting for the ball.'

'Does he come back and help the full-back?'

'Absolutely not. He's there to supply Crowey with crosses.'

'It's off the wall,' Bob laughed.

I explained the game plan to the players. There was only five minutes gone when Liam O'Brien, sitting next to me on the bench, started roaring at Davy to get back to defend.

I said, 'Shut fucking up, Liam, will you?'

Ten minutes before half-time Darren won the ball and swivelled his whole body to drill it to to Davy, who crossed the ball for Crowey to score. It went exactly as we planned it. A few minutes after that, Crowey got a perfectly good second, but it was disallowed for off-side. Then he brought a world-class save out of Georg Koch, the Kaiserslautern goalkeeper. Rehhagel was losing the plot.

The German crowd were on our side, cheering us on for having a go. We won the match. We were the first League of Ireland team to win a match on German soil. We were out, but I was so proud of the players.

I walked out onto the pitch to applaud our supporters. A few hundred of them had travelled. The German fans started chanting, 'Roddy! Roddy! Roddy!'

I remember our kit man, Christy Blackburn, a lovely fella who Pete brought with him from St Francis, stayed sitting at the final whistle. He looked up at Pete and he said, 'Jaysus, Pete, when we left St Francis, I never thought we'd end up in a place like this.'

I felt like a million dollars.

At Dalymount, they weren't chanting, 'Roddy! Roddy! Roddy!' Not by the end of September, anyway. The UEFA Cup was a great adventure, but it drew our focus away from the league. We dropped two points at home against Cork and then we got beaten in Derry. We'd already lost the top spot in the table to Shelbourne when we went to Tolka Park to play them in between the two Kaiserslautern matches.

Winding up other managers had become my stock-in-trade. It has always been part of my nature. But I'd also learned from boxing how trash-talking your opponent could help sell tickets. One man whose skin I loved getting under was the Shels manager, Dermot Keely. I'd say something to the newspapers like, 'I wouldn't let the man manage a blow-football team,' which I didn't mean, but I knew Dermot would take it personally and lose the rag with me. Gerry Ryan had us on the radio before the match and we ended up shouting insults down the phone line to each other.

Dermot's boss, Ollie Byrne, knew the score. He would ring me up and say, 'I'm after saying some scurrilous things about you to the papers, Roddy.'

'What did you say?' I'd ask.

'Get the *Herald* tomorrow and you'll see. Now you have a go back at me and we'll get four thousand in on Sunday.'

Whatever I said about Dermot that week, it didn't work. I was the one who lost it. I got sent off for arguing with the referee and we lost 4–2.

Pat Dolan was another manager I loved antagonizing. Just before we played St Patrick's Athletic that October, I told a newspaper that I was interested in signing Paul Osam. Paul was a brilliant player and a Pat's man through and through – except that he left them once to go to Shamrock Rovers and a lot of Pat's fans hadn't quite forgotten it. One Friday night I turned up at Richmond Park. When the match was over I hung around outside the dressing room and said to a few Pat's heads, 'Can you tell Paul Osam that Roddy Collins is here to see him, please?'

Pat's got beaten that night. The door flew open and all of the players were singing 'When the Saints Go Marching In', like they'd got three points, with Pat in the middle of the circle.

It always made me laugh whenever I heard Pat refer to the club as a family. We played them at home in the second week of October. On the morning of the match I went into the away dressing room with a black marker and I scribbled all over the whitewashed walls. I wrote, 'Anyone who sings and dances after a defeat is hiding a weakness', and, 'Pat's isn't a family – it's a cult', and other things that were calculated to wind him up.

Their players arrived at the ground and disappeared into the dressing room. After fifteen minutes, I'd heard nothing, so I asked Trevor Molloy to go out and see had Pat named their starting eleven yet. A few minutes later, Trevor returned.

'Rod,' he said, 'there's fucking murder going on.'

'What happened?' I asked.

'Someone's after breaking in and writing stuff about Pat all over the walls of the dressing room.'

'Seriously?'

'Pat's crying. He's in bits.'

'No way.'

'The police are in there. They're taking photographs of it and everything.'

The match finished 2–2. By then, Pat had discovered who had vandalized the dressing room. I tried to shake his hand after the match, but he said, 'No, you fucking crossed a line, Collins.'

Not long after that Caroline went into labour. On 26 November she gave birth to our second son. We named him Padraig. He's very different to his brother and sisters in personality and temperament. 'The Quiet Man', I call him. He could go a week without talking, whereas I couldn't go a minute. My da was quiet, and I see flashes of him in Padraig all the time. He's a deep person. You never know what's going on in his head. He's stubborn, like his father, but he's placid in a way that I'm not, and he's kind and soft-hearted like his mother – until he enters the boxing ring.

The day after Caroline arrived home from the hospital there was a knock on the door. It was Pat Dolan, holding a big bunch of flowers.

'Pat,' I said, 'you shouldn't have.'

'Fuck off, I'm not talking to you,' he said. 'These are for Caroline.'

We sat in the conservatory for hours – me, Caroline and Pat, talking about everything under the sun except the League of Ireland title race.

'Caroline, let me ask you something,' he said. 'How do you put up with him?'

Pat had a heart of gold. He was a class act.

Bohemians didn't send flowers to the house. They didn't send Caroline so much as a card. By then my relationship with the club was broken beyond repair, and it seemed not so much a question of whether I was going to be sacked but when. There were rumours that I was gone that November after we lost at home to Shamrock Rovers.

When you're a League of Ireland manager in trouble, there's

always two or three out-of-work managers busy positioning them-selves for your job. I saw all the usual suspects at Dalymount Park around that time, sitting in the crowd near the dugout, trying to get their faces on the telly. Sometime around Christmas, we were strug-gling to beat Longford Town and I thought, This is it, I'm getting the bullet today. Then Tony Hopper, a player the Bohs fans had never taken to their hearts, scored the winner – a very decisive last act for us before he went back to Carlisle.

There were stories at the time linking me to a job in Germany, where I'd apparently impressed one or two people with our victory over Kaiserslautern in September. Eintracht Frankfurt were about to sack their manager, Felix Magath. A Dublin fella named Alan Moore, who worked as a marketing consultant for the club, was pushing my name forward for the job and the papers said I was on a shortlist. But it would have broken my heart to leave Bohs before the end of the season.

I had put together a group of players who I loved being around. They weren't all best buddies, but there were no cliques in that dress-ing room. I arranged two Christmas parties for them that year, both of which I paid for myself. The first, in The Bohemian in Phibsboro, was for the players and their wives and partners. The second, in Fitzsimons in Temple Bar, was just for the players.

At the time, I was minted. Our European journey had made me a bit of a celebrity in the world of Dublin construction and I couldn't keep up with all the plastering work getting thrown my way. I'd turn up on a building site in one of my Louis Copeland suits, my Rolex watch and my brand-new Rover to price a job and men would lean over the scaffolding and shout, 'Come on, Pat's!' and, 'Collins, you fucking wanker!'

God, I loved it.

I had fame. I had money in my pocket. I had a new baby and a wife and family that I loved. And I had a group of players who would have walked through walls for me and I would have walked through walls for them. All I wanted was to give them what they deserved. We started 2001 six points behind Shelbourne. But the season was about to turn on the most incredible ninety minutes of football that I've ever been involved in – a match that I couldn't make sense of at the time and still struggle to make sense of more than twenty years later.

I thought we needed more pace, so after Christmas I bought Mark Rutherford from Newry Town. He was fast like an Olympic sprinter and he'd run all day for you. Then I got Alex Nesovic from Finn Harps, a hard-as-nails striker who'd played in the lower leagues in England and Scotland and would give us a few more goals.

We played Shamrock Rovers on a dark and manky Sunday afternoon in January. Rovers still had no permanent home and were playing their football on the infield of the running track at Morton Stadium in Santry. The pitch was the smallest in the country and the playing surface was like a ploughed field. The match would become known as the Santry Siro Massacre.

Rovers scored after two minutes when we failed to clear a corner. Dave Hill got one back for us. Then we just went at each other. We had chances in the first half – as many as Rovers did. Theirs went in and ours didn't. We were 4–1 down at half-time and the Rovers fans were having a party, singing, 'Roddy Collins is a wanker, is a wanker!' while ours were pouring out of the ground, having seen enough.

Jim Fitzpatrick, my friend on the committee, grabbed me and said, 'Rod, you're going to be sacked when the game is over.'

I went back to the dressing room. I walked into the toilet cubicle and I said a little prayer. I said, 'Give us a little bit of help here, Da.'

Then I took a breath and opened the toilet door. The players were sitting around looking like beaten dockets.

'So we're 4–1 down,' I said. 'They were lucky with two of those goals and we were unlucky with two of our chances. We should be 3–2 up. We're better than them. We're stronger and we're fitter. Trust me, lads, this match is not lost.'

Fifteen minutes into the second half I took off our left-back, Simon Webb, and I threw on Trevor alongside Alex and Crowey up front. I figured I was sacked anyway so I might as well lose while having a go. Almost immediately Mark Rutherford headed a Davy

Morrison cross into Alex's path and Alex scored with a volley. I could see the Rovers players were nervous. They started taking the ball into the corners and there was still half an hour to go. I was looking at Damien Richardson in the other dugout, waiting for him to make a tactical change. We were completely exposed down our left side and I thought he might do something to exploit it. But Damien bottled it.

They had one last chance to bury us when Pat Deans went one-on-one with Wayne Russell, but he hit the post. Then they just fell apart. You could see the fear in their eyes every time Mark ran at them. Davy collected the ball from a long kick-out and fired it past the keeper to make it 4–3 and then Dave Hill, who was a colossus that day, sent Crowey through to equalize. Suddenly, our fans were running back into the ground from whatever pub they had been hosting my wake in. The Rovers players were gone. I could see it. Mark put us ahead with a toe-poke and then Crowey finished them off with his second five minutes from the end.

When the whistle went, I walked onto the pitch and I hugged every single one of my players. They didn't know that they'd just saved my neck. Then I looked over and saw the Amigos, as I called them, standing on the running track – the committee men who would have to wait a bit longer to get rid of me. Jim and Jeff Collins were waiting for me outside in the car. Usually I went to Myo's in Castleknock after a match, but I just wanted to go home. I didn't know what way to feel. I was elated and angry and relieved and sad all at the same time.

I brought in one more player that January. I'd heard rumours that Paul Byrne was unhappy at Pat's and wanted to leave. I went to see him play one Friday night in Richmond Park. Typical Byrnesy, it took him about sixty seconds to pick me out of the crowd.

'Rod,' he called out to me while the game was still going on, 'get me the fuck out of here.'

And I brought him back to Bohs. With his very first touch he scored a free-kick that got us a 2–2 draw against Galway United. But our form was all over the place. We beat UCD, drew with Finn Harps and lost to Cork. By the end of February we were third in the league, a point behind Pat's but eight points behind Shels, with only eight matches left. Everyone thought it was done. I met Ollie Byrne at the FAI Cup draw. He had the league and cup trophies with him. He said, 'Do you want to hold them? It's the only chance you're going to get.'

But then we got lucky. An outbreak of foot-and-mouth disease forced the suspension of the league for four weeks. We used the time to reset and gather ourselves for the run-in. We had a snooker tournament. We went for long walks on the beach. We really got to know each other as a group of men. And the memory of the comeback against Rovers made us all believe that we were capable of anything.

'Right,' I said, when they announced the return of football, 'let's win the league.'

During the break, Jason Cowman had put together a training programme and the players worked like it was pre-season. And the break destroyed whatever momentum Shelbourne had built up. We only lost once between the resumption and the end of the season. I can't pretend that this was down to any great tactical genius on my part. I never concerned myself with the opposition. I never went to watch other teams unless they had a player I wanted to buy or unless I wanted to rattle another manager's cage.

There was a great buzz around Dalymount during the last few weeks of the season. My brother Stephen came to watch us play. Vinnie Jones and Shaun Edwards flew over for matches. Neville Chamberlain came to watch us. Apparently to some people he looked a tiny bit like Samuel L. Jackson, and a rumour swept through the ground that the star of *Pulp Fiction* was at the match. When a reporter asked me about it, I said yes, Samuel L. Jackson was a lifelong Bohs fan. A few years later a Bohs supporter happened to meet the actor in Los Angeles and got him to pose for a photograph with a Bohs jersey. The story became a popular urban myth. But I can reveal the truth. It was Nevy.

The only match we lost during the run-in was against Pat's. If we'd lost the next one against Shels at Tolka Park, the league was over and I was gone. But we beat them and we beat them well. We'd all been hearing stories that their players were fighting among themselves, and that day it was easy to believe. We went into the final game of the season only a point behind them. We had to win in Kilkenny and hope that Shels failed to beat Cork at home.

Before the match I tried to give the Cork players an incentive. In an interview with RTE radio I said that Cork were only tough when they were standing on their own ground. When they came to Dublin, they never had any balls. One of their players told me later that they heard the interview on the bus up from Cork and it made them angry. Bingo. I had them.

We did our part. We tore Kilkenny to shreds and we won 5–0. Word filtered through that Shels were a goal down to Cork. When our match ended, there was still five minutes to go at Tolka Park – the longest five minutes of my life. We went back to the dressing room to wait for the result. I heard a champagne cork pop and I roared, 'Get the fuck out of here with that!'

Then, from outside, we heard our fans roar, followed by a chorus of, 'Championes! Championes!'

It was over. We'd won the league. We all hugged each other and celebrated, then we went outside to celebrate with the fans. I spotted the committee men. They'd been waiting since 1978 for Bohs to win the title. And here they were, champions at last – and the manager who delivered it was a man they didn't want in the job. It must have killed them. Were they supposed to feel happy or sad? I remember Gerry Cuffe walking past me on the pitch. There was no handshake. There was no 'well done'. He just smiled and sort of flicked his Bohs scarf in the direction of my face.

When I was interviewed by Gabriel Egan of RTE, all of my anger came to a seething boil. 'I don't know how we won this,' I said. 'This club is run by Stone Age people.'

And with those words, I sealed my fate.

We still had the FAI Cup final to look forward to against Longford Town the following weekend. We'd beaten Rovers in the semi-final and now we had a chance to take the other trophy that Ollie told me I'd never get my hands on. But first we celebrated the league win.

On the Monday we went to The Belfry in Stoneybatter. All the plasterers and labourers who worked for me got the day off and I put on a free bar for everyone in the pub. Tony O'Donoghue rang me from RTE and asked me to do an interview with him in Dalymount Park. I said, 'Tony, I'm up to my neck in pints. You'll have to come here,' which he did.

Bad teams can win cups but only good teams win leagues. I was thinking I could do it again next season. All I needed to do was add one or two players and we could win four in a row like the great Rovers team of the 1980s. But in the back of my mind, I knew I couldn't put myself and my family through another year of torture. Maybe what I said to Gabriel Egan was an act of self-sabotage. A board member rang. I stepped outside the pub.

'Is everything all right?' I asked.

'No,' he said, 'everything is not all right. As a matter of fact, I think I'm going to have to sue you.'

'Is that right?'

'You defamed the whole board – when you said we were Stone Age people.'

'You fucking *are* Stone Age people,' I said. 'You're a fucking joke. Sue me if you want.'

So that, for me, was the start of cup-final week.

On the Tuesday, we all checked into a golf and country club in Howth. I surrounded myself with good people. Shaun Edwards flew over from England and spent a few days with us. I was determined to enjoy the match. I saw the Amigos hanging around the hotel and I got a sense that the final was going to be my last day out with this group of players. Longford Town were a decent team, managed by the current Ireland manager, Stephen Kenny. They played good football, but I knew we were too street-smart for them. I told Wayne to keep finding Mark with his throw-outs and we'd catch them with a counter-attack. Toccy was so confident that the game was in hand that he went forward and scored the winner.

The following night I celebrated with a quiet pint of Guinness in Myo's. I sat there in a world of my own. Caroline said it was the happiest she'd seen me since we were sixteen. The club had put up two marquees in Dalymount Park to celebrate the double. I had no intention of going, but Caroline persuaded me that I should. I went along and thanked all the players for what they'd given me. But I knew in my heart that I was finished.

I was called to a meeting – another end-of-season review. We won the double. What was there to review? Caroline and I were taking the kids to Florida and I said it could wait until we came home. We were in America when Caroline had a call from her sister, who said, 'It's just been on the radio that Roddy's been sacked.'

It ruined the holiday for me. For three or four days I'd allowed myself to think that maybe I would stay on after all. Lying in the sun, my mind wandered back to all the good times we had and I forgot all about the daily battles with the committee and other figures within the club that wore me down. I'd built something very special at Bohs and I wasn't ready to just walk away from it without a fight.

I went a bit off the wall then. We came home to Dublin and I staged a rally in the boxing gym that Paschal ran on Capel Street. A hundred or so Bohs fans came along to support me and I told them that as far as I was concerned I was still the manager of Bohemians Football Club. I don't know what I was thinking. It was cheap and shabby. My pride was hurt. I should have walked away with my head held high.

A few days later Pete Mahon knocked on my front door and said he'd been offered the job. I said, 'Pete, take it. You deserve it.'

A very special part of my life was over. Now I'd have to follow some other dream.

15

I knew Michael Knighton. At least, I knew *of* him. He was the man with the little Ronnie and the pot belly who was going to buy Manchester United back in the late 1980s. He presented himself to the crowd at Old Trafford in a full United training kit, did a few keepy-uppies, then drilled the ball into the net at the Stretford End. Then it turned out that he didn't have the money after all and I never heard of him again. That was until I went to work for him.

After failing to get Manchester United, Knighton went off and bought Carlisle United. They were bottom of the Football League. He promised that he'd have them in the Premier League within ten years. Nearly ten years later, after two promotions and two relegations, they were near the bottom of the Football League again. Michael had been barred from acting as a company director, which meant he could have no day-to-day involvement in the running of the club.

In the summer of 2001, about a week after I was sacked by Bohs, Tony Hopper rang and asked if I'd be interested in the vacant manager's job at Carlisle. I didn't even think about it. I told him, 'One hundred per cent.'

Tony had recommended me and he told me to ring Knighton's son, Mark, who was running the club for his father. We arranged an interview in the arrivals hall of Glasgow Airport. I flew over with my best pinstriped suit in a bag and I went into the jacks to throw it on me. Mark was only a young fella – I guessed in his early twenties – and was clearly very well educated. We talked about football and about Carlisle United for a couple of hours. They were looking for a manager who could keep them in the Football League next season. I told him I was an expert – I'd helped both Bangor and Bohemians to avoid relegation. He told me I was one of a number of managers on their shortlist. I tried to keep a lid on my excitement.

About two weeks later I was invited over to Carlisle for talks. I'd never set foot in the city before. All I knew about it was that it was up on the roof of England, close to the border with Scotland, and that Caroline and I met a couple of blokes from there in Spain once and they either looked like sheep farmers or were sheep farmers.

Neville Chamberlain's sister Delphine was working as an agent and I asked her to represent me. She collected me at Manchester Airport and she drove me to Carlisle, where I met the chairman, Andrew Jenkins, a local man who made his fortune in the meat business. He showed me around Brunton Park. It was a proper 17,000-seater stadium. I had butterflies in my stomach.

Andrew told me the full score. As the only Football League club in the area, Carlisle United had huge potential, but their financial situation was dire. The Professional Footballers Association had placed an embargo on them buying new players because of an unpaid loan. Soon the club would be in administration and wouldn't be allowed to buy tea bags without permission.

They couldn't commit to a contract and they could only afford to pay me £200 per week. But they would put me up in the four-star Holiday Inn on the M6 roundabout and all of my meals would be paid for, just so long as I ate in Dempsey's Bar and Restaurant, which was owned by two brothers, Jed and Norman, who were lifelong Carlisle United fans.

He offered me the job and I said I'd take it. I'd read in the paper that Michael Knighton wanted Peter Beardsley for the job, but presumably Beardsley wanted more than two hundred quid per week. What I didn't tell them was that they could have got me for cheaper. I'd have done it for one hundred. This was just a stepping stone for me. Manchester United here I come.

A few months earlier, just after the start of the foot-and-mouth outbreak, Caroline's brother Liam and his partner, Rose, had come to our house for their dinner, just like they did every Friday. Liam and Rose were devoted to each other. They had met years earlier at a ballad session in O'Donoghue's on Baggot Street. Liam was there with his brother Mikey. Rose was there with her sister Mary. Mikey got together with Mary. Liam got together with Rose. And that's the way they stayed, two O'Devaney brothers and two Donegal sisters, happily ever after.

Like Liam, Rose suffered from schizophrenia. But they minded each other; Liam had Rose's back and Rose had Liam's. They would sit in their flat in O'Devaney Gardens, chain-smoking cigarettes in front of the fire, oblivious to everything except each other.

Caroline and her five sisters took it in turns to cook dinner for them. Friday was our day to have them because Caroline was working in Bord Gáis and that was the day she finished work early. On this particular Friday, Rose arrived at the house complaining that her stomach was sore. I was out plastering that day. When I arrived home, Caroline took me to one side and she said, 'I think Rose is pregnant.'

I said, 'She couldn't be.'

Liam and Rose had had a baby before. Little Rose was brought into the world out of love, but her parents were in no position to raise a child, so Caroline's ma brought her up instead. When Caroline's ma passed away in 1992, Caroline's sister Martina and her husband Mick took over.

After giving birth, Rose was advised to start taking the contraceptive pill.

'Roddy, I'm telling you,' Caroline said, 'she's pregnant.'

The next day Caroline took her to the Rotunda and it was confirmed. She was six months pregnant. Caroline rang Rose's doctor to find out what was going on. She was told that Rose had stopped taking the pill – as was her right, the doctor explained. Caroline was furious. Rose was very unwell at the time, and certainly wasn't mentally equipped to go through the pain of labour.

I was sitting outside in the conservatory when Caroline arrived home from the Rotunda. I could see she was upset. The baby was due in June and would likely be taken from Rose at the hospital and placed in a foster home.

'Roddy, I don't want the baby being taken away by strangers,' she said. 'This baby is part of our family.'

'It's no problem,' I told her. 'We'll throw the baby in the cot with Padraig.'

'Are you serious?'

'One hundred per cent, Caroline.'

Liam and Rose were agreeable to us raising their child while they remained very much present in her life. But then the HSE told us it wasn't that simple. They had to satisfy themselves first that Rose was incapable of looking after a baby. When she walked into the oxygen room with a lit cigarette and nearly blew up the Rotunda, I think they got a better handle on the situation. But even after that, we were warned that the process of fostering the baby was a long road strewn with bureaucratic obstacles.

We didn't care. We went to Florida that summer, knowing that within weeks of coming home there would be a second baby in the house along with Padraig, who was still only seven months old. Lauren was born on 10 June 2001. The delivery was horrendous. Caroline held Rose's hand for the entire thing and the experience will remain implanted on her brain for ever. Rose had no real understanding of what was happening to her, just the pain she was going through, and Caroline begged the doctors to give her a Caesarean section.

Lauren was eventually born. She was a gorgeous little baby. She was going to be raised with a Daddy Liam and a Daddy Roddy and a Mammy Rose and a Mammy Caroline. We knew that we had years of HSE home visits and meetings with social workers ahead of us before we formalized the arrangement, but becoming parents again at the age of forty had made us feel twenty years younger. We were fizzing with energy. We were ready for this. Of course, that was easy for me to say. I was about to leave Caroline with five children while I moved to England to manage Carlisle United for £200 a week.

My ambition at that point was huge. I wasn't going to be satisfied with just keeping Carlisle in the Third Division that year. I was going to get them promoted to the Second. Then I was going to move to a Premier League club. So confident was I that I scorched the earth behind me. I had a thriving plastering business, employing twenty-eight men, with offers of work coming in all the time. And I handed it over to Rambo Smith, my pal and right-hand man. I didn't want any ties to home. In my head, I was never coming back to Dublin. I told Caroline that I'd spend the first few months finding my feet, then we'd buy a house over there and she could move over with the kids.

And as usual, Caroline said, 'I believe in you, Rod. Go for it.'

On my first day at work I was collected from the airport by Neil Dalton, the Carlisle United physio, who drove me straight to the training ground, just behind the stadium. The whole way there I was thinking about how I was going to introduce myself to the players. I'd spent enough time in the lower leagues of English football to understand the terrain. This wasn't Bangor and it wasn't Bohs. Third Division dressing rooms were hard, cynical places, filled with young fellas who thought they should be somewhere better and older fellas for whom the dream was dead but who would break your legs to make their next mortgage payment.

I was coming from the League of Ireland. They didn't take it seriously at all. They called it a pub league. Players in England still tended to judge managers by how many internationals caps they'd won. They would have loved Peter Beardsley. But I had no international caps. The highest-paid player at Carlisle was on £2,500 per week. Most of them would have known that I was doing the job for next to nothing, all of which made it even more important for me to establish my authority from moment one.

When I arrived, Billy Barr, the caretaker manager, was taking training. There were quite a few reporters there. I called Billy over. 'Billy,' I said, 'what are you doing?'

'We're doing a pressing session,' he told me. 'The lads in the orange bibs are trying to get the ball back.'

I whistled and told everyone to gather round.

'I'm the new boss,' I said. 'You've probably read it in the papers. Billy tells me that's a pressing session. If that's a fucking pressing session, then I understand why you're bottom of the league every year. What I just watched there was a fucking joke.'

It was a roasting hot day and I was sweating in my linen suit. I took the jacket off me, threw it on the touchline and took control of the session. The players put a bit more urgency into it. I worked them hard. When we'd finished, I called them over again.

'Right, lads,' I said, 'this team is going fucking nowhere. Desire, passion, work rate, honesty – if you haven't got those things to start with, you won't be fucking here long.'

I copped one of the players smiling at me.

'The fuck is so funny?' I asked him. 'What's your name?'

'Mark Winstanley,' he said.

'Sorry, who?' I asked him again – it was an old Billy Young trick.

'Mark Winstanley,' he said.

'You fucking see me after training,' I told him.

It turned out that I'd chosen to make an example of the wrong man. When Mark came to me after the session, I asked him what he was laughing at. 'Am I a fucking joke to you or something? Paddy the fucking Irishman?'

'I wasn't laughing,' he said. 'I smiled – because no one has ever spoken to the lads like that. And it needed to be done.'

Mark was a centre-half who was pushing on for thirty-four. He'd played more than four hundred league games for Bolton Wanderers, Burnley and Shrewsbury Town before coming to Carlisle to finish his career. He was a solid, clean-living pro who trained hard and then went home to his family every day. During my first season at Carlisle, he would be my Dave Hill.

Most of the players put in an effort at training as I tried to get my bearings. We were doing a running session one morning. There was a blond, good-looking giant of a lad who I noticed busting his gut. I pulled him aside and I asked his name.

'Luke Weaver,' he said.

'See you, Luke? You're exactly what my team needs – a big, strong centre-forward who puts himself about like I did in my day.'

'Er, thanks, gaffer,' he said.

'I want to make you the focal point of our attack,' I said. 'I'll help you to score a lot of goals for us this season – do you hear me?'

'I do, gaffer.'

It was only later on, when I looked at a team shot, that I discovered he was our goalkeeper. Either he was too embarrassed to tell me or he thought I was a mad Paddy.

We played our first pre-season friendly against Accrington Stanley and I found out that day who was with me and who was going to be leaving the club. There were three or four senior players who the others looked up to but who clearly didn't respect me. The main man among them was Lee Maddison, a left-back with a set of teeth like Robert Mitchum and a permanent smirk on his face.

I persevered through the next three weeks. Our first match of the season was against Luton Town at home. We had a decent crowd. The fans had been through the wringer with the club but they were prepared to give the new man in the dugout the benefit of the doubt. Luton were managed by Joe Kinnear. The difference between us and them was far more than just the two goals we lost by. They were a solid bunch of pros who were proud to play for Luton Town and were going to get them promoted that year. Our dressing room was full of players who were only there because they didn't make it somewhere else and were disappointed to discover that this was their level.

I had a serious battle on my hands. I knew I couldn't improve the technical ability of the players I'd inherited. Most of them had been around the block too many times for that. The only thing I could improve was their effort – and against Luton that was almost completely absent. There were three or four players who I thought were deliberately swinging the lead.

On Monday morning, two days later, I did my analysis of the match for the team. I didn't see any sign of remorse out of the mutton-heads, as I called them. These were the ones who were walking around the city with their chests out and collecting the big wages, so I pointed to each one in turn and said, 'You, you, you and you – I'll see you here at eight o'clock in the morning. Bring your runners.'

The next morning, when they arrived at the club, I was sitting on a mountain bike in the car park.

'Right,' I said to them, 'we're going to go for a run around the town. Change into your gear, then follow me.'

I set off on the bike, with the four boys running behind me. We covered every single inch of the city centre and I made sure we were seen by as many people as possible. Carlisle is a tight community. If someone sneezes on one side of the city, they'll know about it on the other side within an hour. Suddenly, everyone was talking about the new manager and how he'd publicly shamed four of his most senior players by making them run up and down the main street.

It might have meant something if I'd gotten a positive reaction out of the players. But by the end of October we'd lost seven and drawn four of our first thirteen matches and we were bottom of the table. One thing was certain – we weren't getting promoted. The fans were already losing faith, so I did what I did at Bangor and at Bohemians. I went to talk to them.

The Carlisle United and Cumbria Independent Supporters Trust was a group of disgruntled fans who were boycotting our home matches in protest at the way Michael Knighton and his family had run the club. I asked if I could address a meeting one Saturday lunchtime in October, just two hours before we played Jan Mølby's Kidderminster Harriers. The meeting took place in the Sands Centre, a 1,400-seat theatre in the centre of the city, where, according to a poster outside, Val Doonican was due to play the following night. The room was full. The atmosphere was far less fractious than it had been in the Orange Order hall or the bar in Dalymount Park. They were reasonable, knowledgeable football supporters who'd just come to the end of their tether. They made it clear that they supported me, but they did not support the owners of the club. But it was a fine line that I had to walk. I was employed by Carlisle United, which was 93 per cent owned by Michael Knighton. If I publicly criticized him, I knew I'd be sacked, but I wanted to get the fans back onside. I reminded them that Knighton was serious about walking away and was looking for a buyer. I asked them to end their boycott.

'You're choking the club by staying away,' I said. 'Bury the hatchet, come back and support the team. That would bring money into the club and if that money isn't made available to me, I'm off.'

They said they'd heard it all before. They were promised a new start when I was appointed, yet here they were, the bottom team in the English League again.

'Have me back here in eight weeks,' I said, 'and if we're still bottom, you can put me in stocks and throw rotten tomatoes at me, I don't care.'

I thought that if public shaming was good enough for players who weren't doing their job, then it was good enough for me.

'But there's no way the club will be relegated,' I added, 'no way we will be in the Conference.'

I was accused of being a mouthpiece for the owners.

'No one writes my scripts,' I told them. 'It's just I'm not into being part of a lynch mob against Michael Knighton. Now, if you don't mind, I've got a team to go and manage.'

I don't know how Val Doonican got on the next night. But I got a standing ovation.

I was in my office one day, a few weeks into the season, when the phone rang and it was Dermot Keely, the Shels manager.

'Have you any money over there?' he said with typical bluntness.

'Yeah, we've loads,' I told him, even though we hadn't a penny. Under the terms of the embargo, we had to plead our case to the Football Association if we wanted to sign a player. But I wasn't telling Dermot and Ollie that.

Then he got to the point. His striker Richie Foran had been sent off again the night before. It was either the seventh or eighth time in his career and he was still only twenty-one.

'I think referees have it in for him,' he said. 'Either way, he's finished here.'

I played Gaelic football with Richie's da, Podger Foran, at O'Connell's GAA club and Richie had worked as a labourer for me on the building sites. I told Dermot I was interested. Ollie Byrne, the Shelbourne CEO, rang me back within the hour.

'Howiya, Rod?' he said. 'I hear you want Richie Foran?'

'I didn't before,' I told him, 'but I do now. Dermot said you're prepared to let him go.'

'Don't mind Dermot. You can have him for a hundred grand.'

'Ollie, leave it with me. Look, just send him over and I'll see what I can do.'

I rang Mark Knighton. 'There's a kid in Dublin,' I said, 'who will single-handedly keep us up. He'll score goals. But he's also one of the best defenders of set-pieces in the game because he's fearless.'

He said he'd see what money he could get. The next day Richie arrived over with Dermot and Mick Lawlor, who was acting as his advisor. I took Richie out onto the pitch. He was blown away by the ground.

'Richie,' I said, 'whatever way the negotiations go, don't go back on that flight tomorrow.'

'I'm going fucking nowhere,' he said.

Mick talked terms with Mark Knighton and Richie was happy with the deal. Now it was just a matter of persuading Ollie to let him go. Dermot was sitting in my office when he made the call to Ollie, who I could hear on the other end of the phone saying, 'Have you got the fucking money?'

'Roddy needs to talk to you about that,' Dermot said. 'He's only got fifteen grand to give you today. They'll pay the rest in instalments.'

Ollie lost it. Dermot had to hold the phone away from his ear.

'I want the fucking money,' Ollie roared.

'Look, you know what Collins is like,' Dermot told him. 'He's a fucking gangster.'

I was thinking, Yeah, I'm still here, Dermot, thanks a bleeding lot.

'He's a fucking cowboy,' Ollie fumed.

I didn't care. It was all sticks and stones to me. I was getting one of the best strikers in Ireland.

Ollie rang me at least once a week for the next year.

'That fifteen grand was in fucking euros,' he'd say. 'It was supposed to be in fucking sterling. And I'm flying over there to get the rest of it. Do you know who you're fucking dealing with? I'm Ollie fucking Byrne. I've done prison time.'

Ollie had been in Mountjoy in the 1980s for handling stolen cigarettes. He often mentioned his prison record but left out the detail.

I don't know how much money he got for Richie in the end. But Ollie was right. Richie was worth £100,000. He scored sixteen goals for us that year and helped me keep my promise to the supporters that we wouldn't be in a relegation fight by the end of the season.

I'd hired Bugsy Cunningham, my old teammate from Mansfield, as my assistant manager. I'd persuaded him to give up his soccer academy in Derry to become my assistant on the promise that we'd be at a Premier League club within five years. We were staying in adjoining rooms in the Holiday Inn.

I brought a few more players in. Because of the embargo, I had to take them on loan. And because we had no money, I had to rely on the good nature of other clubs to continue paying part or all of their wages. Niall Quinn told me there was a great Dublin kid in the reserves at Sunderland named Brendan McGill, who could do a job for us on the wing. I drove to Bury with Bugsy to watch him play, but we were late and he'd been subbed off at half-time. I met him. He was tiny.

'He's like a fucking jockey,' I told Niall. 'You're going to get me sacked.'

'Trust me,' Niall said. 'He's two-footed, he's got loads of pace and you can't get the ball off him.'

We got Giller on loan. He was everything that Niall said he would be. But when I rang Peter Reid, the Sunderland manager, to ask if the club would continue to pay his wages as part of the deal, all I got was an earful of abuse.

'Who the fuck do you think you are?' he asked. 'You're not in fucking Ireland now.'

Fuck, I thought. Giller was already training with us. He was living in digs up the road from the club. We couldn't afford to pay him, but I was annoyed at the way Peter Reid had spoken to me. So I phoned him back.

'Look, I made a genuine mistake,' I said. 'I'm not here to do anyone a bad turn. I'm just trying to do my job as a football manager under circumstances you wouldn't believe. But don't ever fucking speak to me like that again.'

There was silence on the other end of the line.

'Listen, mate,' he said, 'I was having a row with one of my players when you rang and you got the brunt of it. Don't worry, I'll carry on paying the lad's wages – and here's my mobile number if you ever need anything.'

I was taken aback by the decency of a lot of managers and their readiness to help. I travelled up and down the country to watch matches. Often, I'd see Alex Ferguson, Sam Allardyce, Peter Reid and David Moyes having a cup of tea together in the corner of the boardroom, and I got to know them a little. They must have decided between themselves to help me. Allardyce, the manager of Bolton Wanderers, had started his managerial career with Limerick and he had great time for League of Ireland people. He loaned me Mattie Glennon, one of his backup goalkeepers, and I put him straight in the first team. Moyes, who was the manager of Everton, let me have Leon Osman, a midfielder, on loan. Ferguson offered me a striker and gave me his number in case I ever needed any help from him.

Kevin Keegan, the Manchester City manager, did me a favour by not lending me a reserve team player of his who'd caught my eye. 'I wouldn't do it to you, Roddy,' he said, 'because you're only starting off. He's a party animal. He'd drag you down.'

I enjoyed making contacts, watching matches, working the phones, reading scouting reports and generally navigating my way into the job. By Christmas I had a team that was recognizably mine – a solid group of men who wanted to play for Carlisle United.

But I missed home. I missed my family. For the first few months, I didn't get home at all. It was the longest that Caroline and I had been apart from each other since I was playing for Mansfield Town. Our lives were a lot different now and I felt bad for dumping everything on her.

The plan we had for her and the kids to move to Carlisle had been put on hold because the HSE didn't want baby Lauren taken outside the state. They also insisted that Caroline take time off work to bond with her. Her bosses were initially unwilling to give her maternity leave because she hadn't actually given birth to Lauren. It was very stressful because we couldn't afford for Caroline to give up work. I was sending home whatever money I could, but it was difficult when I was earning only £200 per week. Eventually, her bosses agreed to give her paid leave, which came as a huge relief.

After I'd settled in, Caroline came to Carlisle for weekends and stayed with me in the Holiday Inn. She would arrive exhausted from playing the roles of both mammy and daddy. Sinéad was nineteen and going to college, but the rest of them were still kids. Niamh was thirteen, Roddy was seven and Padraig and Lauren were just babies, who needed her attention all the time. I would have a list of places we were going to visit, but Caroline would pull the curtains and sleep for a day and a half.

I came home once or twice a month. I'd fly to Dublin on a Saturday and return to Carlisle on a Monday morning. On Sunday night I would feel physically sick at the thought of leaving. Stevie Spicer would drive me to the airport and I would cry all the way. I'd fly to Glasgow, where Dave Rogers, my centre-half would pick me up. I always gave him my car for the weekend to visit his girlfriend, Kirsty, in Scotland. He'd drive me to Carlisle, then I'd start thinking about the match on Saturday.

We'd beaten Kidderminster Harriers thanks to a goal from Richie Foran in his first game for us, but we won only one of our next nine matches, and I was becoming as impatient as the fans with Knighton's failure to find a new owner for the club. I asked the supermarket tycoon Albert Gubay to consider buying it and he flew over in his private jet to take a look. Albert had little or no interest in running a football club, but he saw great potential for development in the 124 acres of land that surrounded Brunton Park. That was until his surveyors discovered that it was all swampland.

One weekend, just before Christmas, I came home to see Caroline and the kids. I was driving past Myo's in Castleknock when I spotted a jeep in the car park belonging to a builder who owed me five grand. I thought, There's a few bob for Caroline before I go back to England. I went into the pub. He gave me a cheque and I had a pint of Guinness with him. And that was the moment when John Courtenay walked into the pub and into my life.

Courtenay was a multi-millionaire who'd made his money in the fitted-kitchen business and through his ownership of the Umbro franchise for Ireland. We were on nodding terms, although I'd always thought of him as a bit of a bullshitter ever since Stephen beat Chris Eubank and he started telling people that he was a cousin of ours. He was a loud-mouthed, bombastic sort of character, full of his own importance.

'How are you doing over in England?' he asked, joining us uninvited.

'Yeah, all right,' I said, because we'd just beaten Scunthorpe 3–0. 'I think we may have turned a bit of a corner.'

'Much is that club worth?' he asked.

'I don't know – maybe a million or two,' I said. 'All I know is, if it was run properly, it could be an absolute gold mine. We're getting by on crowds of 4,000 or 5,000, but we could be getting three times that amount. It's a First Division club that just happens to be trapped in the Third.'

He took a long drag on his cigarette.

'If I buy that club,' he said, 'will you sign a five-year contract?'

'Are you serious?' I asked.

'I'm gen-u-inely serious,' he said.

Suddenly it didn't matter to me that Courtenay was full of shit. I allowed myself to believe he might be the white knight that Carlisle United was looking for.

'Absolutely, I will,' I told him.

'Can you set up a meeting between me and Michael Knighton?' he asked.

I said I would. I arranged it for the first week in January 2002 in a coffee shop at Leeds Bradford Airport. I said to Courtenay, 'When Michael gets here, we'll do the pleasantries, then you leave me alone with him for a few minutes, will you?'

Courtenay agreed. Michael arrived and I made the introductions, then Courtenay said he needed a slash and excused himself.

'Michael,' I said, 'this man is serious about buying the club. I'm just letting you know now, if you act the bollocks with him, I'm off.'

Courtenay came back and the two of them talked about money. When the meeting ended, we both shook hands with Michael and he left. I told Courtenay about the warning I'd given him.

'I know what you said,' Courtenay told me. 'Sure wasn't I hiding behind that pillar listening to every fucking word.'

There were many warning signs with Courtenay.

We played Leyton Orient at home that Saturday and Courtenay flew over to watch the game. I'd gone to great lengths to turn the visitors' dressing room into a kip – the same as I did at Dalymount. I slapped cheap white emulsion on the walls and I switched off all the radiators. I watched the Orient players get off the bus in their silky red tracksuits, listening to their Discmans. Londoners, I thought. Soft fuckers. We tore into them and scored five goals in the first half. There was excitement in the air that day. Somehow, the story of the meeting at Leeds Bradford Airport got leaked to the Carlisle *News & Star* and suddenly the entire city knew about the mystery Irish benefactor who was going to save the football club. It was the start of a new year and it felt like the start of a new era. The word went around that John Courtenay was at Brunton Park and the crowd started singing his name.

I was sitting in the dugout. I looked over my shoulder. Courtenay was standing at the front of the directors' box, drinking it in, his shoulders pinned back and his chin in the air, looking like a Roman emperor. I thought, There's no way he's walking away from this now. He'll buy this club even if it means selling everything he owns.

Everyone got a boost. I could see the change in the dressing room. The players were excited. They were thinking that all their problems were over. They wouldn't have to worry about getting paid. The embargo on buying players would be lifted. We'd be able to do simple things that we hadn't been able to do – like have a pre-match meal together.

Bugsy and I had really found our feet in Carlisle. We moved out of the Holiday Inn and into a little rented cottage, where we lived like Darby and Joan. Bugsy cooked, hoovered and ironed for us, and he watched *Braveheart* every single night.

After destroying Leyton Orient, we went on a bit of a roll. Richie Foran was banging in the goals. We got ourselves off the bottom of the table. We beat Hull City, Rushden & Diamonds, Exeter City and Rochdale, and I was named Division Three Manager of the Month for January. We lost only one match between Christmas and the first week in March. For once the fans were facing into the spring without the stress of a relegation battle. They were still chanting the name of their new saviour and this was feeding Courtenay's ego.

'They're pronouncing it Courtney,' he complained to me one weekend. 'It's Courten-ay.'

I could see him getting more and more carried away with it all. He loved showing his face in the dressing room after matches. He was getting off on it. But, at that point, I didn't care if it was the devil himself who was taking over. All I wanted was Knighton gone so that the club could get out of administration and I could start buying players.

I was absolutely convinced that I could get the team promoted next season if I had the right support. But the negotiations between Courtenay and Knighton for the sale of the club were still dragging on. Then another man entered the picture. Brooks Mileson had made a fortune in construction and ploughed a lot of money into non-league football. He was from Sunderland but lived in Carlisle, and now he was reported to be interested in buying the club.

Courtenay told me that Knighton was messing him around and that he was going to pull out of the deal. On 6 April, we lost 1–0 to Shrewsbury Town. After the match, I did an interview with Radio Cumbria and I threatened to quit if Knighton was still the owner of Carlisle United when we played again.

That night I was driving down to Liverpool to see my pal Mikey, Caroline's brother, who was over for the Grand National at Aintree. I was in the car with Bugsy and Dave Rogers, who asked me to drop him to Liverpool for the weekend. My phone rang. It was Michael Knighton. He'd obviously heard the interview.

'How fucking dare you speak about me like that?' he said.

'You promised me that you wouldn't act the bollocks,' I reminded him. 'This deal should have been signed months ago. You're nothing but a bollocks.'

'You're fucking sacked.'

'Oh, am I?'

'Yes, I'm sacking you.'

'You're not sacking me because I'm fucking resigning.'

'You can't resign because you've already been sacked.'

Then he hung up on me. About five minutes later the news came on Radio 5 Live that I'd been sacked by Carlisle United. Michael certainly moved fast when it suited him.

I left Dave Rogers at the side of the road, turned the car round and drove back to Carlisle with Bugsy. We went to the Beehive, which was our local pub.

'What are we going to do?' Bugsy asked.

'What do you think we're going to do?' I said. 'We're going to go home – we're sacked.'

Poor Bugsy. All the promises I'd made him and now he was going home to Derry with his tail between his legs.

We packed up all of our stuff, threw it in the boot of my car and drove the two and a half hours to Stranraer, where we caught the overnight ferry to Belfast. Bugsy's brother collected him while I drove to Dublin to tell Caroline all about the latest twist in the career of Roddy Collins.

A few days later I had a phone call from a mate of mine in Carlisle. 'Rod,' he said, 'there's posters all over town saying there's a warrant out for your arrest.'

It turned out that the club had reported me to the police for having stolen my company car because I'd driven it back to Dublin, and now it was the front-page story in the *News & Star*.

Weeks passed. There was no sign of me being extradited to England. Carlisle United ended the season with two draws and two defeats and finished seventeenth. Two more wins and we would have finished in the top half. But then it wasn't *we* any more. That part of my life was over. But the job I'd done in just one season had got me noticed. According to the newspapers, Sheffield Wednesday, Port Vale and Macclesfield were all interested in me. I told Caroline not to worry. I wouldn't be out of work for long.

A few weeks later the phone rang. It was Courtenay. The sale was finally going ahead, he said. He was about to become the new owner of Carlisle United Football Club and he wanted to know if I'd come back as the manager. I felt sick to my stomach. By then I'd seen enough of Courtenay to know that I didn't like the man.

'I've the deal over the line,' he said. 'There's a flight over in the morning. I could put you on it.'

My ambition overruled my gut instinct. Against my better judgement, I said yes.

16

All of my good work at Carlisle United had been undone by the time I arrived back at Brunton Park. When the season ended, Michael Knighton had released most of the playing staff. By the time I was reappointed in July there were only six footballers left for me to work with. The heart of the team that I was sure would get promoted the following season – including Mark Winstanley, the rock at the centre of my defence – had been ripped out. I had to start all over again. And I didn't have a lot of time. The first match of the 2002–3 season was only four weeks away. I signed fourteen players in two weeks. It was very late in the day to be looking for the choicest cuts.

I still managed to get some very good players in. I got Dessie Byrne from Wimbledon and Trevor Molloy and Brian Shelley from Bohemians. I brought in Leon Osman on loan. He was a central midfielder who went on to play more than 350 games for Everton, but at that time he was a teenager who was coming back from a knee injury. He was a brilliant kid, always smiling, with a great attitude. And I also signed Willo McDonagh, the seventeen-year-old son of my old friend Whacker McDonagh, who had great potential and who I knew would watch my back in the dressing room.

We played Hartlepool on the first day of the season. In the week of the match, I listened to the hype on the local radio station and I felt sick to the pit of my stomach because I knew the players I had. The boycott of the ground had ended and we had 15,000 fans there to see us get beaten 3–1. It could have been much, much worse.

We went on a bit of a run then. We beat Southend United away 1–0 – Southend missed about four sitters – and we beat Lincoln City away, despite having two players sent off. Then we drew with Bristol Rovers at home. For three days we were top of the Third Division, but I knew it was a false position. I looked at my players and I thought, He'll never score like that again. He'll never clear the ball off the line like that again. He'll never pull off that many saves again.

In interviews, I was asked about making the play-offs, but I made sure to stress, 'Any points we can accumulate now will go towards keeping us in the league.'

I could also see that I was going to have a bigger fight on my hands than the one against relegation. It was only the middle of August and John Courtenay was already becoming a problem. Richie Foran was one of two players sent off against Lincoln. After getting the red card, he'd gone to watch the rest of the match in the executive box, where he was accused of spitting on the floor. He was asked to leave. When Courtenay intervened, arguing that it was only a concrete floor, he was asked to leave too. I turned round to see something I'd never seen in all my years in football: the chairman was rolling around on the ground, beating the head off one of the stewards. The referee stopped the match and I had to jump a wall to try to pull them apart. The police arrived. Courtenay was placed under arrest and led away in handcuffs. On the way home we had to take a detour past the police station to collect him. I had to sign a form to get him released. He walked out of the station like Gerry Conlon. All the players cheered as he climbed onto the bus shaking his fist in the air.

I was mortified. I wanted Carlisle to be about something more than drunken Paddies getting involved in brawls. Football club chairmen tended to be well-educated men who wore shirts and ties, spoke well and knew how to conduct themselves in public. Courtenay thought decorum was a deodorant by Lynx.

It was going to be hard for me to maintain discipline in the dressing room when the man who was in charge of the club was making a public disgrace of himself. But it was already clear to me that buying Carlisle United was Courtenay's mid-life crisis. He was like the Pied Piper, wandering from pub to pub with a little comet-trail of hangers-on following behind him. From the Beehive to the White Horse to Freddie Fat Fingers, he bought drinks for everyone and acted like he owned the entire city.

I could have lived with the embarrassment, but then he started bringing my players on the lash with him. I went into the club at my usual 7.30 a.m. one Monday to watch a video of our match the previous Saturday. As the players were arriving for their team talk, Bugsy pulled me aside and said that two of them were drunk.

'Do you mean hungover?' I asked.

'No, they're still pissed,' Bugsy said.

I called the players in. I could smell the drink off them. I suspended them for two weeks, fined them and sent them home to sleep it off. The next day they came to me and explained what happened. They'd been in bed at 10 p.m. when Courtenay knocked on the door of their digs to tell them he had a lock-in in one of the local pubs. 'He's the chairman,' one of them said. 'We didn't feel like we could say no.'

I went to see Courtenay, who was sitting in Michael Knighton's plush former office at the end of the corridor.

'Am I a fucking eejit or what?' I said.

'What are you fucking talking about?' he asked, looking up from his computer.

'You were out drinking all night with two of the lads.'

'So? They're not playing until next Saturday.'

'The preparation starts on Monday morning.'

'Ah, will you lighten up. They're only fucking kids.'

'And not only that, John, you knew I suspended the two lads and you never came near me once to say what happened.'

'I'm not a bleeding rat.'

'John, if this is the way it's going to be, I might as well pack my bags and go home. And you might as well get the rest of your money, put it in a hole in the ground and set fire to it.'

But I was talking to the wall. We had become a drinking club. And as we did, we found our true level. Between the end of August and the middle of October we lost eight of our nine matches.

Our season was being charted for a fly-on-the-wall documentary that would eventually be called *The Rod Squad*. A small TV crew spent the entire season shadowing me, recording what they thought was going to be the story of two call-it-as-you-see-it Dubs bringing success to Carlisle United. But already I knew it was going to be the story of a manager desperately trying to keep the club in the Football League and almost losing his mind in the process.

At least I had Caroline and the kids with me now. We all moved into the Holiday Inn and we lived in two adjoining rooms on the second floor. Caroline and I slept in one room and Niamh, Roddy, Padraig and Lauren slept in the other. When I hear now about homeless families forced to live in hotel accommodation, I can completely empathize with them. It was a boring, rootless existence, especially for the children. They ate their breakfast every morning sitting in a dining room filled with businessmen and travelling salesmen. Roddy kicked his little football up and down the corridor just for the want of something to do, then when he got given out to by the staff, he took it outside and kicked it around the car park, with the cars and trucks roaring past. On a Sunday we went to the club. Caroline washed the family laundry in the kit room while I went out onto the pitch with young Roddy and he took shots on me in goal.

We couldn't rent a house because I had no bank account. And I couldn't open a bank account because I had no wage slips. I didn't receive any salary for the first two months of the season because I hadn't agreed a formal contract with the club. Courtenay had some fella selling old Umbro stock for him on a market stall somewhere in South Wales and he was throwing me the odd £100 out of that.

Then, one day in the middle of September, Kathleen, a lovely girl from Sligo who worked on reception at the hotel, called me over and said she was dreadfully embarrassed, but we were going to have to leave. The club hadn't paid the bill. That night we played Rotherham away in the League Cup. I did my team talk, then we went out onto the pitch. I spotted Courtenay leaning against the dugout. I said to him, 'Can I've a word?'

He stuck his chest out and said, 'Yeah, what?'

'When am I going to start getting paid, John?' I asked.

'Don't start getting fucking awkward with me,' he replied.

'I'll give you fucking awkward,' I said. 'I've moved my family over here. I still haven't been paid a penny and we're being thrown out of our hotel tomorrow. Either start paying me or I'm fucking gone.'

I was finally given a contract. It was for five years. The club agreed to pay me £1,500 per week – the first decent money I ever earned out of football – plus a bonus of £15,000 if we reached a cup final. We moved out of the hotel and into a bed and breakfast. It sounds even worse, but at least we had the use of a kitchen, and Caroline was able to cook, which was something she loved to do. She would make a big stew. Dessie Byrne, who was desperately homesick, would pop in regularly to see if there was anything in the pot and ask Caroline for advice about his romantic life.

I felt guilty, knowing that we were living this way because of me. But I was convinced I could make a success of football management. I was getting good notices. I was listening to the radio one day and Lawrie McMenemy said that Roddy Collins had done really well at Carlisle United and was one for the future. A few weeks into the season, when we'd been top of the table, Barry Fry had sent a fax congratulating me on the job I was doing. Compliments like that could keep me going for weeks, and I needed them that winter as we dropped down the table like a stone.

The drinking culture in the dressing room was being talked about in the local community. It wasn't just the Irish fellas who were gargling, but it was the Irish fellas who were getting noticed because of the stigma of the drunken Paddy.

After one defeat, I told the players to cut out the drinking because we were getting a bad name around the city. If they had to have a drink, I told them, have just one or two pints in the Beehive, a quiet, family-run pub where I knew the lounge staff would keep an eye on things for me. I was in bed one night when my instincts told me that something wasn't right. I put the blue light on, as I called it: went out on patrol to find out what was going on. I walked into Mood nightclub in Botchergate to find half my players in there. Richie Foran, Mattie Glennon and a few others were sitting at a table and you couldn't have put a matchstick down for all the drink that was on it. The rest of the players scattered when they saw me coming. It was 1.30 a.m. and we had training the next morning. The red mist descended. I grabbed the table and I turned it over, sending all of their drinks crashing to the floor. The three fellas got up and ran for

233

it. There was a young fella who'd written me a letter begging me for a trial. He was throwing shapes on the dancefloor with a cigarette in one hand and a Bacardi and Coke in the other. He got a kick in the arse and was told not to come back to the club. Then I went to the bouncers. I had £100 in my pocket. I handed it over and said, 'I'm sorry about that. Will you give that to the staff to clean up the mess?'

One of the bouncers was a Carlisle United season-ticket holder. He said, 'It was about time somebody did that.'

But I knew I was fighting a losing battle. As their manager, I could turn over a table of drink every night of the week, but footballers know that their real boss is the one who signs their cheques – and he was telling them that it was fine for them to be out on the beer, especially if he was leading the party.

In the background, Caroline and I had an ongoing battle with the HSE to hold on to Lauren. They had allowed us to take her out of the country, but we were still subject to ongoing interviews and surprise visits from social workers. I remember one in particular. She wasn't much older than our eldest daughter, Sinéad – and certainly not old enough to remember when Ireland was an economic basket case. She said to us one day, 'What if it all collapses?' meaning the house of cards that was my football management career. She may or may not have known that we'd just lost to Shrewsbury Town, our third defeat in a row.

'If it collapses,' Caroline told her, 'we'll do what we've always done – we'll rebuild.'

I was so proud of her. But the entire experience of fostering Lauren was more traumatic than anything I've ever faced in football. Two social workers flew over one day and interviewed me in the club boardroom and it felt like a police interrogation.

It was excruciating, knowing that everything I said was being written down and that the consequence of a 'wrong' answer could be that we would lose our daughter.

Courtenay and I were on a permanent war footing with each other throughout that season. He hated me and I was embarrassed by him. The documentary brought out his worst instincts. When the production company had first pitched the idea to us, he rubbed his two hands together and said, 'There goes my anonymity in Dublin!'

Despite the programme being called *The Rod Squad*, he thought it was going to be all about him. He loved the cameras even if the cameras didn't necessarily love him back. He tried to create an image of himself as this wisecracking Dublin character, even though he was really just doing a bad impression of me. One day he came in with a giant bag of grass seed and started scattering it around the pitch. 'That's Tipperary seed,' he said, 'the best in the fucking world. That's why the horses from Tipperary win all the classics.'

Very quickly he went from telling the groundsman how to cut the grass to telling me how to pick the team. He said to me one day, 'I want you to play Willo McDonagh on Saturday.'

Willo had only just turned eighteen. His da was one of my best friends and I felt a special duty to protect him. I told Courtenay he wasn't ready.

'Well, I was drinking with his da the other night,' he said to me, 'and I told him he was getting a game – so put him fucking in.'

I didn't.

Then the local radio station started using Courtenay as a co-commentator on its matches. Unfortunately, he didn't know the first thing about football. He used to stand at the door of the dressing room and listen to my half-time team talks. If I said we needed to tighten up in midfield and concentrate our attack down the left channel, Courtenay would run back upstairs to the commentary box and repeat it like it was an observation he had made.

Another time I walked into the dressing room and found him standing where I usually stood, in front of the blackboard. I said, 'John, get the fuck out.'

'You what?' he said.

'I said get fucking out,' I roared, walking him to the door and slamming it shut behind him.

While our form in the league was poor, we had a few good results in the LDV Vans Trophy. From experience, I knew that if you wanted to secure a decent position in the league, you're better off getting out of the cup competitions as quickly as possible. But Courtenay was absolutely fixated on winning it because he wanted the glory of a trophy in his first season.

In December we were due to play Wrexham twice in four days – first in the quarter-final of the LDV, then in the league. Courtenay came to see me before the first match and said, 'Who's going to play?'

I told him I was going to leave out most of the first team and save them for the league game on Saturday.

'Don't you fucking go there,' he said. 'We're two matches away from a final at the Millennium Stadium.'

'If we stay in this competition,' I told him, 'we're going to end up in a relegation fight, John. We need the points.'

'Fuck the points,' he said. 'I need this to wash me linen.'

That was when I first realized that money was an issue for him. Either he wasn't as rich as he claimed to be or Carlisle United had turned out to be an even bigger money pit than he might have feared. Around the same time, he started trying to ingratiate himself with the local business community to try to find someone to share the financial burden. At the start of 2003 I noticed one or two new faces hanging around the directors' box. One was Fred Story, the biggest builder in Cumbria, and then someone from the local Pirelli tyre plant, then someone else who owned a building supplies company.

One evening, Bugsy and I were summoned to a meeting in Courtenay's office. When we got there, the three blokes were sitting there with him. They started asking me questions relating to team matters – players I selected, tactical decisions I made. Then Fred Story said something smart to me. It was like being back at Bohemians again. I was thinking, Who the fuck *are* these boyos?

'Don't be getting all defensive,' Courtenay said to me. 'It's just our results have been poor.'

We put Wrexham out of the LDV. Then four days later, exhausted, we lost to them at home in the league after conceding a winner with three minutes to go.

'John,' I said, 'I told you that this was going to happen if we stayed in the cup.'

After the meeting he said to me, 'Are you coming for a drink with us?'

'No,' I said, 'I'm going home to Caroline.'

Home was now a four-bedroom house that we'd bought just after Christmas with a £2,000-per-month mortgage that I was becoming increasingly worried about as the mood around the club changed.

'You never come for a fucking drink with me,' he said.

'Who the fuck are those lads to ask me about my managerial tactics?' I asked.

'They're the new board of directors,' he said. 'They're all throwing in a few bob.'

It was just as I'd thought. Courtenay had bought Carlisle United to feed his monstrous ego. Now he was broke and he wanted to pawn the whole thing off on someone else.

I sacked two players. They deserved it. They turned up drunk at training. I told them they'd never play for Carlisle again and I stuck them on the transfer list. Courtenay begged me to give them a second chance because it was his fault. He'd brought them out drinking. Against my better instincts, I agreed. I remembered Dermot Keely doing something similar with a player at Sligo Rovers and I lost a lot of respect for him. And, similarly, my authority as a manager was fatally undermined once I went back on my word. I was made to look weak. Footballers notice these things.

At the beginning of March we beat Shrewsbury Town over two legs to win the semi-final of the LDV Trophy. In the four weeks leading up to the final, no one seemed to care that we were in danger of relegation. Despite my best efforts, all of the focus was on the final against Bristol City at the Millennium Stadium. I could sense that I was losing the dressing room.

The final was on Sunday, 6 April. On the way to Cardiff I arranged for the squad to stay over in Celtic Manor, a luxury golf and spa hotel that I remembered from my time at Newport. It was the start of the week, so I told the players that they could have a few beers. During the course of the night, Richie Foran got a few drinks in him and called me a wanker in front of the other players.

'What did you call me?' I asked.

'I said you're a wanker,' he said. 'Someone in the club slagged me off in the *News & Star* and I know it was you – you fucking wanker.'

I hadn't a clue what he was talking about.

'Get up to bed,' I said.

Brian Shelley, who was already in trouble with me, was rooming with him. He offered to take him. I sat there for half an hour, seething at him for daring to speak to me like that. I went upstairs to confront him. Shellyer opened the door.

'All right, boss?' he asked.

'Where's that little bollocks?' I said, pushing past him.

Richie was asleep in the bed.

'I need to have a chat with you,' I said. 'Get up.'

He got out of the bed.

'I'm disgusted with you,' I said. 'I've been friends with your da since we played Gaelic football together. I was at your christening. I brought you over here and gave you an opportunity when nobody wanted you. And you call me a wanker in front of everyone.'

'You slagged me off in the paper,' he said.

Then he punched me in the face. It was a hell of a dig as well. Richie could look after himself.

'You little fucker,' I said. Then I took off my shirt, which I had the habit of doing in times of confrontation. I don't know why.

I squared up to him in the style of a boxer. We had a straightener. Richie was trying to dig me in the head, while I concentrated on body shots because I didn't want to knock him out or even mark his face, what with the final being televised. Poor Shellyer was hiding behind the sofa in the room, begging us to stop.

'Please, lads, don't do this,' he said.

'You're fucking next,' I told him.

Eventually, Richie gave up. He said, 'I've enough, Rod. I've enough.'

I went back to my room, washed myself down, put on a clean shirt and went to the bar for a lager shandy with ice. About twenty minutes later, Richie appeared beside me.

'Rod, I'm sorry,' he said, all sheepish. 'Can I have a lager shandy?'

'Sit down,' I told him, 'you fucking eejit.'

'I read a thing in the paper,' he said, 'and I was told you were slagging me off.'

I had a good idea who told him.

'Richie, I'd never badmouth any of my players,' I said, 'let alone you.'

'So am I dropped for the final, am I?' he asked.

'Shut up, you fucking dope. Get up to bed.'

We patched it up, but I could see that the air of authority I once had over the players was gone.

We walked out at the Millennium Stadium in front of 60,000 fans. None of our players had experienced an atmosphere like it before. Bristol City were chasing promotion to the First Division, while we were down at the bottom of the Third. There was a big deficit in class between us, but we put up a great fight until we tired and conceded two goals in the last twelve minutes. And Richie didn't let me down. He was brilliant.

Courtenay got the result he wanted – £700,000, according to the *News & Star*. But it was only after the final that he started to become concerned with how perilously close we were to losing our league status. He'd come into the dressing room after a match and watch the other Division Three results come in on the TV. 'Fuck's sake!' he'd shout. 'Exeter are after winning!' – like that was somehow within my control. But then I'd look around and discover that he was doing it for the benefit of the documentary cameras.

We were running out of time to save ourselves. We went to Wrexham and we were 3–0 down at half-time. I had a little ritual where I went into the toilet cubicle to compose my thoughts. Little Roddy tried to follow me in. He was upset. I said to him, 'It's going to be grand, Rod.'

When I came out of the cubicle, he was walking around, assuring each player, 'My daddy said it's going to be grand.'

It broke my heart in two. I took off Richie Foran and Peter Murphy. We ended up losing 6–1. Courtenay was furious afterwards.

'The fuck are you at,' he screamed at me, 'taking off two of our best players?'

'The match was lost,' I said. 'I was saving the lads for next week.'

'That was a fucking humiliation.'

It turned out that Courtenay was embarrassed that his team were slaughtered in front of Alex Ferguson, who was there to watch his son Darren play for Wrexham.

Our second-last game of the season was against Shrewsbury Town at Gay Meadow. There were 7,000 fans there. The place was packed to the rafters. One of us was going to be relegated that night. We needed to win to be safe. The tension was unreal. Kevin Ratcliffe, the former Everton and Wales defender, was the Shrewsbury manager. After we did our team talks, he invited me into his office. He looked about ten years older than he did at the start of the season.

'Oh, well,' he said, 'one of us is getting the bullet – probably tonight.'

'How are you fixed?' I asked.

'I'll be all right,' he said. 'I've a bit of property in Portugal and a few quid. What about you?'

'Ah, yeah, I'm sorted,' I lied. 'Here, you wouldn't have a drink in here, would you?'

He opened his desk drawer and pulled out a bottle of brandy. He poured us each a shot. We knocked them back and we hugged each other.

I had a row with the fourth official that night that became one of the most famous scenes in *The Rod Squad*. I knew the official well. He looked impossibly young for the job he was doing and I used to say to him, 'Does your ma know you're out this late?' Against Shrewsbury, he started complaining that I was stepping outside my box and I ended up having a screaming match with him that was almost nose to nose. At the end, I said, 'I'll tell your ma on ye!'

I wasn't anywhere close to as worked up as I appeared on the telly. I was trying to let my players see that I wasn't worried, even though my stomach was doing backflips. After half an hour, we went a goal down. But then Brian Wake scored a hat-trick for us and we ended up winning 3–2. I'd told the players beforehand that, if we won, they should keep the lid on their joy until they were back in the dressing room. The year before, we'd relegated Halifax to the Conference.

Richie scored the goal that put them out of the league. I remember seeing the devastation on the face of their manager, Neil Redfearn, and their players. The players promised me there would be no displays of triumphalism, and they were as good as their word. They walked straight off the pitch and back to the dressing room. I locked the door and then we had our moment of celebration.

The next thing I knew, Courtenay was kicking the door, shouting, 'What the fuck is going on? There's four thousand of our supporters out there – go out and celebrate with them.'

I shouted, 'Fuck off, John,' through the door.

A couple of weeks later I had a letter from Shrewsbury Town, thanking the players for behaving with such dignity and restraint. I didn't see Kevin Ratcliffe after the match. A few days later he was gone from the club and he never worked as a football manager again.

People often ask me if I regret doing *The Rod Squad*. Am I embarrassed now by the things I said on the programme: that I was going to manage Manchester United one day, that I was going to manage Ireland? And the answer is no. The man you saw on TV is exactly the man I am. I wasn't hamming it up for the viewers back home.

I was away when the documentary was shown, so I only heard about the reaction in Ireland from friends and family. People told me they loved it. And it made me well known outside the world of League of Ireland football. I wasn't just the brother of Steve Collins any more. When I went back home, strangers in the street shouted lines from the programme at me: 'I'll tell your ma on ye!'

We went to Spain for three weeks that summer. When we came back, Lauren had to go into hospital. She had been born with a cleft palate and she was having an operation to repair it in Temple Street Hospital. Caroline and I took turns to sleep on the floor beside her bed until she was well enough to be discharged. Then we all headed back to Carlisle – the entire family this time. Sinéad was about to do the final year of her Science degree in Maynooth, and she transferred to Newcastle University so that she could be with us. What I didn't know was that we wouldn't be there long enough for her to attend a lecture.

When you get sacked as a football manager, it never comes as a complete surprise. You pick up on a change in the general mood. You notice signals. You walk into a room and the conversation stops. Someone who you got on well with before suddenly can't make eye contact with you. Someone who used to respect you speaks sharply to you. Someone on your staff is suddenly walking around the place with a confidence you've never seen in them before.

The first inkling that I was for the door came when I was on holidays in Spain. A friend of mine at the club rang me to say that Courtenay was having regular three-hour meetings with Billy Barr, who was the caretaker manager when I arrived. When I returned from Spain, I wanted to sign Stevie Livingstone from Grimsby Town. Stevie was a big centre-forward who could also fill in at centre-half. I got a bit of pushback from Courtenay. He wanted me to hold off. I thought, Is that because he knows I'm not going to be here?

In the end, I signed him. Then he got sent off in our first league match against York City. As he left the pitch, I could hear Courtenay roaring at him from the directors' box. We played really well with ten men but we lost 2–1. Afterwards, Courtenay barged into the dressing room.

'What the fuck was all that about?' he said. 'Them fucking York players are only getting £400 or £500 a week. I'm paying £800 or £900.'

I said, 'John, relax, will you? It's only the first match of the season.'

Four days later we got beaten by Paul Merson's Walsall, who were in the First Division, in the first round of the League Cup. I was suspended for the match and was sitting in the stand next to Courtenay. He spent the match acting like he was the manager, roaring at Paul Raven, a defender I'd signed from Grimsby along with Stevie: 'Tuck in, Raven, for fuck's sake!' even though he hadn't a clue what it meant. We got beaten by Yeovil, then by Bristol Rovers at home. A man who I knew was a drinking buddy of Courtenay's shouted at me, 'Fuck off back to Ireland on your donkey and cart!'

In the summer I'd signed a former Manchester City winger named Paul Simpson, who'd most recently been the player-manager at

Rochdale. People told me I was mad. He was thirty-six and clearly had ambitions in the game beyond his playing career. 'He'll take your job,' I was told. But I went ahead.

'If he can do a better job than me,' I said, 'he's welcome to it.'

Our fourth league game of the season was against Boston United. There were two elderly couples who used to stand on a grass bank and watch all of our training sessions. I used to chat to them while the players did their warm-up. On this particular day, I noticed that they couldn't look at me.

I said, 'Is everything OK?'

I saw that one of the women was crying.

I pulled Richie Foran to one side.

'What's going on?' I asked.

'I don't know,' he said. 'There's a few rumours going around. Are you going to be all right, Rod?'

'Don't worry about me. I've a four-year contract. I'm going nowhere.'

Courtenay disappeared that week. The most attention-hungry chairman in English football turned into a recluse overnight. I remember finally getting him on the phone on the morning we played Boston United away.

'Is everything OK?' I asked.

'Sound as a bell,' he said.

'There's an awful stink of something around the club. I need you to do something for me. I need you to come into the dressing room and tell the players that I have your support – because there's an awful lot of rumours going around, John.'

'I'll be there.'

I did my team talk. Courtenay didn't show up for it – he said he was stuck in traffic. As we were leaving the dressing room, I noticed Paul Simpson shouting his mouth off – 'Come on, lads, let's facking do it today!' It was all to impress Courtenay, who'd arrived late. And I saw the full picture. Paul was the next manager.

We lost 1–0. The home crowd were singing, 'Sacked in the morning, you're getting sacked in the morning . . .'

I got into a row with the referee and he sent me off. I left the pitchside area. I remember leaning on a gate and just breaking down. A newspaper photographer took a picture with a long lens, me with tears in my eyes, looking like a beaten docket. I went back to the dressing room. I screamed, 'They're not going to fucking beat me!' and I punched a door, which I thought was plywood but was actually made of mahogany.

Then on Sunday, bizarrely, I had a call from Keith Duffy out of Boyzone. He was in Carlisle to open a nightclub.

'I've never met you before,' he said, 'but I'd love to have a pint with you.'

Which put him in a minority of one at that time.

I went along to the nightclub with Caroline and Sinéad. I had a couple of shandies – my hand was all busted up – and the night ended in a sing-song.

'Jaysus, Keith,' I said, 'maybe I should do what you do – it looks easier – and you can manage Carlisle United.'

At the end of the night I said goodbye to him and he said, 'Best of luck tomorrow, mate.'

It was like everyone in the world knew what was coming.

I got up the next morning and put on my best Louis Copeland suit. Sinéad drove me to Brunton Park. I saw the Rolls-Royces and the Jags belonging to the directors in the car park. I said to Sinéad, 'Tell your ma I'll be home early. The hit squad are waiting.'

I walked into the club. Sarah on reception couldn't look at me. I went down to my office. Bugsy was there before me. 'I was thinking over the weekend,' he said, 'we can turn this around.'

Bugsy was still in denial. The next thing, Sarah rang to say that I was wanted in the boardroom. I went along. All of the directors were sitting there, most of them looking down at the table.

'This is not working out,' Courtenay said.

'We're only a month into the season,' I told him. 'Putting together a squad takes time.'

'The crowds aren't turning out,' he said.

Courtenay had this phrase: 'I don't see supporters – I see pound notes.'

'The crowds will come back,' I said. 'Trust me. I know this business.'

'The players don't like you,' Fred Story piped up.

'Is that right?' I asked. 'What do you want me to do about that?'

'Step down,' he said.

They wanted me gone, but they didn't want to pay out the remaining years of my contract. I'd spoken to Brian Delahunt, my solicitor in Dublin. His advice to me was, 'Cement your feet to the floor and don't leave until they sack you.'

'You're going to put everyone at the club out of work,' Fred said, trying to shame me into going. 'You're a pariah in this town.'

I felt the cold rush. I wanted to turn over the table, but I managed to keep the urge in check.

'So what are you going to do?' Courtenay asked.

'What am I going to do?' I said. 'I'm going to take training. Then I'm going to start thinking about Cambridge United on Saturday.'

'Are you not hearing what we're saying to you?' Courtenay said. 'You're not wanted here.'

'Then you're going to have to sack me,' I told him.

'Right,' he said, 'I will. Clear out your office and fuck off!'

I went and told Bugsy the news. We both broke down. I cleared out my desk, then I went outside. It was a beautiful, sunny morning. Paul Simpson was taking training. The players were playing some game and they were laughing and cheering. For them it was a new start. For me it was like I'd never, ever been there.

I remember thinking, That's football.

17

George Reynolds was a safecracker who was born into extreme poverty in Sunderland between the wars. He did prison time in the 1960s and 1970s but then went straight and made a fortune from kitchen countertops. The so-called 'Chipboard King' was among the hundred richest men in England, with his own yacht and a fleet of luxury cars.

Like a lot of rich men, he also bought a football club – Darlington FC, who were in the Third Division – and was trying to turn them into a Premier League side. He heard about my sacking and rang me the next day to say he wanted to talk. He sent his driver to bring me and Caroline to Witton Hall, his £7-million mansion on the edge of Witton-le-Wear. As the car crunched its way up the gravel driveway, Caroline said, 'It's like the house in *Gone with the Wind*!'

George was a brilliant, flamboyant character and he had big, hare-brained plans. Despite an average home gate of 2,500, he was going to build the club an enormous 25,000-seater stadium called the Reynolds Arena. His dream would eventually cost him his entire fortune and send him back to prison for tax evasion. For some reason he liked me – he'd actually made inquiries about me after I was sacked by Bohemians. He asked how much I'd want to manage Darlington FC. I told him £50,000 a year.

'And what would you guarantee me for that?' he asked.

'I'll get you to the play-offs,' I told him.

'And if you don't,' he said, 'will I get £25,000 back?'

'Do you want my kids knocking on your door for bread?' I asked him.

'I'd rather they were knocking on my door,' he smiled, 'than mine were knocking on yours.'

He said he wanted to take my proposed appointment to the board of the club. He gave me his business card – it said, 'George Reynolds – Gentleman, Entrepreneur, Adventurer, Maker of Money and Utter Genius' – and said he'd be in touch. I never heard from him again. I suspect he rang John Courtenay and asked for a reference.

Caroline and I spent a couple of weeks thinking about our next move. We had a mortgage of £2,000 per month and no money coming in. But I had a decent reputation in England. A lot of clubs change their managers between the start of the season and Christmas. I was sure I'd get something. But then I was looking at Padraig and Lauren – two little toddlers – and I saw this sadness in them. And I started to wonder were any of us actually happy. I'd dragged Caroline, Sinéad, Niamh and Roddy away from their friends and the life they knew in Dublin for this.

I said to Caroline, 'It's time to go home.'

It was the middle of September 2003. Sinéad was about to start the final year of her degree at Newcastle University. Fortunately, Maynooth agreed to let her transfer back. Then we rang Niamh's and Roddy's old school principal in Castleknock Community College and he said he'd find places for them. We packed everything we owned into the back of a removals truck and we went back to Dublin to do what Caroline told the social worker we'd do – rebuild.

We were completely broke. We had a home in Dublin that was paid for and a mortgage on a house in the north of England that we were now trying desperately to sell. I dug out my hawk and trowel and I went back to the only other thing I was qualified to do. A fella I knew had the construction contract for a building on Fleet Street in Dublin and he said he'd give me a start for £150 a day. By then, *The Rod Squad* had just gone out on Setanta Sports. Within an hour, the word was out that Roddy Collins was plastering on the site. Suddenly men were roaring from the scaffolding above me: 'Collins, you gobshite! You said you were going to manage Man United one day! You said you were going to manage Ireland! You fucking eejit, you!'

I'd set myself up for a fall. Now I was just trying to get a few bob together for my family. I was never precious about work. I'd have done anything to put food on our table. But by lunchtime, I was getting absolutely ripped apart, so I walked off the site and never went back.

The issue of compensation from Carlisle United rumbled on for months. Just before Christmas I got a call from Ollie Byrne. I met him for a cup of tea in a little café next to a laundrette on Richmond Road in Drumcondra. He asked me how I was getting by and I said I wasn't. A year before, he'd offered me the Shelbourne job after I was sacked by Carlisle the first time and I'd told him his club was too small for me. Now I'd have marked the pitch for him.

'You've a gang of kids,' he said, 'don't you?'

'Yeah,' I said, 'five.'

He reached across the table and stuck €500 in my shirt pocket.

Around the middle of December a meeting was arranged with John Courtenay in the Westbury Hotel in Dublin to discuss the terms of my severance. We sat with our solicitors on either side of a big long table. The balance of my contract was worth over €200,000. They were offering €7,000 – 'For the Christmas,' Courtenay smirked. I was holding a Waterford Crystal glass. I nearly crushed it in my hand.

I asked could I speak to him outside alone.

'Don't fucking insult me,' I told him in the lobby. 'You owe me two-hundred-and-odd grand.'

'How much do you want?' he asked.

'Two-hundred-and-odd grand.'

It took about sixty seconds to agree a deal to end my relationship with Carlisle United. But it wasn't the end of my relationship with Courtenay. Shortly after that he told a friend of mine in a pub one night, 'I kept that cunt out of work in England – and I'll keep him out of work in Ireland as well.'

The upside from doing *The Rod Squad* was that it made me a media figure in Ireland. I started writing a weekly column in the *Irish Daily Star*. I was also offered work as a TV pundit with RTE. My first job was a live match in Cork, which is where I was driving in the summer of 2004 when Ronan Seery rang.

Rocky, as everyone knew him, was the chairman of Dublin City

FC, formerly Home Farm Everton, who were trying to create an identity for themselves in a city that already had four big League of Ireland clubs. They had no permanent home and no real fan base, which meant no regular income. They were bottom of the Premier Division and they were heading for relegation. And they needed a manager.

I said I'd take a look. I went to see them training and could feel myself getting sucked in. I told Rocky that I'd take charge, but as a consultant. Being the manager would have meant giving Carlisle back the company Merc, and I didn't know if the job would last more than a few weeks. From the start I could see that the club was a shambles. They had far too many players and few of them were good enough.

I told Rocky that I needed to bring in a few men of the road, players who were maybe coming to the end of their careers but were the kind of street-smart old pros we needed for a relegation battle. I got Carlton Palmer, who had played in midfield for Sheffield Wednesday, Leeds and England. We became friends when I was at Carlisle and he was player-manager at Stockport County. He agreed to play for me, more as a favour than anything else. We couldn't afford to pay him much, but he didn't need the money. He brought his mate Efan Ekoku, a striker, who'd played for Wimbledon and Nigeria. The Skylon Hotel agreed to put them up for free and I got sponsored flights to bring them over for matches.

I read an article later that said 'flamboyant' Roddy Collins bankrupted Dublin City by bringing in big-name has-beens on massive money. But the fellas were only on a few hundred quid a week and I'd saved the club a fortune by clearing out a load of players.

What I didn't realize was the extent of the financial trouble the club was in. Rocky and those around him were well-meaning football people, but Dublin City FC was a pipedream. There was talk of a new stadium and of following the Rosenborg model of the small club that punches far above its weight. Within a few months the talk had turned to the more familiar ground of not having the money to pay the players until the end of the season and withdrawing from the League of Ireland before our fixtures were completed.

Along with Terry Eviston, my assistant manager, I had a crisis meeting with Rocky at which he pulled €40 out of his pocket and told me tearfully that it was all the money he had left in the world. And it was around that time that I was offered the Shamrock Rovers job. It placed me in a very difficult position, because Rovers were Dublin City's relegation rivals. Initially, I told Rovers that it would have to wait until the end of the season. But then I heard that Dublin City were getting ready to pull the carpet from under me anyway. So with only three weeks of the season left, I said yes to the Rovers job.

Rocky was absolutely livid. On the day that Rovers made the announcement, he went on *Liveline* on RTE radio and lumped me out of it for betraying the club. It allowed him to present me as the villain when the team got relegated. But I knew the truth. The Dublin City project was doomed from the start.

Not that Shamrock Rovers were on firmer ground. The club was €2.5 million in debt, their plans for a new stadium in Tallaght had stalled and they'd come close to being relegated for the first time in their history. It was a lot for a manager to deal with in his first season at a club.

Added to that was the fact that most of the Rovers fans hated me. To them, I was a Bohs man. The manager who had led their hated rivals to the league and cup double. The manager who had masterminded the Santry Siro Massacre. The man with the big mouth in the Louis Copeland suits and the brown-and-white spats. A mate of mine in Bohs said to me, 'If you don't win every single match, they'll fuck you out. And they'll probably fuck you out even if you do.'

The first man I saw when I took training was Trevor Molloy. I'd given Trevor a three-year contract at Carlisle then terminated it because I didn't think he was living the way a professional footballer should. He looked at me and asked, 'Am I all right, boss?'

I said, 'No problem with me, Trevor,' and I gave him a hug.

There were only two or three matches left in the season, but it was enough for me to suss out who was for me and who wasn't. I cleared out a few of the old faces, players who I didn't feel were doing it for the club, then I brought in a few players, mostly Irish fellas who'd come to the end of the road in England. I got Willo McDonagh from

Carlisle United and Mark Quigley on loan from Millwall. I also got Paddy McCourt from Rochdale.

I've already mentioned that Marc Kenny and Paul Byrne were two of the three most gifted players who ever played for me. The third – the best of the bunch – was Paddy McCourt. He was the nearest thing to George Best I ever saw. I used to come home from training on a high after watching him. Years later, when he was in his thirties and nearing the end of his career, I helped get him a deal at Luton Town. The younger players there were in awe of him. They'd text my son Roddy to say, 'You'd want to see what Paddy did at training today.'

That he never ended up a household name in England was down to bad coaches who didn't know how to use his talents, which were many. He had two brilliant feet. He could beat four or five players and score a goal at the end of it. He could ping a pass sixty yards. He was as strong as a bull. He could jump higher than a player who was four or five inches taller than him. He had a great footballing brain and he was the calmest man I've ever seen under pressure. And yet managers got rid of him because he didn't track back and he couldn't tackle.

The first time I saw him was when I was the manager of Carlisle and he came on for Rochdale as a sub against us, a teenager with a skinhead who immediately dropped his shoulder, beat three men and nearly scored. I said to Bugsy, 'Who the fuck is that?'

'That's Harry McCourt's little brother,' Bugsy said.

I'd played against Harry in the Irish League.

For all his talent, Paddy hadn't been able to nail down a regular place. I was trying to sign him for Carlisle United the week I got sacked and my first priority when I got the Rovers job was to get him. I went to see him play for Rochdale against Blackpool. I took young Roddy with me. He was ten years old at the time.

'Who are we here to see?' he asked.

'See can you guess,' I said.

The match was about sixty seconds old when a ball came out of the sky and Paddy took it down and put it through a player's legs with one touch.

'Ah, *him*,' Roddy said.

Paddy put on an absolute masterclass in the first half. As he was walking off the pitch at half-time, I nabbed him. 'The fuck are you doing?' I said to him. 'They're never going to let you leave if you play like that.'

Thankfully, Paddy downed tools in the second half. I don't think he left the centre circle. The next day, I signed him.

That night, Roddy and I were at a loose end. Bradford City were playing at home, so we drove up there on a freezing cold night. Jason Gavin was playing. I couldn't believe it. He'd played as a centre-half for Middlesbrough and once put in a man-of-the-match performance against Manchester United.

'What's the story with Jason?' I asked Colin Todd, the Bradford manager. 'Is he injured?'

'No,' Colin said, 'he's not getting in my first team. I don't want him.'

'Much is he on?'

'Two thousand pound a week.'

'Would you loan him out to us if we paid half his wages?'

Rovers didn't have a bean, but I knew that for Jason Gavin they'd find the money from somewhere. Colin agreed. Jason wasn't interested in coming back to Ireland, but I persuaded him that it was a chance to kick-start his career and we agreed a deal with his agent and his da in Darkey Kelly's pub in Christchurch.

I wanted to present the image that Shamrock Rovers were back in the big time. We went to Spain for pre-season training and we took a drive down to La Manga, the famous football academy where the Spanish team trained. As luck would have it, I ran into Colin Clarke, the former Northern Ireland striker, who was there with Dallas Burn, the MLS side he coached. Colin said they had two training pitches booked for the afternoon and we could have one. We'd brought balls with us on the off-chance. We trained for a bit, then the next day we played a friendly against a local team, who tried to break one or two of our players up, so I took them off the pitch for their own protection. But we took a team photo that I sent back to the *Irish Daily Star*, along with the story that we were preparing for the new season at the most prestigious training base in the world.

In a normal year, all other things being equal, that Rovers team would have finished in the top three. But it's difficult to ask your players to give their best when you have no wages for them.

The club was broke. Finding money to pay them often meant persuading a local pub or shop owner to cash a cheque and agree not to lodge it with the bank for a week or two. The rest of the time I was having to perform a loaves-and-fishes routine with what little money we had. Luckily, we had a great bond in the dressing room and the players agreed to be paid according to the greatest need.

Mark Rutherford had four kids and was at college, so I tried to make sure he never went without. Players like Marc Kenny, Trevor Molloy, Willo McDonagh and Mark Quigley regularly told me that they could wait for their money. Still, it went against all my principles to send the players away with no wages at the end of the week.

Some of our players were only on £50 a week anyway and they were getting lambasted by the fans. We failed to win any of our first five matches.

One night we played Finn Harps away and we had no money for a pre-match meal. One of the committee men did a whip-round in the local pub to buy the players burgers and chips for the bus journey home. You had to keep reminding yourself that this was the most famous club in Irish football.

We were forced to leave our training base in Three Rock Rovers and some nights ended up training on a patch of ground in Marlay Park in Rathfarnham. The warden came over and told us that ball games weren't permitted in the park. I tried to explain to him that we were Shamrock Rovers.

The club was full of good people like John Noonan, John Breen, Tony Ennis, Paul Doyle, Tony Maguire, Mick Kearns and Mick McCarthy, who did everything in their power, including dipping into their own pockets, to keep the show on the road.

It wasn't enough. In April 2005, just a few weeks into the season, the High Court appointed an examiner to Rovers, giving the club ninety-one days to map out a plan for its future.

Then, in May, the club got docked eight points for submitting the wrong accounts with their application for a licence the previous season. It was a devastating blow. We only had nine points at the time.

It changed the whole dynamic of our season. We went from being a mid-table team that was building for next season to bottom of the table with just a single point.

When the examinership ended, a group of supporters calling themselves the 400 Club announced that they were going to take over the running of the club. Brooks Mileson, who had almost bought Carlisle United ahead of John Courtenay, wanted to throw some of his fortune at a League of Ireland club. I arranged a meeting between him and some members of the 400 Club. He asked them what they planned to do to make Rovers self-financing going forward. They started talking about shaving heads for a fundraiser. I was so embarrassed. Brooks thought they were a joke. He said to me, 'Bring me back to the airport.'

We had some good results that summer and clawed back the eight points we were docked. In September, we beat Bohemians at Daly-mount. I wound the Bohs fans up by sending out a bagpiper to play on the pitch before the match. Earlier in the year we'd beaten Shelbourne at Tolka Park and Ollie Byrne finally lost it with me. In a radio interview, I'd made some comments about his club's financial position that turned out to be a little too close to the bone. I was talking to the Shelbourne full-back Owen Heery when Ollie walked up to me and punched me in the side of the head, then tore my shirt. I didn't mind that so much – I could take a punch and Pat Fenlon, the Shels manager, gave me the loan of a shirt – but then Ollie called me 'a thug' in the newspapers.

It was a very sensitive and highly stressful time for Caroline and me. We were fostering Lauren, but we were suddenly subjected to a new round of interviews and home visits from social workers, who were often just kids themselves, laying down the law to us about how to parent a child. Lauren shouldn't be calling us 'Mammy' and 'Daddy', they said – it should be 'Auntie Caroline' and 'Uncle Roddy'. And if she came to us in the night after having a nightmare, Caroline could take her into the bed, but I had to leave the room immediately. There was already tension between me and the social workers when the business with Ollie made the newspapers.

I made a complaint to the gardaí and Ollie was charged with

assault. When the case came before the Dublin District Court, I told Ollie that all I wanted out of him was an apology.

'I'm not apologizing to you, Collins,' he told me. 'You *are* a fucking thug.'

But when I explained the situation with Lauren, I watched his eyes fill up with tears, then he walked into the courtroom and apologized for the assault. I accepted it and acknowledged that there had been some degree of provocation. The charges were struck out and that was that.

The pressure of being the manager of Shamrock Rovers was huge. There was a section of the supporters who were impossible to please. I was on holiday in Marbella with Caroline just before the season started. I was sunbathing one day when a shadow fell over me. It was a Rovers fan.

'You'll fucking listen to what I have to say,' he said. 'I pay your fucking wages.'

'Fuck off,' I told him, 'you fucking clown.'

The abuse was worse than anything I ever heard in the North. I was a wanker. I was a paedophile. I was a wife-beater. During one match I left the dugout and told a fella to stay in his seat afterwards and we'd have it out. Of course he legged it. I was glad. He was huge.

At the same time John Courtenay was going around telling people that he would pay the wages of the next Rovers manager if the club sacked me.

When the examinership ended, I was ordered to put all of the players on the transfer list. David Mooney went to Longford Town. Jason Gavin went to Drogheda United. Mark Rutherford went to St Pat's. Paddy McCourt, our top scorer, who won the PFAI Young Player of the Year award that season, went home to Derry City. Poor Paddy couldn't even face me. He told me afterwards that he cried on the bus home.

As bad as things were, I still felt we could stay up. That summer I signed Tony Sheridan, the former Coventry midfielder, who was playing in the Leinster Senior League. He had a sun holiday booked and I couldn't ask him to cancel it, not for the £50 a week we were paying him. He arrived home from Lanzarote on a Saturday night.

We played Bray Wanderers away the next day and I don't think we had two substitutes. Shero was in bits. I said to him, 'Please, will you just sit in the dugout for us? It's embarrassing – we've only kids.'

With ten minutes to go it was 2–2 and I asked him to go on.

'Fuck you, Roddy,' he said. 'I'm fucking dying here.'

'Just go on and get us a goal,' I said.

So he went on. That was Shero. A man. And he got us a winner. He took the ball on the edge of the box and bent it into the top corner, then he ran all the way to the dugout to celebrate. As I hugged him, he said, 'I can't go back out there, Rod. I'm bollocksed.'

Most of the 400 Club lads that I met were spoofers who knew nothing about football. They started giving me verbal and written warnings about my conduct. They said I'd missed a reserve-team match. They said I left Richmond Park before the final whistle on the night we lost to Pat's to take part in a white-collar boxing event – which I didn't, I stayed until the end. They said I'd publicly criticized the way the club was being run, which was true. They said there were times when they found me uncontactable on my mobile phone. They said I'd allowed the players to train in unofficial kit and now they were being threatened with legal action by Umbro Ireland – in other words, John Courtenay.

One night, at a reserve-team match, I was handed a dossier of pages detailing all of their issues with me. It was reported that night that I was suspended pending an internal investigation, which was vague enough to leave a stain on my character. Did I rob money? Was I drunk on the job? Did I molest someone? My ma rang me in tears, saying, 'Roddy, what did you do?'

They thought that Terry Eviston, my assistant, would take the job, but Terry quit out of loyalty to me. So they hired Alan O'Neill, the former Rovers goalkeeper, who I played with at Dundalk, to manage them for the two-legged relegation play-off. As fate would have it, it was against Rocky Seery's Dublin City FC, who were now managed by Dermot Keely. I offered to talk to the players beforehand and give them one of my famous pep talks, but I was told to stay away.

Dublin City were a terrible team. But Rovers lost the first leg at Dalymount Park 2–1, and three days later they drew 1–1 at Tolka.

For the first time in their history, Shamrock Rovers were relegated. Four days later I got the sack. I took a claim for unfair dismissal and Rovers ended up having to pay out my contract in full. But I would much rather have been the manager who kept them up.

I remember seeing a photograph in the paper of Rocky Seery at the final whistle in Tolka Park, smiling at the camera and punching the air, savouring his moment of revenge. Maybe he deserved it.

I was damaged goods after Rovers. I applied for a few jobs in England, including Stockport County and Bristol Rovers. The first interviews always went really well, then their enthusiasm for me would die.

In Ireland, I couldn't even get an interview. Every time I applied for a job I was quietly told the same thing. I was toxic. Through Umbro, John Courtenay was one of the biggest financial supporters of the FAI and was great buddies with John Delaney, the FAI's chief executive. No one wanted to make an enemy of him by hiring me.

In early 2007 the Shelbourne job became vacant. Ollie offered it to me in Fagan's in Drumcondra one night. This time I nearly took the hand off him.

A press conference was arranged for Tolka Park on a Monday morning. The night before, I got a call from Ollie asking me to meet him in the Red Cow Hotel. When I arrived I knew that something was wrong.

'Rod, I'm sorry,' he said. 'Courtenay said if I give you the job, he's going to call in his loans. And we haven't got the money to pay him.'

Ollie died not long after that. I didn't know at the time – and maybe he didn't either – that he had cancer. He was hospitalized that summer. He was found to have a tumour on his brain and it was inoperable. I went to see him in the hospice in Harold's Cross where he spent the last few weeks of his life. I pushed him around the grounds in a wheelchair and it broke my heart to see the fire that burned so fiercely in him being slowly extinguished. I held him in my arms and we both got emotional. When I said goodbye to him that day, I knew it would be for the last time..

Ollie died in the middle of what was a very dark period of my life.

I was unemployable. For two and a half years, I didn't leave the house for any meaningful purpose. I had no reason to get up in the mornings, so I didn't bother. I stopped caring about my appearance. I ate rubbish all day, every day. My weight ballooned to seventeen stone. I stopped laughing. I couldn't see the joy in anything. And I spent more time thinking about John Courtenay than was healthy. I tortured myself wondering how my life might have turned out if I'd never gone into Myo's that night.

Courtenay didn't have one good day at Carlisle after he sacked me. Paul Simpson turned out to be less than the football genius that Courtenay thought he was going to be. The team lost fourteen and drew two of his first seventeen matches as player-manager and they dropped out of the Football League at the end of the season. Courtenay ran out of money and handed over the keys of the club to the other directors. Then he moved back to Dublin.

He was still badmouthing me all over town and promising that I'd never work again. I followed him home in his car one night. I was going to knock lumps out of him. That was how dark my life had become. The only thing that stopped me was seeing how pathetic he looked. I thought, Football has done that to him. And the saddest thing of all was I couldn't see that it was doing exactly the same thing to me.

Caroline would say to me, 'Roddy, you have to stop this. You have five children. You're going to be no good to them if you wind up in Mountjoy.'

It all came to a head one day when Courtenay's face popped up on the television and Padraig said, 'I hate him.'

To hear a little boy talk about hatred was too much for Caroline.

'We've never used that word in this house,' she said to me. 'The only reason he knows it is because of you. Roddy, you need to go and talk to someone.'

Jim Fitzpatrick, my ally from my time at Bohs, had told me about his friend Laurence Kettle, a Capuchin monk who worked with the poor in South Korea. He suggested I talk to him. Jim rang me one day to say that Kettle was home from Korea, so I went to see him.

Laurence looked like Padre Pio with his big grey beard. I sat down with him. There was a serenity about the man – I suppose I'd call it holiness – that I'd never experienced in another human being before. He asked me how I was feeling and I told him I was angry and I felt that way all the time. He asked me what was the source of that anger and I told him it was a man who destroyed my career as a football manager. He gave me a set of rosary beads. He said, 'Every time you feel angry, take them out and say a few prayers.'

I took the beads, even though I thought it was a bit off the wall. But over the next few weeks, whenever I felt the bile rise in me, I took them out and said a little prayer to my da. I continued to see Courtenay around Castleknock. Sometimes I'd walk into Myo's and he'd be sitting having a drink with John Delaney. I'd slip my hand into my pocket and finger the beads and try to ward off dark thoughts.

Six months went by and Laurence was home from Korea again. I dropped around to see him. He asked how I was feeling.

'The same,' I told him. 'Actually, no, a bit worse.'

'Would you like me to hear a confession of your life?' he asked.

I started talking, reluctantly at first. The next I knew I was telling him everything. The whole time he sat looking at me with this peaceful smile on his face. Nothing I told him seemed to shock him or move him in any way. It took about an hour for me to unburden myself of everything.

At the end, he said, 'You allowed someone to put hatred in your heart,' and that brought me to tears. 'But you've just cleaned yourself out. Now go and fill yourself up with goodness.'

I can't say it was an alleluia moment for me. But over a course of months, whenever I felt angry, I reminded myself of his words, played the beads through my fingers and slowly let go of my hatred for John Courtenay.

As I started to get back to my old self, I suddenly had all of this energy, but it was manic, unfocussed energy. I got it into my head that I should make the downstairs of our home open plan, so I knocked down a wall that I shouldn't have knocked down, then I had to put in steel girders to support the weight of the floor above it. I remember wrapping tinsel around them that Christmas.

Then I decided to build a brand-new house on a bit of land at the side of our house. I got up one morning, took a shovel and started digging the foundations in the lashings of rain. The neighbours thought I was a lunatic: 'Collins is digging a hole in the garden with his shirt off again.'

I got the foundations dug. After about a week, I got bored and gave up. Caroline said to me one day, 'Roddy, you need to put your time into something productive – something you love.'

'I love football,' I told her, 'but no one will give me a job.'

'Well, what else do you love?' she asked.

'I don't know,' I said. 'Boxing.'

And *that* was the alleluia moment. I rang John Prunty, a business-man I knew who owned a load of premises in Coolmine Industrial Estate.

'John,' I said, 'have you any units free up there?'

'Yeah, I've one lying vacant,' he said. 'What do you want it for?'

'I'm going to set up a gym,' I said.

I decided to call it The Bronx Sporting Club. And that was when my mid-life crisis started to get really interesting.

18

The Bronx Sporting Club was my salvation. No matter what else was going on in my life, when I turned the key in the door every morning I felt like I was stepping into another world.

It was more than just a gym: it was a social outlet for people, many of whom were going through difficulties in their lives. There was one chap who'd been widowed in his twenties and had two young daughters. He was about four stone overweight and in a terrible state. In the two years he was coming to the gym, I watched him become a different man, physically and emotionally.

I allowed a local addiction-support group to use the unit to train. One afternoon a week the place was full of people who were addicted to everything imaginable – drink, drugs, food, sex, gambling. There was one lad who was addicted to armed robbery.

'They your car keys, Rod?' he asked me one day, eying them on the counter.

'Yeah,' I told him.

'Don't leave them lying around. I look at them and in my head I'm already planning a heist.'

There was a boxing ring in the centre and the walls were lined with old fight posters that I'd collected over the years. The equipment was rough and ready. There were heavy ropes that I got from Guinness. There was sand in muslin sacks of different sizes. There were car batteries that served as kettlebells.

Word spread. Soon, a lot of GAA clubs started coming in – Bridget's, Plunkett's and Na Fianna. Jason Sherlock, the Dublin footballer, trained with us. Kieran McGeeney, the captain of Armagh, boxed in the ring and used the equipment. He was one of the fittest men I ever saw. A few of the Meath players came in one night.

I started a football clinic, offering advice to local clubs. I hosted a strongman competition. I was in my element.

The gym was full all the time. I opened at ten o'clock in the morning and pulled the door closed at nine o'clock in the evening. We had solicitors, bricklayers, accountants, bank robbers, IRA men, teachers, GAA players, all mingling together.

Then I came up with the idea of putting on boxing shows in the gym. The first one was called the Good Friday Disagreement. I chose the date because the pubs were shut. I got a gang of fellas who had beef with each other – some I knew from the gym, some from the pub and some who were just living around the area – and I matched them up. The deal was that they each had to sell twenty tickets at €20 a pop and that whatever issues they had with each other were settled in the ring wearing gloves and ended with a handshake. I sold 250 tickets for the first show, but I could have sold a thousand. There were hundreds of people locked outside, begging to be let in.

I put on another show called the Valentine's Day Massacre. By then it was a slick operation. An electrician we called Vavo, who boxed on all of the shows, put a rig with lights on it above the ring and I got Johnny Lyons from 98FM to perform as the emcee. I refereed most of the fights and made sure nobody got badly hurt.

I had no bar licence, so everyone would bring their own drink. I built a balcony in the place and roped it off as a VIP area, although it almost ended in disaster when I watched it sag under the weight of too many people. An engineer who used to go to the shows brought in a lorryload of steel acrows to prop it up.

It wasn't gangster stuff. Most of the grievances were petty. Blokes would come to me and say, 'There's a lad badmouthing me around Clonsilla. We're going to have it out,' or, 'There's a fucking eejit who was trying to chat up my missus for half an hour. I'm going to punch the head off him,' and I'd say, 'Here you go – twenty tickets. Bring the money on the night. You follow the rules of boxing and there's to be no trouble afterwards.'

It wasn't just grudges that were settled on those nights. There were some brilliant boxers on the shows. There was a lovely bloke called Wayne Doherty, the local bread man, who was utterly fearless and had this all-action style that sent the crowd wild. There was a lad named Mark Kennedy who would get in the ring with anyone, and his brother, Ray, who looked like the American boxer Eric 'Butterbean' Esch. But it added to the atmosphere if there was some needle between the two men in the ring.

There were no winners or losers. After three three-minute rounds – or five three-minute rounds if I felt the two fighters could take it – I raised the hands of both men. In the seven unlicensed shows I promoted, we only had two knockouts. At the end of each night we put on music and the ring became a dancefloor. Everyone would go across to Molloy's Liquor Store in the industrial estate and come back with cans and bottles and everyone would stay until the early hours – all the fighters mixing with each other and talking over their fights blow-by-blow.

Wayne Doherty – or Dottsy, as we knew him – was a brilliant bloke who started helping me to run the place. He was one of my bouncers at the shows. But there was never any trouble and the audience policed itself. One night a plainclothes detective came in and said to me, 'There's going to be murder here tonight.'

I said, 'Why?'

'Well,' he said, 'you see that lad down there and that lad over there? Well, that one shot that one's brother.'

'Holy fuck,' I said. 'Leave it with me.'

I went downstairs and spoke to the two boys. I said, 'Are we going to have a problem here tonight?'

They said no, they were just there to watch the boxing.

Another night, there was a Traveller on the bill – a lovely fella who used the gym regularly. He had a crew with him from England and one of them was drunk and harassing women.

'You're off the show,' I said. 'Your mate's acting the maggot.'

He was already in his gear, getting ready to box.

'I'll sort it,' he told me.

He took your man outside, knocked him out cold with a single punch, threw him unconscious into the boot of his car, drove him home, then returned within half an hour to fight at the top of the bill.

The shows became a huge social event. Men and women would dress up like they were going to a fight in Caesar's Palace. The buzz of those nights helped me rediscover my love of life. I was frozen out of football – maybe for ever – but the Bronx Sporting Club saved me.

One Christmas I decided to throw a party as a thank-you to the regulars. I booked a DJ and bought ten barrels of Guinness and Heineken on the cheap from a fella I knew in the North. When I asked him for an invoice, he laughed and said, 'There'll be no invoice, Roddy – if you know what I mean.'

I guessed it meant the barrels had found their way to me via a channel that wasn't 100 per cent kosher. I stashed them in a storeroom that I was using as an office. One day, I was leaving the gym to go to RTE to do some punditry work, all dressed up in my shirt and tie and best suit. When I stepped outside, the car park was swarming with gardaí. I ran back inside.

'Lads,' I said, 'if anyone has an arrest warrant out for them, you better get the fuck out of here now. We're about to get raided.'

Two or three of the lads scarpered through the side door. I asked a few of the others to help me hide the barrels of drink. We got them out the side door and stashed them in the laneway at the side of the gym. I went inside and waited for the gardaí to come through the door. But nothing happened. When I went back outside, they'd gone. There was only a woman there who had a little boy with Down's syndrome. He used to come in to watch the fighters train.

'Are you, er, coming in?' I asked, nervously looking over her shoulder.

'No,' she said, 'the Garda band is playing a Christmas concert in the unit next door.'

I had had a visit from the gardaí when I was putting the finishing touches to the gym. I was laying the wooden floor when two of them arrived on bikes and asked me what I was doing. I told them I was opening a boxing gym.

'A bit of advice for you,' one of them told me. 'Don't let the Travellers in – because they'll have you tormented.'

I hadn't opened the doors three days when the first van pulled up outside. There were three men, led by Simon O'Donnell. He was a plasterer, as was his father, who I'd worked with a few times. All of his brothers – Pat, Jason and Arthur – boxed and they were great kids.

'We'll be booking the ring every Tuesday night,' Simon said, pulling a wad of notes out of his pocket. 'I'll pay you now.'

'I'm not quite ready to open yet,' I told him, 'but you'll be the first in when I do.'

Simon called in every day, checking on my progress, even offering men to help me finish the job.

I've always had huge respect for the Travelling community, which is something I got from my da, who felt they were unfairly maligned by the settled community. He used to bring Christmas presents to the Traveller kids in Dunsink Lane, many of whom were living under tarpaulin covers that were hung from sewer rods. When I was in my twenties, I worked alongside Travellers on the market stalls. I boxed with Travellers. I laid tarmacadam with Travellers. I plastered with Travellers. I loved the way they lived their lives and their honour code. I even appreciated the element of roguery that some of them brought to business.

Simon came in regularly and sparred with another Traveller, Simon Reilly. They used to knock lumps out of each other and they were still the best of friends. I put them on the top of the bill on one of the shows and it was one of the best fights I've ever seen.

Inevitably, the word got around that Steve Collins's brother was running a boxing gym that welcomed Travellers with open arms. Soon, more and more of them began to show up. Members of the Stokes family. The McDonaghs. The Wards. The Quinn McDonaghs. The Joyces.

The various families came in on different days. Most of them signed in using fake names. They didn't want members of the other families to know they were training, especially if they had a fight coming up. They started asking me for advice – on diet, training, boxing styles – which was how I got drawn into the world of bareknuckle fighting. I wasn't exactly keen to get involved. I'd seen videos of Travellers engaged in fights that went on for hours and they were way too brutal for my taste.

Against that, I had no income, apart from what little I earned from the shows and punters coming in to use the equipment. At the height of the Celtic Tiger, when the banks were keen to throw money at people, I'd remortgaged the family home in order to build the gym and I had a big loan to repay. So I said yes. I knew that men calling each other out is a part of Traveller life. They needed a trainer and I needed the money.

That's how I got sucked into this mad world of feuding families and long drives to secret locations and holdalls full of banknotes. And, in one case, guns.

It was a fight between Martin Stokes and Cowboys Michael McDonagh. I trained Stokesy, who was a brilliant lad, small but with a big heart and a giant ego. He used to fight in fluorescent shorts to show off his tan. He'd won Irish titles in the ring as an amateur. But when he told me he was fighting Cowboys Michael, I told him to pull out. I'd trained Cowboys Michael for a previous fight and I knew it was a mismatch.

'I can't pull out,' he said. 'I've already called him out. You have to train me. You cannot let me down, Rodney.'

For some reason, none of them could ever get my name right.

So I trained him – most of it involved teaching him how to protect himself, because I knew Cowboys Michael was out of his league.

On the day of the fight I was sitting in a black S Class sports Mercedes on the M50 with a bunch of English boys I'd never met before and no idea where we were headed. The rumour was Cavan. I was sitting in the middle of the back seat with a bag containing the wraps and other bits and pieces. There was very little conversation in the car, just directions being discussed on the phones. The tension was unbelievable.

At that point I'd been present at a lot of bare-knuckle fights and I knew how it all worked. But there was something about the atmosphere that day that was different. Everyone seemed more on edge than normal. I looked over my shoulder and noticed that there were dozens of wagons following behind us. The fight wasn't going to remain a secret for long.

We'd only just pulled into the site when the gardaí arrived in three cars with their sirens wailing. The doors of the Merc were thrown open and the fellas scarpered, slamming the doors behind them. Before I could move, they'd activated the central locking, trapping me in the car. I tried to open the door, but the alarm went off.

I thought, Oh, fuck! How am I going to explain this? I was an RTE pundit at that time. A TV celebrity with a house in Castleknock. What a story this was going to be when the newspapers got a hold of it. I was thinking, Maybe I can say I was kidnapped.

For some reason, the Guards never came near the car. I was poxed. I found out afterwards that there were two sawn-off shotguns under the front seats and £100,000 in the boot.

The boys regrouped and the convoy headed for a site in Navan, where the fight eventually took place. That's when I discovered the reason for the tense atmosphere. Half the Dublin underworld was there. Most of them I knew from town. Some of them I knew from the papers. I'd never seen them at a bare-knuckle fight before and I had no idea why they were there.

There was also a big English lad – not a Traveller – who was walking around, mouthing off, off his head on coke. I watched him take a sawn-off shotgun out of the leg of his tracksuit bottoms and hide it behind a shed. I thought, If he takes one step towards that shed, I'm running straight through that gap in the fence.

The fight was a horrible mismatch, and to this day I kick myself for not doing more to persuade Stokesy not to fight. He got battered that day. But he wouldn't give up. He was too brave for his own good. I wanted to stop it but I wasn't even supposed to be there. The rule was that the fighters weren't permitted to have their trainers present. I had a baseball cap on me and the black-rimmed glasses that I'd started wearing for my short-sightedness. I had my head down, trying to be invisible.

A copper sidled up beside me.

'Well, Steve,' he said, mistaking me for my brother, 'you could have done a better job with the disguise.'

'You've got to stop this,' I said to him.

'It's too late for that,' he said. 'There'd be killings.'

I took Stokesy to the hospital afterwards to have his face stitched.

It wasn't always like that. Most of the bare-knuckle fights I worked on were even contests that ended with two men shaking hands at the end and everyone driving away happy with the outcome.

One day, I had a knock on the door from a very well-to-do Traveller who bred horses.

'Rod,' he said, 'I'm in a terrible situation. My son's been called out by his brother-in-law and he doesn't want to fight, but he has no choice. His mother's very worried.'

'I can't teach him how to fight,' I told him. 'But I can teach him how to run away. To throw punches while back pedalling. He'll get a couple of smacks and then the two will shake hands and it'll be over.'

So that's what happened. The kid got out of there unhurt and with a draw.

When I was approached about training a bare-knuckle boxer, the first thing I asked was the nature of the dispute between the two men. Was there beef between the two families or was it a simple call-out? Then I'd draw up a diet and training programme for the fighter. They always asked, 'What time should I get up? What time should I go out and run?'

A lot of the boys had watched the *Rocky* movies way too many times and wanted to do the things they'd seen Sylvester Stallone doing in the montage sequences. I always had a job explaining to them that that kind of training was pointless for bare-knuckle fights, which are never high-energy contests. A busy base-knuckle fighter is one who throws three accurate punches in a minute.

They would put in a savage amount of work in the gym, often to Survivor's 'Eye of the Tiger', which they would just keep playing on repeat. But coming from a macho culture, they couldn't get their heads around the danger of overtraining and the importance of rest days. There were times when I'd watch a fella spar and I could see straight away that he was tired.

'Get out of the ring,' I'd say, 'and come back tomorrow when you've had a rest.'

'I don't need a rest,' I'd be told. 'I'm not paying you good money to tell me to rest.'

'If you're paying me to do something, let me do it right.'

I always saw it as my first duty to protect them. If I thought a fighter wasn't ready the day before a fight, I'd get him a letter from a physiotherapist to say that he'd damaged ligaments in his hand or fractured his wrist.

The best bare-knuckle fighter I ever saw was Paddy 'Jaws' Ward from Galway. Jaws didn't engage in any of the flashy or macho bull-shit that other Travellers got involved in. He boxed in jeans, black leather shoes and a vest. He beat a lad called Barney McGinley in what had been the biggest fight in the west of Ireland for years. Barney knocked on my door one day and told me he wanted me to prepare him for a rematch. I watched the video of the fight online.

'Barney, this is a very difficult situation,' I told him. 'You got hit way too many times with his right hand.'

My da used to say that if you get hit by the same punch twice, it's a coincidence. Three times – get out of the business.

'I'll pay you any amount of money you want,' he said. 'I'll move over here from England and train with you for three months.'

I told him no.

Under me, the Travellers trained in ways they'd never trained before for bare-knuckle contests, with an emphasis on fitness and mental preparation. I did cardio work with them. I did thirty-minute pads sessions with them without a break. I worked on their psychology. If a fighter was the subject of a call-out, I reminded him that the pressure was on his opponent and showed him how to use that knowledge to his advantage. I persuaded them not to reply to videos that their opponents posted online and to maintain a respectful silence until the day of the fight.

The first Traveller I trained for a bare-knuckle fight was Michael Quinn McDonagh, who was due to fight Paul Joyce in England in the summer of 2008. It was a big fight. Both sides were throwing in £60,000.

I knew the Quinn McDonagh family well. They were from Dunsink Lane and my da bought carpets off them. Their father was an old-style 'tinker', in that he traded in pots and pans. All of the children in the family boxed, but Michael lived in the shadow of his brother, James Quinn McDonagh, one of the greatest bare-knuckle fighters of all time.

It was James who approached me and asked me to train his brother. Michael didn't have a fraction of James's ability, but he wanted the same recognition. At the time, he was one of the subjects of a documentary film called *Knuckles* about the fighting tradition among the Travellers. I agreed to train him on the condition that there was no filming in the gym and that I didn't appear in the documentary. I was working for RTE at the time and didn't need the publicity.

Michael was one of the hardest trainers I ever worked with. He followed my directions. He ate what I told him to eat. Carbs before exertion days. Protein on rest days. I did a lot of strength and conditioning work with him. I got him super-fit for the fight. On his last day of training, I put him in the ring with twelve different spars, three minutes each, no breaks, each of them wearing giant 24-ounce gloves. He couldn't have been in better shape.

On the day of the fight, the tension was unreal. I was collected at Stansted Airport and driven to a pub called the Post Office Arms in Hemel Hempstead, where I was to await a phone call. Michael was going to send someone to try to sneak me into the fight. I was eventually picked up and driven to the Cherry Trees site, where it was going to happen.

It was a boiling hot July day. I was watching from the back with a baseball cap on me so as not to be spotted. I was nearly suffocating in the heat.

Paul Joyce was an absolute giant of a man, six-foot four and twenty-four stone. Legend had it that he used to train for fights by eating five Big Macs a day, which I knew gave us one advantage. I noticed, too, that there was a slight hill on the site. I told Michael, who was giving away a lot of height to Paul, to take a few steps backwards onto the hill, which would mean that Paul would lose an inch or two and would also be facing into the sun. The two men fought for an hour and a half, with a police helicopter circling overhead. Michael knocked Joycey down, but he couldn't finish him off. At the end, neither man was badly hurt. They shook hands and agreed to a draw. Both sides went home with their money.

Michael had a dark side to his personality. I saw it in the gym one day when we were sparring together and a clash of heads opened up a cut just above my forehead. Michael saw the blood pouring down my face and went into an absolute frenzy.

A few years after I worked with him, I read in a newspaper that he'd murdered his wife, Jacqueline. I had no idea what was going on behind the scenes. It sickened me to my stomach to read about it.

One day in the autumn of 2006, Caroline and I came home from a weekend break in Liverpool. I opened a bottle of wine and said, 'Let's finish out the weekend in style.'

Our eldest daughter, Sinéad, said to Caroline, 'Ma, will you come to the shops with me?' and I could see that she was trying to get her on her own. I rushed to every father's first conclusion.

'Are you pregnant?' I asked.

Niamh – our eighteen-year-old daughter – said, 'No, Da – it's me.'

To say we were shocked wouldn't even come close to covering it. Niamh had got a great Leaving Certificate and had just started her studies in Maynooth.

Caroline – always the calm, pragmatic one – said, 'It's fine. Take a year out and then we'll look after the baby while you go to college.'

It took me a day or two longer to come to terms with it. But when I did, I was fine. On 3 June 2007 Niamh gave birth to a little boy. He was a gorgeous little thing – a Collins through and through.

'Roddy's a good name,' I said to her.

'Da, I'm not calling him Roddy,' she said. 'You already have your Messiah.'

We started throwing names backwards and forwards. What about Callum? What about Finbarr?

'What about Donnacha?' I said.

I was a huge fan of Donncha O'Callaghan, the Munster and Ireland rugby player. I'd never met him. I just thought he was brilliant.

'Donnacha,' she said. 'I love that name.'

One Saturday night, a while later, Caroline and I were in Renards when the Irish rugby team walked in. I'd a good few drinks on me and I cornered Donncha O'Callaghan and told him that we had a little grandson, less than a year old, who was named after him. He seemed delighted.

'Shane's a great name,' he said.

It was only then that I realized I was talking to Shane Horgan.

They were happy times. I still couldn't get an interview for a football job, but the gym had given me a new lease of life and I was also having fun with my status as a minor celebrity.

By that stage, I'd appeared on a few reality TV shows. One was *The Restaurant*, an RTE show in which I had to produce a three-course dinner to impress food critics Tom Doorley and Paolo Tullio. My fellow celebrity chef Bill Hughes made bruschetta. I thought a bruschetta was a miniature dog. I made the only thing I'm capable of cooking – an Irish stew. When Tom tasted it, he copped the main ingredient immediately.

'It tastes of oxtail soup,' he said, wrinkling up his face in disgust, 'from a packet!'

When they were asked to guess the identity of the mystery chef, they said I must be a caber tosser. I went home with one star out of five but a cheque for €1,500 in my pocket.

Then Louis Copeland persuaded me to duet with him on *Charity You're a Star*, something for which I've never forgiven him. The show was filmed in front of an audience of nearly 2,000 people at The Helix. I said I'd do it as long as we could sing something by Frank Sinatra, but Louis insisted that we perform 'Swinging on a Star', a Bing Crosby song from the movie *Going My Way*.

'We'll do Sinatra in week two,' he promised me.

But there was no week two. We came out dressed in matching striped shirts, looking like a couple of deckchairs, and we were awful. Brendan O'Connor, one of the judges, said we were like two drunks at a wedding. We ended up in a sing-off with John Aldridge, who had one of the worst voices I'd ever heard – and we still got slung off.

I continued to train the Travellers. One day I had a call from James Quinn McDonagh.

'Robbie,' he said – he always called me that no matter how many times I corrected him – 'we need you and we need you badly.'

I arranged to meet him and a few family members at the Papal

Cross in the Phoenix Park at eleven o'clock on a Sunday morning. He and I broke away from the others to talk.

'I'll tell you what it is,' he said. 'The McDonaghs and the Quinn McDonaghs are going to fight the Nevins. One full day of it and we'll put this thing to bed once and for all.'

I trained four McDonaghs and four Quinn McDonaghs in the gym for six weeks leading up to the fight, with the *Rocky* music always blaring. They were great blokes. There was one of them whose name I never knew, but they all called him 'Big Trousers', because his shorts were pulled up to about six inches below his armpits. I made the mistake of calling him 'Big Trousers' one day, not knowing that it was a name they called him behind his back.

'Where did you hear that one?' he asked. He wasn't very happy.

The fellas trained hard, but the fight never happened for one reason or another. They paid up and they left.

Around that time Drogheda United were in financial trouble and I offered to bring a team of former League of Ireland legends to United Park to play against a Drogheda selection to raise some money. The Drogheda supporters had adopted the chant 'Roddy Collins is a wanker', and as part of the half-time entertainment I offered to box any supporter who didn't like me for sixty seconds on the pitch. Three got gloved up. I was knocking these three muttonheads around the centre circle when I started to feel a bit odd. I knew I was fit, but I felt exhausted and I had this strange sensation in my chest and the back of my throat, like I'd breathed in sherbet. But then it went away.

One night shortly afterwards, Caroline and I went out for a few drinks in town. The next day I popped out to buy a newspaper and I suddenly felt very badly hungover. I did something that I'd never done in my life. I went for a cure. I rang Caroline from Myo's. I was sitting at the bar with a pint in front of me.

'Caroline,' I said, 'I don't know what's the matter with me. I just felt I needed it.'

'Have a pint or two,' she said, 'and come home.'

Then, one frosty morning in January 2009, I was in Porterstown Park in Castleknock, doing a workout with four Traveller brothers from Athenry on the old 400-metre track on which Eamonn Coghlan used to train. One of the fellas was a lazy fucker and I'd come to the end of my rope with him. 'I'm going to race you,' I told him, 'and if I beat you, I'm not training you any more and you're not getting your money back.'

So I raced him and I very nearly won. But when I pulled up, I had the same strange sensation I'd experienced at United Park.

Because of my da's history of heart trouble, Caroline had been at me for ages to get myself checked out. I was now forty-eight, almost the same age at which my da died – after running in a park. When I arrived home, Caroline decided that it was enough of a sign. She said, 'Come on, we're getting you checked out right now.'

I put my suit on and we went to Blanchardstown Hospital. The doctor who examined me asked if I'd had any chest pains or shortness of breath. I told her no.

'But your father died young,' she said, 'didn't he?'

'How did you know that?' I asked.

'My mother is from the Cabra Road.'

She told me they had a bed for me and they wanted me to stay until they'd performed a battery of tests. I was given an electrocardiogram, which showed up nothing unusual. Then I was told to run on a treadmill so they could monitor my heart when it was under stress. After about sixty seconds, the doctor told me to stop and drink some water. Then she said she was calling an ambulance to take me to the Mater.

I was in shock.

'I don't need an ambulance,' I said. 'I'll drive down.'

'Don't move,' she said. 'It's on the way.'

The ambulance took me to the Mater Hospital, where I had an angiogram. Then they told me they were going to insert a number of stents into my heart to open out my blocked coronary arteries.

I remember lying there, staring up at the bright light and hearing a voice say, 'Jesus, we've a bit of work to do here.'

I was conscious for the whole operation and I'll never forget the pain. When they were putting the last stent in, my heart went into trauma. I pulled the oxygen mask off me and said to the surgeon, 'Please stop!'

He said, 'Bear with me, I'm nearly finished.'

After the operation, a consultant came to see me. He said, 'You were just days away from the big one.'

'Big one?' I asked.

'A heart attack – and you wouldn't have recovered from it.'

He asked me if I'd been feeling tired recently. I remembered a few weeks earlier falling asleep in the car in the middle of the day while waiting at a railway crossing.

'I'm not surprised,' he said. 'Your blood was trickling around your body.'

I was told that I had to change everything. I was grossly over-weight. I had to cut out the Big Macs, the chipper food and the Indian takeaways. I was also told to take it easy – at least for the next few weeks. Within three days of going home I was back in the Bronx Sporting Club – until Caroline rang Orla, my doctor, and told on me. Orla told me that if I fell back into my old habits, I wouldn't see my fiftieth birthday the next year. That brought me quickly to my senses.

It turned out the Drogheda United fans didn't think I was a wanker after all. The club was looking for a new manager at the start of the 2009 season and the supporters made it clear that they wanted me. I was only out of hospital about a month when I got a call inviting me to an interview in the Halfway House on the Navan Road.

I was buzzing leaving the house that night. I'd been given a second chance at life and now I was about to get back into football. I arrived fifteen minutes early and I was sitting there suited up when Dermot McKenna, a Drogheda committee man, walked through the door twenty minutes late.

'Howiya, Rod?' he said.

'Howiya,' I said, looking over his shoulder. 'Is there anyone else with you?'

'No, it's just me,' he said. 'The thing is, we're looking for a man-ager but, you'd probably be too expensive.'

'Well, you won't know that until you've talked to me,' I said.

A very strange conversation followed. It didn't feel like a job inter-view at all.

'If we decided not to go with you,' he said, 'would you advise us on who we should go for instead?'

I felt like such a dope for getting dressed up. After a while, he said he had to rush off because he had to meet someone in town.

I was in the Phoenix Park the next day, walking with Caroline, when the secretary of Drogheda rang to say they'd decided to go with Alan Mathews instead.

Suddenly, it was as if all of the energy had been sucked out of my body. I sat down on the grass. Despite all the frustration I'd experienced in football, I'd never felt as low as I did at that point. I was like a deflated balloon.

'Caroline,' I said, 'will you go and get the car, because I can't get up.'

She got the car and managed to get me to stand up and get into it.

'Don't give up,' she said. 'Someone out there will give you a job.'

And she was right. A few weeks later, I got a phone call that would change the direction of my life again. I was going back to football management. Not in Ireland, or in England – but in Malta.

19

The phone call came out of nowhere. I thought it was a wind-up.

'Roddy, this is Alan Moore,' the voice said.

The only Alan Moore I knew had played in midfield for Middlesbrough and had just retired out of Sligo Rovers.

'I'm involved with a club called Floriana FC in Malta,' he said. 'They're looking for a new head coach and they'd love to talk to you.'

'Would you ever fuck off!' I said, thinking it was the fellas in Walsh's, then I put the phone down on him.

He rang me back and assured me that it wasn't a joke. He told me that he was the commercial manager who tried to put me in the Eintracht Frankfurt job when I was the Bohemians manager. He said he was now working for the most successful club in Maltese football and they were very interested in me.

'Tell them to e-mail me,' I said.

Within an hour I got a message from a man named Tony Zahra, the president of Floriana FC. We then spoke on the phone and he invited me and Caroline over to Malta to meet him. On Friday of that week, we flew to Valletta. We were put up for the weekend in The George, a spectacular boutique hotel in St Julian's, just north of the capital, with a swimming pool on the roof.

I went to meet Tony. He owned several hotels in Malta as well as a car-rental business and he was the president of the Malta Hotels and Restaurants Association. We talked football. He had a couple of fellas with him, including one of the directors, Joe Cauchi, and the club secretary, Dione Borg, who asked me about some of the scurrilous things written about me by Rovers fans in my Wikipedia entry.

I thought, Wiki-fucking-pedia? Are you having a laugh? He might as well have been asking me about graffiti in the men's jacks.

'It's all false,' I said.

We got over that and we agreed a deal. As the head coach of Floriana FC, I'd be paid €50,000 per year. The job came with a brand-new company car, and half of the rent on our house would be paid by the club. They would also subsidize Roddy, Padraig and Lauren's education at an international school in Valletta.

I went for a walk with Caroline on the beach of St George's Bay. It was a scorching hot day. The sun was beating down. Caroline said, 'Roddy, is this really happening to us?'

We came home. I said a sad farewell to Dottsy and big Mark Kennedy and Vavo and Stokesy and Simon O'Donnell and all the fellas who trained in the Bronx Sporting Club during the almost four years I was frozen out of football. Then I locked the unit up for the very last time. I was back.

A press conference to announce my new role was held at the Maltese Embassy on Leeson Street in Dublin. 'They tried to keep me out of work in Ireland and England,' I told the reporters, 'but they never thought of Malta.'

I flew out the next day, with Caroline planning to follow a week later with Roddy, Padraig and Lauren. I was presented to the Floriana supporters that evening. It was the kind of reception that managers got in Spain and Italy. More than 3,000 of them turned up to cheer as I stepped out onto the balcony of a building to wave to them. I thought, This definitely beats being called a wanker.

All of the Floriana players had jobs or were in college. Training, I was told, was at seven o'clock in the morning and then again at five o'clock in the evening. What I saw the first time I watched them train didn't impress me at all. They had a lot of skill, but physically they just weren't there at all. It was low-energy, tippy-tappy football. Everyone had time to take the ball down and decide what they were going to do with it.

I shouted, 'Stop! Stop! Stop!' and I called all the players together. 'If you want to play for me, you won't be playing like that. Why are you giving him time on the ball? Close the space – force him to make a quick decision. I want to see you do everything faster.'

They quickened the pace. After half an hour, Orosco Anonam,

our Nigerian-born midfielder, asked me if he could speak to me in private.

'Coach,' he said, 'if they play like this, men will die.'

I'd forgotten that most of the matches in Malta were played in temperatures of up to forty degrees Celsius. I had to apologize to the players.

Malta was one of the best places I'd ever lived. Caroline loves Caravaggio and the island was full of his art. It was also full of churches, and we tried to see as many of them as we could. We found one in St George's Bay where we decided that we would one day renew our wedding vows.

We were only there a couple of weeks when I got a phone call with devastating news from home. Wayne Doherty – the local bread delivery man who trained in my gym, boxed on my shows and filled in for me behind the counter when I was busy – had been shot dead outside his home in Dublin. He'd intervened in a row between two of his neighbours. Typical of Dottsy to try to make peace between them. He took a blast from a shotgun and he was killed instantly. Dottsy was only thirty-one and left behind his wife and two kids. His loss was so tragic and so pointless and it still saddens me all these years later.

We didn't win a single match in pre-season, but I wasn't concerned. I didn't know any of the players and I was still deciding who my best eleven would be. There were ten teams in the Maltese Premier League. All of them played in the Ta' Qali National Stadium in Valletta, which hosted five matches every weekend – one on a Friday night, two on a Saturday and two on a Sunday.

Just before the season started, Tony Zahra called me into his office. He said that someone claiming to be from the FAI had contacted the Maltese FA to say that I stole money from two football clubs in Ireland.

I was floored. I thought, Why won't the bastards leave me alone?

'Who was it?' I asked. 'And what clubs?'

'I don't know,' he said. 'This is what they reported.'

I told him it was lies.

That night I went back to the Radisson Blu in St Julian's, which was our home for the first few weeks we were there. I bumped into

Jim Boyce, my old chairman at Cliftonville, who was now a vice-president of FIFA. He was in Malta for a conference.

'Roddy, what about you?' he asked.

'I feel sick, Jim,' I said, then I told him what had happened.

'I'll ring the Maltese FA tomorrow morning,' he said, 'and I'll tell them a story – that when you discovered you hadn't the legs to play for Cliftonville any more, you gave your signing-on fee back, which you didn't have to do.'

Jim made the call the next morning and I never heard a word about it again.

The big derby in Malta is Floriana v. Valletta. I was unfortunate that the match came so soon into the season. We got absolutely destroyed, 6–0. We had some bad luck that day. We should have scored first. Then our centre-half – our best player – did his cruciate. But the simple truth was that they were better than us. They had Jordi Cruyff, the former Man United player. I still didn't know my best eleven. The same supporters who had turned out to welcome me when I arrived now booed and whistled me. Then they all walked out with fifteen minutes still to play.

I always feel crap after a defeat. Whether it's 1–0 or 10–0, it's all the same. I went back to the dressing room and told the players that we were beaten by a better team, but we'd improve. I said I'd see them all for training at seven o'clock the next morning.

Then I was summoned to a meeting, which turned into an interrogation that was far worse than anything I'd experienced at Bohemians or Carlisle. In the room were Tony, Joe and Dione. The first thing I was told was that Floriana had never lost to Valletta by such a margin before. I told them I was as disappointed as they were, but it was still early in the season.

'But why the fuck six?' Tony asked.

'Why *not* six?' I replied. 'They were better than us.'

'Why did you not put everyone behind the ball at 2–0?'

'Because I'd rather lose a match trying to win than lose trying to keep the score down.'

'This will be in the history books,' Dione said.

'If I'd known it mattered that much,' I told him, 'I'd have put six bricklayers on at half-time.'

The upside was that they accepted we needed new players. The way transfers worked at Floriana was that I, as head coach, identified the type of player we needed – a striker with pace, a hard-tackling midfielder – and Peter Agius, whose title was manager, went out and bought someone. But if the player turned out to be no good, it was down to me.

Peter, a brilliant bloke, decided to bring back Brian Said, a big centre-half, and a favourite of the fans, who helped shore things up at the back for us. Our form started to improve. We lost only one of our next seven matches.

For a few months, Caroline and I felt like we were living in paradise. We had the perfect life. I finished work at 10 a.m. every day, then I came back to the rented house we were living in and we went rambling for hours, enjoying the sun and the scenery, before I returned to work in the evening. We were eating healthily and the kids absolutely loved it. Roddy was sixteen and was developing as a footballer. I'd given him his debut for Floriana in a couple of pre-season friendlies and he did great. It all felt too good to be true. And then it turned out that it was.

I never really knew who was in charge at Floriana. Tony was the overall boss. But all the talk was about mystery Russian investors who were going to pour millions into the club. Alan Moore had the title of International Development Officer. He'd signed a partnership agreement with FC Volga Ulyanovsk, who were going to send us players. There was supposedly money coming too. It became a running joke that whenever I asked for something, I was told: 'The Russians are coming!'

The €50,000 to cover my salary was in an escrow account. At the start of October I was summoned to Tony's office again. He was a straight talker – a bit of a rogue, but my kind of rogue.

'Rod,' he said, 'you know I don't like surprises. Which is why I feel I have to tell you that the €50,000 is running out.'

'What?' I said. 'How? I've only been here three months.'

It turned out that the money in the account was to cover not only my salary but other expenses as well.

'How long can you keep paying me for?' I asked.

'A couple of months,' he said.

It suddenly dawned on me that this was just the League of Ireland except with better weather. It was Shamrock-Rovers-on-Sea. I couldn't listen to any more promises that the Russians were coming. It was all bullshit. I couldn't put my family through another ordeal of settling in a country and then having to go home. It broke my heart to tell Caroline that this dream life of ours was exactly that. Castles in the sand.

'You'd better pack your bags,' I said.

Once again we rang the children's old schools in Dublin and they said they would find places for them. Caroline and the kids went back home, but she persuaded me to stay on for a while longer. She thought it would be good for my CV if I saw out the season. The team had turned a corner and the fans suddenly loved me again.

I got slung out of the house because the rent hadn't been paid by the club. The landlord wouldn't let me in to get my clothes until he got what he was owed. Then the car was taken off me.

I mentioned in my column in the *Irish Daily Star* that I was home-less, walking everywhere, and I'd been wearing the same lime-green tracksuit for two weeks. Then I got a phone call from Ray Byrne, an absolute gentleman who part-owned a hotel in Valletta called the Venetia. He very kindly offered me a free suite there, with all my meals paid for.

And then, out of the blue one day, Tony Zahra stepped down. I had no idea what was going on behind the scenes, but everyone at the club said not to worry. The Russians were coming.

Alan turned up one day while I was giving a team talk. There was a Russian fella with him and he had a backpack. I grabbed it and I said, 'This better be full of money! The Russians are finally here, lads!'

Needless to say, the backpack wasn't full of money.

I was so lonely without Caroline and the children. I was nipping home for two or three days every couple of weeks to see them and combining it with a bit of work for RTE. The travelling was exhausting.

One night in November I was in the studio doing an end-of-season wrap-up show when – out of absolutely nowhere – I said that the manager of a team that lost that week would probably 'bate the head of the missus when he goes home tonight'.

It was the stupidest thing I've ever said in a lifetime of saying stupid things. The words were out of my mouth before I realized I'd said them. I was jaded, tired and engaging in pub banter. But from the dead silence in the studio, I knew that I was in trouble. They went straight to an ad break and I was told to get out of my seat. When the programme returned, I was gone from the screen. I sat in a dark corner of the studio, listening to Tony O'Donoghue apologize for my remarks and I knew my career as a TV pundit was over. I was sick with myself.

I decided that I couldn't continue this way. The worst of it was that things were going well on the pitch. We went on a bit of a run. We beat Birkirkara and Hibernians and no one talked about the defeat to Valletta now.

But without Caroline and the children, I didn't want to be there any more. In December, I told Peter Agius that, when the season reached the halfway point, I was going home.

'Don't worry,' he said, 'when the Russians get here, we'll get you a new apartment.'

'Peter,' I said, 'I can't take my kids out of school again and ask Caroline to move back here on the strength of more promises. I'm sick of hearing that the Russians are coming.'

My last match as head coach of Floriana was a 2–1 victory over Msida St Joseph that moved us up to fifth place in the table. I made sure to get my wages before the match. I met Joe on the street and I said, 'Give us me money,' and he paid me in cash.

I was flying home the next morning and I wasn't coming back.

Just as the end was coming in Malta, I had a call from Tom Coughlan, the businessman, property developer and owner of Cork City, yet another football club that was in dire financial trouble.

Clearly, I had a type.

He asked me how things were going in Malta and I said not too well as it happened. He asked if I'd be interested in managing Cork City. It was in the middle of December 2009 and I was flying home that weekend. We arranged to meet in the Shelbourne Hotel. We couldn't have chosen a less discreet venue. The Irish soccer writers were having their Christmas do in the hotel and so the secret was out.

Managing Cork had long been an ambition of mine. I always loved going there both as a player and as a manager, because you always knew you were going to get a match and probably get lumps kicked out of you as well.

Tom told me that when he first took over the club in 2008, he mentioned to John Delaney he had a shortlist of three managers – Roddy Collins, Alan Mathews and Paul Doolin.

'Collins?' Delaney said. 'Don't touch that fucker with a bargepole.'

Tom followed Delaney's advice. But now he had no qualms about hiring me because he had the same antagonistic relationship with the FAI as I did. They had just charged him with bringing the game into disrepute over his running of the club and he would soon be banned from all football-related activities for a year.

Two days before Christmas I signed a twelve-month contract to become the manager of Cork City for the 2010 season. Almost immediately, Tom received a letter from the FAI to say that I couldn't take the job because of a new rule in the League of Ireland: all managers had to complete a coaching course and get a UEFA Pro Licence. I rang Packie Bonner, the technical director of the FAI, and asked him for help. Packie said he could not help me.

I'd been involved in League of Ireland football for over thirty years. I'd *won* the League of Ireland. There was nothing any jumped-up PE teacher with a laptop could teach me about managing a football team. But I had no choice other than to register for a course to get my Pro Licence.

There was another problem. Floriana had complained to FIFA about Cork City poaching their coach and were demanding €100,000 in compensation.

Cork City didn't have €100,000. They didn't have a bean. And the idea that I'd been 'poached' was laughable. I was moving to a club in a far worse financial state than Floriana.

It was the same old story except worse. Ireland, like much of the world, was in the throes of an economic collapse. Banks were failing. There were no money trees left to shake. Football suffered like everything else.

Tom was a good man. He was doing everything he could to try to keep the club afloat while dealing with his own financial troubles. I backed him publicly and that was what essentially sealed my fate.

Tommy Dunne, who I'd played with when he was a kid at Dundalk in the early 1990s, had finished his playing career in Finland and come back to Ireland to be the assistant to Paul Doolin, the previous Cork manager. Tommy was planning to go back to Finland, but I persuaded him to stay on as my assistant manager.

When I took training for the first time, I knew straight away that I didn't have the dressing room on my side. Most of the players wanted Tom Coughlan out. I couldn't blame them. They were full-time professionals and a lot of them were waiting on wages. Their morale was on the floor. As we went through pre-season, I tried my best to motivate them, but I was wasting my time. One or two of them acted the bollocks. We played a friendly against a junior club and someone in the dressing room recorded my team talk on their phone and posted it online.

Tom put me up in the show house of an otherwise vacant housing development. I shared it with Tommy Dunne and young Roddy, who trained with the first team. Anthony 'Bisto' Flood, who I'd signed from Shelbourne, was also there along with one or two other players. There was no money and we lived on a shoestring. We bought food from the local supermarket that was stickered yellow because it was about to go off and Tommy made a dinner for us every night.

We tried to focus on the new season, although we didn't know if we were going to be a part of it. Tom Coughlan went to the High Court to try to overturn the FAI's ban on him, but the judge threw it out and he resigned as the chairman. In the background there was a battle going on for the ownership of the club similar to the one at

Rovers. A supporters' trust, led by Jonathan O'Brien of Sinn Féin, wanted to take control of the club.

The whole thing came to a head on 23 February 2010. Tom was in the High Court in Dublin seeking a stay on an order to wind up the club. We would know the outcome by midday. The fellas trained that morning in Carrigaline with this giant sword hanging over them. Looking at them, I could see that they'd had enough. They were jogging around the place with their heads down and their shoulders slumped. Mark McNulty, the goalkeeper, was about to be the father of twins. His face was sheet-white with worry.

I called off training. I said to the players, 'Let's go for a walk instead.'

I saw a steeple in the distance and I said, 'Let's head for that church and we'll say a prayer.'

Unfortunately, I misjudged the distance. It took us about two hours to get to the church and the fellas moaned the entire way. Footballers will run for you all day long, but they don't like walking.

I was telling them, 'Whatever happens, we have our health. I've been through this with Carlisle, Rovers, Floriana. Someone will come up with money. There's no way there's going to be no football team in Cork City.'

We eventually reached the church and we all went in. I lit a candle and said a prayer: 'Please, God, let everything be OK.'

The players were looking at me like they thought I was a spacer. When I left the church, no one followed me. Greg O'Halloran, one of the Cork defenders, came out and said, 'The lads are bollocksed, Rod. They want to know can we get a minibus back?'

'A fucking minibus?' I said. 'We haven't the price of a loaf of bread.'

On the walk back to the training ground, Greg pointed out his old school to me. I said, 'Go in and tell them that the Cork City team is outside.'

The next thing, the kids started flooding out of the school, all cheering and chanting, 'Cork! Cork! Cork!'

And it was a brilliant moment because I could see in the faces of the players just how much they loved playing for the club. And then we got back to the training ground to find out that Tom's request for a stay had been denied. It was over. I got very upset that day.

But I was right when I told the players that there would still be a Cork City. The supporters trust, who called themselves FORAS, put together a rescue package for the club. I was in the car with Caroline on the way to Cork for a meeting with them when I got a call from Jonathan O'Brien.

'Where are you?' he asked.

'I'm just pulling into Douglas,' I told him.

'Don't bother,' he said. 'We don't want you. We're going with Tommy Dunne instead.'

I thought, Tommy Dunne? My loyal lieutenant, who I'd shared a house with for the past seven weeks? I was absolutely raging with him. I rang him, still sitting there on the hard shoulder.

'The fuck is going on, Tommy?' I said.

'What do you mean?' he asked.

'You were going back to Finland when I met you.'

'Well, they asked me if I was interested in the job.'

'But you're not qualified to do it. Why don't you work as my assistant for a year or two?'

'Look, Rod, I want to have a go at it. I've a family. You understand.'

I understood only too well.

I was gone from Cork without managing them for a single competitive match. When the press asked me for my reaction, I said they'd employed a boy to do a man's job. It was a low blow and I shouldn't have said it. But I meant it at the time.

The first time I ever became aware of John Delaney was in the summer of 2002. I'd just been sacked by Carlisle United for the first time. Roy Keane was sent home from Ireland's World Cup training camp and I was one of hundreds of fans who took part in a protest outside the offices of the FAI in Merrion Square.

I remember watching the news around that time and this fella with wavy hair was talking about doing everything in his power to try to get Roy back in the squad. Apparently, he was the treasurer of the FAI. He talked about being a football person, which was funny because in all of my years in the game I'd never laid eyes on him before. I knew his father, though. Joe Delaney had also been the treasurer of the FAI, and resigned in the wake of the so-called Merriongate World Cup ticket scandal.

John Delaney was on TV quite a bit that year. I'd spent enough time around football to know a spoofer when I saw one. And that's what I saw when I looked at Delaney – a complete and utter charlatan, leveraging off Roy Keane to try to create a name for himself.

I went back to Carlisle then and I mostly missed Delaney's ascent to the top of the FAI. I knew that a lot of good football men like Brendan Menton and Fran Rooney got shafted along the way. Delaney was finally named Chief Executive in 2005. I was at Shamrock Rovers and it was around the same time that John Courtenay, the FAI's main financial backer, was offering to pay the salary of the next manager if the club sacked me. I often saw the pair of them drinking in Myo's in Castleknock, thick as thieves.

I was very critical of the FAI in my weekly column in the *Irish Daily Star*. I described the League of Ireland as a shambles, which is what it was. Every season three or four clubs looked like going to the wall. Footballers were going without wages. Supporters were having whip-rounds to get the players their dinner from the chipper. And when I travelled around the country, I could see that the facilities were the same as they were when I was going to League of Ireland matches as a kid.

At first, Delaney tried to get me onside. I watched him do this to a lot of his critics over the years. He gave people bits of work just to soften them up. Roy Keane couldn't stand the man, but he went to work for him eventually, when he took the job as Martin O'Neill's assistant manager to the Irish national team, which disappointed me hugely, because I thought Roy was too smart to get sucked in.

Twice I had calls from the FAI asking if I'd like to have dinner with Delaney. I said the same thing both times: 'Only if it's to celebrate his retirement.'

We had a couple of unpleasant exchanges in public then. I was at an FAI Cup final, in a marquee with Turlough O'Connor having a glass of wine and talking about old times, when Delaney arrived over. He was wearing some kind of coat with a cape on it.

'Are you enjoying the FAI hospitality?' he asked, then he walked off like a child.

At another do in Croke Park, I was sitting at a table with Paul Lennon and a few of the other football writers from the *Irish Daily Star*. Delaney came over, acting Mr Big with everyone there.

'And Mr Collins,' he said to me, responding to something I'd written about him in the paper, 'can I just say to you that I do love Irish football.'

Of course, we all found out years later just how much he loved it.

There was another night I remember when Caroline and I were at an RTE Sports bash in the Mansion House. Delaney was there with Pat Hickey, his great mate from the Olympic Council of Ireland. Pat was waving me over but I just ignored him. Then he came across and said, 'John wants you to meet some people.'

Delaney was locked. His hair was all over the place and his shirt was sticking out of his trousers.

I said, 'Let him bring them over to me, then.'

A minute or two later, Delaney arrived over with a couple of cronies. He put his hand on my shoulder, then sneered, 'This man is going to be the manager of Ireland one day.'

I said, 'Get your hand off me, you fucking eejit. You're making a show of yourself.'

As the years passed, he appeared to be getting richer while the League of Ireland was getting poorer. He was living in a mansion, driving around Castleknock in big cars, and always seemed to be buying rounds of drinks for football supporters. Meanwhile, the people who really loved football were putting their holiday savings or money set aside for a new kitchen into League of Ireland clubs to try to keep them alive. I saw it at Dublin City. I saw it at Shamrock Rovers. I saw it at Cork.

It's like Irish football operated in two different dimensions. In one, it was players eating yellow-stickered meat and getting thrown out of public parks by the warden. In the other, it was champagne and opulence.

I knew what was going on years before the house of cards fell down. I wasn't the only one, but Delaney had managed to bully almost everyone into silence.

After a year's suspension, RTE had taken me back as a pundit.

Ryle Nugent, the head of sport, called me in and said, 'Just remember to mind your manners.'

It was six months after the job with Cork ended and I needed the work. But there was a new mantra that you had to listen to before you went on air now: 'Don't say anything about John Delaney. And don't say anything about the FAI.'

Delaney had used threats of legal action to shut everyone up. But I wasn't going to be silenced by him, a man who never had a sleepless night worrying about how he was going to find the money to pay players.

I'd given my life to football. I broke my leg four times playing it. Caroline and my children suffered for it. I uprooted them and brought them to Mansfield, to Newport, to Carlisle, to Malta, then I brought them all home again every time it fell apart. I played for peanuts and I managed for peanuts – and those were the weeks when I got paid at all. I gave up my plastering business for football. I was now unemployed and broke and potentially losing my house because of football. But I did what I did because I loved the game. And I wasn't going to let this impostor shut me up.

After Cork, the phone went silent again. I went to Belfast to do the Pro Licence course so that I was suitably qualified to be a football manager. I spent the rest of 2010 doing punditry on RTE and Newstalk, writing my column for the *Irish Daily Star* and training Travellers for cash. I was also tipping away at the house that I'd started building five years earlier when I was slung out of Rovers. As one of the neighbours said to me, 'The Taj Mahal went up quicker than that place.'

My daughter Sinéad was married to Alan Byrne, who was playing for Monaghan United in the First Division. In 2010, they got to a promotion play-off against Bray Wanderers, but lost in a penalty shoot-out. Alan put his kick over the bar. We still joke that they're still searching Bray Head for the ball.

Mick Cooke, the manager, decided he'd taken the team as far as he could and stepped down. Jim McGlone, the chairman, asked Alan if his father-in-law would be interested in taking over. I met him in Myo's. We had a cup of coffee. He said I had the job and left.

The team trained in the Phoenix Park and used the dressing rooms that belonged to the Garda GAA Club. The place was manky. Caroline and I spent the weekend sweeping and scrubbing every inch of the room until we could see our reflections in the tiles. Then I asked the groundsman to cut the grass. The players arrived for training for the first time with me as their manager. I could see they got a lift straight away.

Monaghan United was a brilliant club and Jim was the best club chairman I ever worked under. We were all on small money, but everyone got paid on time and Jim never questioned me about results. Before every match, he asked me who was in the team. When I told him, he'd laugh and say, 'None of us can guess from week to week what you're going to do,' and then he'd go off shaking his head.

We were getting home crowds of fifty or sixty people – and, as I used to say to the players, 'four cows on a hill, who turn away when they see you running out onto the pitch'.

But Jim and the committee worked hard to raise money through social events and renting out the all-weather pitch, which was the club's only real asset. When you went to see Jim in his office, he always had the heating and the lights off, because he was saving every penny he could for the players.

Mick left me with a great little team. Then I nearly pulled off the greatest coup of my career by stealing future Dublin football legend Paddy Andrews right from under the noses of the Dublin County Board. Although the truth is that I did steal him. Paddy was great friends with my daughter Niamh. One Sunday morning, about halfway through the season, I was driving through the Phoenix Park and there was Paddy, coming off a night out, looking down in the dumps. I pulled in and offered him a lift. It turned out he'd been dropped off the Dublin panel by Pat Gilroy. I said to him, 'Why don't you go back to soccer?' because Niamh told me he was a great player. 'You see that Shane Long? There's no reason why you can't do what he's doing.'

'Do you think?' he said.

'Trust me,' I told him.

I got him back to the house, gave him a cup of tea and persuaded him to sign for Monaghan United. Then I gave the story to the papers. The next thing, Paddy was at the door, begging me to rip up his registration. 'I'm going to get fucked out of Bridget's,' he said.

I ripped it up. Paddy went on to win seven All Irelands with Dublin. Imagine the what-if story he'd have to tell today if he'd listened to me.

We were going great that summer. By August, we'd put ourselves in a good position to at least get into the promotion play-off.

Around that time I was invited to appear on Des Cahill's Saturday afternoon sports show on RTE Radio. It was the day of the FAI's AGM, from which the press had been excluded. I said that if John Delaney was a bit more transparent in his dealings, he might get more respect in the game. I also criticized the way the League of Ireland was being run and the standard of facilities at grounds all over the country, which I said were 'shabby' – which they were and still are eleven years later.

The next thing, a letter arrived from the FAI disciplinary committee. I was charged with making 'disparaging comments' about the FAI. I was given the option of a €1,000 fine or a six-match touchline ban.

I thought, No way, I'm not accepting this. Monaghan United were flying and people were starting to remember that I was a very good football manager. I wasn't paying any fine. But to manage my team, I needed to be there in the dressing room.

I received the letter at 5.30 p.m. We had a game that night against Waterford United at home. I was forced to watch it from the terrace. We won 3–1. There's a great photograph of me celebrating in front of a giant flag with Bart Simpson on it. I was screaming, 'Fuck you, Delaney, and your fucking ban!'

Afterwards, I decided to appeal the decision. I knew I had no chance of winning, but I wanted to see the whites of Delaney's eyes to show him that I wasn't going to be intimidated by him.

I put together a team for my hearing. Fran Rooney, Delaney's predecessor as chief executive, had as little time for him as I did. Fran was a Cabra man and he drank in Myo's. He was qualified as a barrister and he specialized in contract law. I asked him to help and he agreed.

The appeal hearing was set for the FAI's headquarters in Abbotstown. Fran helped me put together a crack legal team that included three barristers: Paul Callan, Vincent Martin and Séamas Ó Tuathail. It was a pretty heavyweight team to fight a €1,000 fine, but it felt great to look Delaney in the eye and let him know that he wasn't going to bully me into silence.

Vincent Martin was unbelievable. It was like watching Gregory Peck in *To Kill a Mockingbird*. Ireland were playing a Euro 2012 qualifier against Slovakia at the Aviva Stadium that night and a lot of the FAI boys were looking nervously at their watches as the hearing started to edge into the early evening. There was a long drawn-out discussion about the correct interpretation of the word 'disparaging'. Dictionaries were sent for.

I'd have happily paid the €1,000 just to watch how Delaney reacted when someone stood up to him. He thrived on fear. A fella who worked for the FAI used to ring me regularly, whenever I criticized Delaney in my newspaper column, and say, 'Fair play to you, Roddy. He's a bully and he needs people like you to stand up to him.'

I saw the same fella in Abbotstown on the day of the hearing. I said hello to him and he nearly had a stroke.

'Jesus Christ,' he said, 'don't let people see you talking to me.'

I lost the appeal. But it didn't matter. I didn't pay the fine and I never served the suspension. And I'd made my point to Delaney.

We should have been promoted as champions that year. It would have been some achievement, given that we were competing against Cork City and Shelbourne, who had a few bob. If we'd beaten Cork in October, we would have finished top, but it was one of those matches determined by small margins. Seanie Brennan missed a tap-in by inches. His brother Ryan missed a chance by inches. Then they both got sent off in the second half. We lost 3–1. Cork won the league and Shelbourne finished second. We were two points off the top, and had to play Galway United home and away for a place in the Premier Division.

We won the first leg in Gortakeegan 2–0. Then, three days later, we went to Terryland Park for the return. There was a big crowd in Galway. We were all thinking the same thing. An early goal for them and it was going to be a long night. Our players had lost a shoot-out the year before. And for the first time I saw the fear in their faces. It was the same fear I saw in the faces of Bohemians players when we went to play Cobh Ramblers in 1999. The nerves were sucking the life out of them.

I decided not to say anything in the dressing room beforehand. I turned to Seanie Brennan, the joker in the team, who does the best Roddy Collins impersonation you'll ever hear.

'Seanie,' I said, 'you do the team talk today.'

Which he proceeded to do.

'Just pretend you're oul' chisellers again,' he said, 'playing an oul' ball game on the streets of Cabra. Jumpers for goalposts. Next goal wins. Forty Coats and Bang Bang and oul' Lugs Brannigan looking on. And don't be worrying if it doesn't work out. No one's going to put you in front of a firing squad and yisser missus will still love you. Just go out and give it yisser best – not just for the supporters, but for them four cows on the hill.'

The players were laughing when they left the dressing room. Then they went out and beat Galway 3–1. I was so proud of them.

As we celebrated on the pitch afterwards, I spotted a familiar figure walking towards me. It was Keith Duffy from Boyzone. He had his son with him. The last time I saw Keith was the night before I was sacked by Carlisle United, when we sang karaoke together. He chose very strange times to make cameo appearances in my life.

As I hugged Keith, I spotted Jim McGlone and his wife behind the goal. As chairman of a club with an average home gate of fifty people, promotion to the Premier Division was both his greatest dream and also his greatest nightmare. I've never seen a man look so happy and so terrified simultaneously.

It was as if he was thinking, 'Thank you – but what the hell did you go and do that for?'

20

During the Celtic Tiger years, my bank manager was my best friend in the world. We had a great relationship. I used to call into the branch to have coffee with him, then in the course of the conversation I'd suggest an oul' top-up – 'What'll we say – ten grand this time?' – and he'd say that was no problem at all.

Then, one day in late 2008, he told me there'd be no more oul' top-ups. There was this thing called the credit crunch. I said I'd never heard of it, but it sounded like a chocolate bar.

How we laughed.

I was never especially smart with my money. I have a mate who's a multi-millionaire. He lives in a mansion in Castleknock and he drives around in a Maserati when he's not riding around on a Harley-Davidson. We both started out contracting around the same time.

One day I said to him, 'Where the fuck did I go wrong?'

And he said, 'Do you remember the good old days when we were earning two grand a week? Well, you were spending four.'

And it's completely true. For Caroline and me, that's what money is for – it's for making life a bit happier for you and those around you.

When we had the cash, we took the kids on big holidays to Florida and we brought home clothes and extravagant presents for everyone. Caroline and I went to Vegas and we had the time of our lives. Some weeks, one of us would say we hadn't seen Vinnie Jones or Shaun Edwards in a while, so we'd book a flight to London that weekend. We'd go into town and Caroline would buy a couple of dresses from Brown Thomas and I'd drop a few grand in Louis Copeland.

Any excuse we could think of, we'd rent a marquee and throw a party for fifty or a hundred people. We'd get crates of wine and champagne, a couple of Portaloos and a live band. It's a wonder that any of the neighbours are still talking to me.

They were brilliant days, especially during the construction boom. Blokes who'd struggled for years to find work on the sites were suddenly drinking Veuve Clicquot on their ten o'clock tea break. I did it myself. I was the one pouring it. We really lived it up during those years. And at the end of it, like a lot of people, we hadn't two pennies to rub together.

I've been broke in my life and I've been loaded. It's taken me until my sixties to discover the happy medium between the two. When we were at our most well-off, we were mortgage-free and there was €50,000 in the attic. Don't bother, there's nothing there now. It's long gone. But I used to lie in bed at night, staring at the ceiling, happy to know it was there. It was treated like an ATM – the kids even referred to it as the hole in the wall:

'Da, can I get a new pair of runners?'

'Yeah, go up and get it from the hole in the wall.'

When the economic crash happened, Sinéad – who was just starting out on her married life – said to Caroline, 'What are we going to do?'

And Caroline said, 'We'll do what we did in O'Devaney when times were tight. We'll go without, we'll make less stretch further and we'll look after each other.'

Much of what I owed I'd borrowed to put into the Bronx Sporting Club, which was now gone, and the second house, which I'd started working on with great gusto and then abandoned.

I still wasn't getting a lot of work in football. I didn't get any wages for most of my seven weeks in Cork and I wasn't on much money at Monaghan. The inevitable happened. I defaulted on my loans and the bank came down on top of me.

They wanted me to sell the house to pay them what I owed them. I said no, they couldn't force us out of our family home. They said we could sell it and buy a cheaper one in Longford. I said we weren't moving to Longford. Our children were in school in Dublin.

This went on for about two years. One night, I couldn't sleep. Everything was just getting on top of me. I had the idea that if I could finish the house next door, everything would be OK. I got up at 3.30 a.m., put on my work clothes and started beavering away on the house. I worked until 6 p.m. with a break for breakfast somewhere in between. I got a lot done. The only problem was that I couldn't get out of bed for the next two days, but it was a start.

Then I went to Supermike DIY builders providers in Clonsilla. I knew Mike Whelan, the owner. I told him I was in a deep hole and I asked him if he'd let me have materials on account. He told Chris, his son, Aine, his daughter, and Brian, the manager, to give me anything I needed.

Then I went to Brian Arkins of BA Engineering, a friend I knew through football. He gave me steel, then he put me in touch with a lad who said he'd do the doors for me and would be happy to wait for his money.

Old friends came and pitched in. Tommy 'Donkey' Daly reappeared. He fitted the fireplace. I offered to pay him.

'After all the work you gave me over the years?' he said. 'Don't insult me.'

John McEvoy, a millionaire roofing contractor and one of my oldest friends, put the roof on for me and wouldn't take a penny. Johnny Melia, an old pal from Rumours, did all the electrical work. A pal of mine, Bob O'Leary, provided all the plastering equipment I needed. James Jordan, another good friend of mine who's in the carpet and flooring business, carpeted the hall, stairs and landing and said, 'That's your house-warmer, Rod.'

In 2017, twelve years after I started digging a hole in the ground to try to work out my anger towards John Courtenay, a brand-new house stood on the spot. And it's the house that we call home today.

At Monaghan, Jim McGlone gave me a budget of €4,000 per week for the 2012 season. With that, I managed to put together a team of competent players, who I believed were good enough to keep us in the Premier Division.

We trained in Clondalkin. A fella I knew did me a favour and gave us the pitch for cheap. I did other bits of wheeling and dealing to get us through from week to week. When we played Shamrock Rovers in our first match, I told our supporters to go to The Bell in Blanchardstown for their pints and the manager agreed to feed the players.

But I didn't know the extent to which Jim and the rest of the committee were struggling to keep the club afloat. As always, Jim prioritized the wages above everything else. He made sure the players got paid. When the FAI demanded the affiliation money, the club didn't have it. They were given a deadline by which to pay up or face expulsion from the league.

It was June – just over three months into the season. We had a break, so Caroline and I headed to Spain for a week. I knew at that stage that we were going to be in a relegation battle, but I could win one of those in my sleep.

I was lying in the sun when Jim rang and said, 'Rod, I've a bit of bad news for you. We're pulling out of the League of Ireland.'

Poor Jim was in bits. He said he'd continue to pay me what he could until I found a new job. I said, 'Jim, don't worry about me. I'll tear up my contract now.'

I did some ringing around and found clubs for about half of the players, either in the League of Ireland or in junior football. It broke my heart. The people in charge of Monaghan United were good, honest football people. When I met the players to say goodbye, it was another sad moment, just like Cork.

For the next seven months I was unemployed again. I did a bit of coaching for St Mochta's, a Leinster Senior League team in Clonsilla, because I couldn't bear to be away from football. And I went back to training bare-knuckle fighters for cash. I wrote my weekly newspaper column and did bits of punditry for RTE and Newstalk.

Then, early in 2013, Turlough rang me – as he had a habit of doing when I was at my lowest ebb.

'Rod,' he said, 'Athlone Town are looking for a manager.'

The club had been stuck in the First Division for seventeen years, and thirteen successive managers had failed to take them up. It appealed to me because it was Turlough's home club and I knew how much it meant to him. It also meant a lot to me. I spent some of my happiest days as a footballer at Athlone Town, not including our humiliation against Standard Liège, of course. There was also the fact that I'd helped send them down in the relegation play-off while playing for Home Farm Everton.

The job came with two provisos, Turlough said. The first was that

I had to take his brother, Michael – Socksy – as my assistant manager. The second was that half of the players I fielded had to be locals, although I admit that I put a generous interpretation on what was considered 'local' to Athlone.

I put together a squad of twenty-six players. There were some very good teams in the First Division in 2013, including Longford Town and Waterford United, but I figured we could at least keep pace with them. Then, if it looked like we were going to make the play-off, I could maybe bring in a few marquee players during the transfer window.

I accidentally happened upon a diamond formation in a pre-season friendly against Tullamore Town. We didn't have a lot of players with pace, so I tried out the diamond because I thought it would help us keep the ball. We used it against Bradford City in another friendly and they couldn't get the ball off us.

Setanta was filming a second season of *The Rod Squad*. But the series ended up with me being unveiled as the new manager of Athlone Town and promising to succeed where more than a dozen managers before me had failed in bringing the club back to the Premier Division.

If I was going to do it, I thought it would happen through the play-offs. At one point that summer we were four points off a play-off place but also three points away from relegation. One night John Hayden, the chairman, called me off the training pitch. He was worried about our league position. As a barrister, John represented the DPP. He was tough and he was straight.

'John, I promise you,' I said, 'we're not going down. Get me two or three players and I promise you we'll get to the play-offs.'

I got three players, one of whom was Enda Curran, a striker from Galway. He scored four goals in eight games for us, including winners against Finn Harps and Mervue. We started climbing the table and suddenly it looked like we might even go up as champions.

We were blowing teams away and it was like a throwback to the old days. We were getting crowds of 2,500 and 3,000 again. For the last two or three home games of the season, the town was buzzing. When we beat Waterford United 1–0 at home, we were champions with three games to spare.

I'll never forget the scenes on the pitch afterwards. People told me that they thought Athlone Town would never be a Premier League club again. The whole town got a lift. Caroline and all the family were with me that day. It was the first thing I'd won in football since I did the double with Bohs twelve years earlier. I can honestly say it was one of my best ever days in football, not just because I loved the club, but because I knew how much it meant to Turlough.

After winning the First Division on a shoestring, it didn't matter what John Delaney or John Courtenay thought of me any more. I was back in demand as a manager. Bohemians – who had a new committee in place – asked John Hayden for permission to speak to me but he refused.

I wanted to leave Athlone. The club didn't have the money to push on the following season. I didn't want to deliver them to the Premier Division only to spend the next year desperately trying to keep them there. I wanted to go out on a high, so I asked John to let me go and he agreed.

There were two Premier Division clubs who I knew were interested in me – Sligo Rovers, who'd finished third the previous season, and Derry City, who'd finished fourth.

I met a delegation from Sligo in the Castleknock Hotel on the morning of the FAI Cup final. There were about six of them. They were all nice blokes but they seemed to know more about football than Alex Ferguson and I thought, Why don't you just manage your own team?

I went from there to a meeting with Sean Barrett, the CEO of Derry City, and Peter Wallace, one of the club's directors. We went to the cup final together. I had the impression that Sean wasn't wild about me, but I got on great with Peter. I always loved Derry City, especially the passion of the Brandywell crowd. I got excited talking to them. They had big ambitions and they matched mine. My plan was to bring in my old mate Bugsy Cunningham, who was from Derry, as my assistant and together we'd build a team capable of winning the Premier Division.

The next day I got a call to say the job was mine if I wanted it. They offered me a twelve-month contract with a good salary, plus the use of a car, a mobile phone and the rent paid on a house in Derry.

The only stipulation was that I had to take the former Derry City captain and fan favourite Peter Hutton as my number two. And I had five minutes to make up my mind. That's when I should have said no – when I still had some leverage. But I did the Michael-Collins-at-the-Treaty-talks thing. I thought if I could get my feet under the table, then I could get what I wanted down the line.

What I didn't know was that everyone saw Peter Hutton, not Roddy Collins, as the future of Derry City. I was only there to wet-nurse him for twelve months until he managed to get the experience and necessary coaching qualifications. I twigged it at my very first press conference.

'I'm a bit worried that he's wearing a better suit than me,' I told the press. They all laughed because they thought I was joking. I was when I said he was wearing a better suit. I looked a million dollars in mine. But there was a swagger about Peter that suggested he thought he was more than just my number two.

He was asked more questions than I was that day. It turned into the Peter Hutton Roadshow. He was, after all, 'a Derryman' – which, I would soon discover, was the be-all and end-all as far as the locals were concerned.

The 2014 League of Ireland season was launched at the Aviva Stadium in Dublin. I totally disarmed John Delaney by walking over to him and offering to shake his hand. He asked me how I thought we'd do that year. I told him we were going to win the league. He said nothing and walked off.

There was a club dinner that night for five hundred people in the City Hotel in Derry. Delaney was there, along with the Ireland manager Martin O'Neill – another 'Derryman'. Martin McGuinness was also there. In October 2011, when he ran for the Irish presidency, I went on the campaign trail with him and Gerry Adams in Dublin. He gave me a warm hug and told me he was delighted for me.

I was sitting at a table with Caroline, Sinéad, Niamh and young Roddy. It was one of the proudest moments of my life. People kept stopping by and wishing me the best for the season. I thought, Whatever happens, Rod, you are well and truly back.

Next thing, Delaney got up to make a speech. He said, 'Roddy Collins tells me that you're going to win the league,' and then, with a big smirk on his face: 'You're not going to be here long enough, Roddy.'

I was fuming. I wanted to grab him and throw him out the fucking window. Happily, nobody laughed. It was just John Delaney being John Delaney. The one thing he could never buy with the FAI's money was class.

By that time I'd already started to make my presence felt at Derry. The first day I arrived at the club there were five or six players sitting around the boardroom watching the TV with their feet up on the table. When they saw me, they didn't even stir.

I said, 'Right, lads, get the fuck out. Don't come in here to watch that TV again. This room is out of bounds.'

From their reaction I knew that I was going to have trouble with them.

Derry City was a huge club, but two FAI Cups was the sum total of what they'd won in the past fifteen years and I wanted to send a message that it wasn't going to be business as usual.

I cleared out a few players, including Kevin Deery, a former captain who was a legend at the club. He was also – as everyone was keen to remind me – 'a Derryman'. Kevin had been injured for years. He was out of contract, but the club had kept him on and were paying for the rehab on his knee. I told him there was no future for him there.

Kevin went home and posted a message on his Facebook page that said: 'I've had some amazing times with Derry City but all good things have to come to an end. Unfortunately for myself, it has come to an end partly through injuries and through a manager who's without doubt one of the most hateful men I have come across in football.'

The club issued a statement expressing disappointment with him, but there was no question whose side the supporters were going to take.

I got rid of a couple of others who'd played about twenty matches between them over the past two seasons. Straight away, I'd saved the club about £100,000 a year in wages.

There was £8,000 set aside in the budget to bring the players away for a pre-season tour, which was really a boozy holiday. I pulled the plug on it and told the players that there were to be no drinking sessions during the season. I've always believed that it's training together that creates a bond between players, not drinking together.

'We'll have a drink when we've actually won something,' I said.

I knew I was alienating the players, but they'd get over it.

Originally, the plan was that I would move to Derry with the whole family. But when I realized I was only there to keep the seat warm for Peter, we decided not to take the kids out of school in Dublin again. Caroline would move up with the kids when their summer holidays came. Roddy came with me. He was nineteen now and ready for first-team football.

We lived in a house on Culmore Road opposite Da Vinci's Hotel on the banks of the Foyle. I remember Dodie McGuinness, Martin's sister-in-law, who was involved in the club, helping Caroline to make the house a home. She was one of the leading lights of the civil rights movement. I loved talking to her. She was a brilliant person.

Very early on, I started to feel like I wasn't fully in charge of the club. I remember finding out that we'd signed Mark Timlin, a winger from Donegal, who'd been in the youth team at Ipswich Town. I went to Peter and said, 'Who the fuck signed him?', because I'd already spent a month brining down the wage bill.

'He's only costing us fifty quid a week,' Peter insisted.

The season started. Our form wasn't great. In our first match we played Shamrock Rovers in Tallaght. We were winning 1–0 until they equalized in injury time. Then we lost to Cork City, drew with Drogheda United and St Patrick's Athletic, beat Sligo Rovers, lost to Dundalk and then beat Athlone Town. It wasn't sacking form, but after a month I was already under pressure.

We weren't playing good football. I admit that. I was trying to make us hard to beat, which Derry hadn't been for a long time. The team was a work in progress.

Derry City football supporters are very knowledgeable and they had no qualms about stopping me and telling me where I was going wrong. And there was often this undertone of, 'Who does this Free State fucker think he is, coming up here, throwing out lads from the Creggan, the Bog and the Brandywell? Derrymen!'

That was when the city started to feel really claustrophobic. I remember I was invited to judge a Strictly Come Dancing competition for charity in the Everglades Hotel one night. I was having a slash when the fella standing next to me at the urinal said, 'Well, Collins, when you going back down the fucking Dublin Road?'

I said, 'I'm going on Sunday to watch a match.'

'I mean for fucking good,' he said.

As I walked back to my table, another lad said under his breath, 'Krusty the fucking Clown.'

I said, 'What did you say?' turning around to face him.

'I said Krusty the fucking Clown,' he said.

I took my jacket off.

'OK,' I said, 'I'll give you Krusty the fucking Clown.'

Caroline ended up dragging me away.

We'd only lost two matches all season, but it was the draws that killed us. We weren't creating chances. I admitted after one match that even I wouldn't pay to watch us.

I dropped Rory Patterson, Derry's top scorer the previous season, because I didn't think he was working hard enough for the team. I made him train with the reserves.

I decided that it was time to do something drastic. This was going to be my team or it wasn't. As an assistant manager, Peter Hutton hadn't impressed me at all. I let him take training once or twice while I jogged up and down the sideline. Then he kept asking me when I was going to let him take a team talk. When I finally did, it was all, 'We're in this together,' and other clichés that meant nothing.

We were due to play Shamrock Rovers at home on the second Friday in May. I made my big play that week. The club could either back me or back Peter. I called him in and I said, 'Peter, I've assessed you over the first few weeks of the season and you've no football brain.'

'What do you mean?' he asked.

'I mean you're no benefit to me in the dugout,' I said. 'You don't see what's going on. I want to offer you a new role.'

'What's that?'

'Chief scout.'

His face turned white.

'Are you fucking serious?' he said.

'Yeah, I'm serious,' I told him. 'We're playing Cork next week. I want you to go to Dublin and watch them against Pat's on Friday night.'

The word was all over the city within hours. Peter had been shafted. I got calls from one or two people within the club, asking me, 'Are you sure about this?' and I said I was.

Friday arrived. Peter went to Dublin to watch Pat's v. Cork while we played Shamrock Rovers at the Brandywell. On the day of the match, hardly anyone around the club was talking to me. They couldn't even look me in the eye.

When I named the team to face Rovers, someone in the dressing room started playing circus music on his phone.

Before we walked out onto the pitch that night I turned to Trevor Croly, the Rovers manager, and I said, 'Have you ever heard a manager get booed *onto* the pitch by his own crowd before?'

'No,' he said, 'never.'

'Well, have a listen to this,' I said.

The fans tore into me. I made my way to the dugout. The abuse was bitter and personal. 'You Free State bastard!' they shouted. And, 'Fuck off to your mate in Belfast,' because everyone knew about my friendship with Kirk Hunter.

We played well that night, but we got beaten 1–0. And that was the only detail that mattered to anyone. I did an interview afterwards with Kevin McLaughlin, a local reporter. I got upset and used a lot of F-words. I told him that everyone at Derry had been too nice to each other for years – 'everyone looking at each other, going down to the Brandywell to pick up their few quid' – but that the club was built on quicksand.

'It's not a YMCA,' I said. 'And it's not about personalities for me. It's about winning and playing well . . . If people get hurt and upset along the way, I'm sorry but that's life. Nothing comes easy. Do you think it's easy for me, sitting in that house, looking at four walls, getting abused? It's not.'

The next day, I drove home to Dublin for the weekend. That night I went to the Setanta Sports Cup final in Tallaght between Dundalk and Sligo Rovers. A few of the regular football reporters came up to tell me there was a strong rumour that I was gone.

On Sunday morning, I had a call from Philip O'Doherty, the chairman of the club, who was a brilliant bloke. He asked me when I was coming back to Derry. I told him I'd be back that night because I had training the following morning.

'Can you come up a bit earlier,' he said, 'and come to my house?'

I said to Caroline, 'This is it.'

On Sunday I drove back up and went straight to Philip's house. Sean Barrett was there. Philip made tea while Sean tried to make small talk with me. It was hard for him because he didn't like me.

'Let's get down to business,' Philip said. 'The crowd have turned, Rod, and they're never turning back. You took a gamble on Peter.'

'Yeah,' I said, 'I did. I called it out – it is what it is.'

'Well, what do we owe you?'

'Owe me?'

'To walk away.'

We settled on a figure in two minutes. He was a very fair man. There were things I wanted to say, but there was no point in prolonging it. It was done.

Philip shook my hand. I gave him a hug and told him if ever he was in Dublin to call me. The club released a statement immediately to say that I was gone 'by mutual consent'. It was a boot up the arse, but the money in my back pocket acted as a cushion.

Peter Hutton was announced as my replacement. He got found out in the end. He was sacked a year later.

Derry was my last big job in football. I took the settlement and we used it to furnish the house. Even today, I still tell people, 'Derry City moved us in.'

I wanted to remain in football after I left Derry, but the phone wasn't exactly ringing off the hook. Young Roddy got signed by Luton Town and I returned to my old routine of trying to finish the house and training Travellers for cash while I waited for the right job to come up.

In 2015 I went to England to help out my nephew Colin Mahon, who had his own plastering business but was having difficulty getting paid by a builder. We collected the debt and I stayed to give him a hand with the business. He was renovating an enormous mansion in the Hertfordshire countryside and we were living in it while we did the work.

I was enjoying being a plasterer again – and no one was calling me a wanker or a Free State bastard. I considered going back to contracting myself. Through my old friend John McEvoy, I became friendly with one of the biggest builders in England, who promised enough work for me to employ two hundred plasterers.

'You'll be a very wealthy man within five years,' he said.

My brother Stephen was living nearby in St Albans. Young Roddy was at Luton, less than an hour's drive away. I started to think that we might move over there permanently.

One weekend Caroline came over with Padraig and Lauren. Having previously persuaded her to move to Mansfield, Newport, Carlisle, Malta and Derry, I wanted her to know that this wasn't just another one of my pipe dreams.

The four of us were in the Disney Store on Oxford Street in London when my phone rang. It was Paul Cooke, who was on the committee at Waterford United. He asked me if I'd be interested in becoming their new manager.

'Paul, leave me alone,' I said. 'I'm living in England. I get to see Roddy play every week and I'm going back into contracting again.'

'Please, Rod,' he said, 'we need you.'

Caroline has always been a home bird. 'Go and talk to them,' she said.

I knew that as soon as I did, I'd get sucked back in again. I flew home and drove to Waterford to meet with Paul, John O'Sullivan, a millionaire who was running the club in memory of his late father, and three other board members. Waterford United were in the First Division, but they had big plans for the club. Didn't they all? John offered me a two-and-a-half-year contract on a good wage, along with a car and a phone. I brought in Aaron O'Callaghan, the most knowledgeable coach in the country, as my assistant.

And so I turned my back on my plans to become a wealthy plastering contractor and instead became the manager of Waterford United.

John was a brilliant chairman. Not once was I ever left without wages. His friend owned the Woodlands Hotel and I lived there free of charge.

But once again it was all castles in the air. I was promised that we were going to do things differently, but it turned out the same way it always did. Lots of people were going to put money into the club. By the end of my first season, John was the only man there still putting his hand in his pocket.

I tried to make things happen myself. I leaned on some of my contacts in England to get one or two big-name teams over for a summer football festival that might raise funds for the season. I tried to set up a hospitality lounge in the club. But it was no good.

We finished second from bottom in 2015. In my second season I brought in a few players I was familiar with, including young Roddy. But it was hard to attract good players with no money.

The season was only three or four games old when John came to me and said he was stepping down as chairman. He couldn't put any more money into the black hole. I understood. The game had broken many men but none better than John O'Sullivan.

I was writing about him when I said in my column in the *Irish Daily Star*: 'The game here is fucked without good people who get nothing in return only stress and abuse, and without the players and the phenomenal effort they put in.' I also called the League of Ireland a 'shambles'.

I got a letter from the FAI. I was fined €1,500 and banned from the touchline for six matches. Des Gibson, the sports editor of the *Irish Daily Star*, offered to fund my appeal. He wrote me a cheque and I took it out to Abbotstown. I was told that it was no good because it had to be a bank draft. The next week I repeated my comment about the league being a shambles – 'a fucking shambles', I said, correcting myself – and got suspended for three more games.

For our home matches I got around the ban easily enough. There was a door in the public toilets that led into the home dressing room. It was usually locked, but I had a key and I let myself in and out to talk to the players before matches and at half-time.

With a budget of €300 per week, it was a struggle to find eleven competent players to put out on the pitch. We didn't have petrol money so I put out an APB, asking supporters to give players lifts to training and games. No one at the club got paid for the last ten weeks of the season, but Aaron stuck with me to the end. A man.

I saw out the season until the end of September, when we lost 8–1 to UCD at home. It was one of my most humiliating days in football. Shortly after that, as the committee tried to find a new buyer for the club, the relationship fell apart in bitterness and acrimony.

I wished I'd stayed in England.

A few weeks later, I got a call from Vinny Arkins, Brian's brother. Vinny had spent most of his playing career at Portadown, who were now interested in having him as their manager. The only problem was that he didn't have his Pro Licence yet. He asked if I'd be interested in taking the job with him as my assistant just until he was qualified. I said yes.

I drove up for an interview. Portadown was a predominantly loyalist town. When I played in the North, it was where I received the worst sectarian abuse of all. One of the men on the interview panel was missing half a leg, the result of an IRA bombing. Another had been related somehow to Billy Wright of the LVF. But the interview seemed to go well.

Vinny got called in off the training ground and I was told to wait outside. I went out and sat in my car while I waited for their decision. The next thing, Vinny came running out, looking pale.

'Rod,' he said, 'do you write for *An Phoblacht*?'

'I do,' I told him, 'but it's just a sports column.'

'They're after Googling you,' he said. 'Get the fuck out of here now.'

Things went quiet again.

Then I got a call from David Dully, the secretary of Athlone Town. He wanted to know would I come back to Athlone. They had been relegated again the year after I took them up, just as I knew they would be. There was a big investor in Portugal who was going to put a lot of money into the club.

The Russians, the Chinese, the Portuguese. I'd heard it a million times before. And yet I still said I'd hear what he had to say.

I met Turlough's brother Michael O'Connor and the chairman, John Hayden, in Athlone. These Portuguese investors, they said, were interested in using Athlone as a sort of centre of excellence. They planned to develop the players and sell them on. It was the same thing that Johnny Giles tried with Rovers forty years earlier.

At that stage, there were six young overseas players at the club. I went along to watch them train. They were all great kids, but they couldn't kick snow off a rope.

And, of course, I said yes to managing them.

After two weeks, one of the kids pulled me aside in training one day. He said, 'Boss, can we speak? We are living in a big house down there but we have not enough food to eat. We are hungry.'

'What do you mean?' I asked. 'Are you not getting any wages?'

'No,' he said, 'we are here for the opportunity.'

I thought, What, to play against Cabinteely and Longford Town? Fuck that!

The club, I should add, were very honourable. But the investors, who were responsible for the players, didn't look after their end of things. There were a few guys hanging around who seemed to be looking after the interests of the famous investors. One of them looked like a hitman out of *Gomorrah*. He was a big fat fella with holes in his shoes and he always seemed to be eating. I went up to him one night and I lumped him out of it. I told him, 'Don't show your fucking face around here again if you don't have money for them players.'

I never saw him again.

I rang John immediately after training. He was disgusted. He came straight to the training ground with Socksy to speak to the players. That night they arranged for a local supermarket to supply them with food and the club took over the responsibility of looking after the players until they left.

I stayed for a year. We played twenty-seven matches that season and won only four of them. We finished bottom of the first division. I couldn't believe that this was the same club that Turlough led to the League of Ireland title, the same club whose jersey I was proud to wear. When the season was over at the end of 2017, I left.

And that, I presumed, was that. I was fifty-seven years old and I'd had my fill of football. Our lives in the next few years began to revolve more and more around our grandchildren. Niamh had another boy, Sonny, a little brother for Donnacha. Sinéad had two little girls named Fiadh and Grace. The house was full of children's voices again. I spent most of my time on Padraig and Donnacha's boxing and Fiadh's football.

Then, in 2019, I got a call out of the blue from Declan Roche, a lad from Dublin who was at Celtic when he was a kid and went on to play for Cork City and Shelbourne. He was involved in a company that connected experienced football coaches with clubs abroad. He asked me if I'd ever considered coaching overseas.

'I'd love to coach in America,' I told him.

'What about China?' he asked.

And I got that old butterflies-in-the-tummy feeling again.

'China?' I said.

'That's where I am right now,' he said. 'Roddy, they would love you out here. I could find the right club for you. Money, expenses, accommodation – none of that will be a problem.'

I asked Caroline if she fancied moving to China.

'Yes,' she said – no hesitation.

I suppose it wasn't the worst place I've ever asked her to move for my football career.

We got really excited about starting a new life on the other side of the world. We inquired about taking Mandarin classes. We were all ready to go. Early in 2020 I got a call from Declan to say there was a new virus out of control in China, and they were shutting the borders.

I went and broke the news to Caroline.

We were both disappointed.

'Roddy, she said, 'tomorrow is another day.'

And despite the setbacks, the defeats and disasters we suffered along the way, I realized in that moment that I still believed it. And believing it, for me, is the secret of happiness.

Epilogue

It's March 2022. I'm sitting on a Ryanair flight from Dublin to Luton and I have butterflies in my stomach. I'm going over to watch my son play football. These days, young Roddy plays in the centre of midfield for non-league Chesham United in Buckinghamshire. They're a semi-professional team with big ambitions. Roddy is a leader of men – far better than I ever was. And he's dedicated to a degree that would have put me to shame. He doesn't drink, he eats the right things and he's even more demanding of himself than he is of others.

His brother Padraig came to me last year and told me that he was unhappy in his apprenticeship. He said he didn't want to be an electrician any more. He wanted to be a professional boxer. And I laughed and thought, How mad is that? My two sons are going down the same roads as me and Stephen did forty years ago.

I told him, yes, of course he could give up his apprenticeship as an electrical engineer to become a boxer. I got to follow my dreams – the least I owe my children is to encourage them to follow theirs.

Two nights before I wrote this, Ireland played Belgium at the Aviva Stadium in Dublin. Before the match I was honoured by the FAI for my services to football. And, yes, by all means take a moment if you need it to read that sentence again.

It started with an e-mail to say they wanted to present me with an award. I could have told them what to do with it, but it's a point of principle for me never to refuse a man's hand if it's offered in good faith. I stepped onto a little platform and Gerry McAnaney, the president of the FAI, handed me the medal in a little presentation box. He said he knew I'd had a difficult time of it over the years, especially off the pitch, and he wanted to show me his appreciation. He struck me as a nice man who was being genuine with his words. I told him thank you and I shook his hand.

I'd watched the slow and shameful unravelling of the John Delaney era with a mixture of frustration and sadness. The frustration came from knowing that all of the revelations about the way he ran the FAI just confirmed the things I'd been saying for years. The sadness came from knowing that good football people stood by and did nothing to stop him. A lot of them were happy just to take whatever work he threw their way while telling me in private that I was doing a great thing in standing up to him. Well, I lost ten years of my career doing it.

Of course, it doesn't matter now. He doesn't matter now.

We've commenced our descent towards Luton. I'm excited about seeing Roddy. 'The Messiah', as his sisters still call him. It's great to have him so close again. A few years ago, when he moved to Australia with Katie Fox, his partner, Caroline and I went through something similar to bereavement. Every Friday night we used to have a few glasses of wine and cry our eyes out listening to Colm Wilkinson singing 'Bring Him Home' over and over again. We'd have tears streaming down our faces and I'd be making wild promises: 'I'm going to Australia to get them home, Caroline! I'm going on Monday morning and we'll have them back by next weekend!'

There's another reason I'm excited this morning. Chesham United want to talk to me about taking some kind of role within the club, maybe as a director, maybe as director of football. Like I said, they have big ambitions. They want to be playing in the National League – the old Conference – within five years. They're about to start work on a brand-new stadium. Bob Breen, who I brought into Bohemians as commercial manager in 2000, is the head of the project.

They're serious people. They know my background is in construction and in football, and they think I might have some expertise to offer them in both areas. They're interested in learning what I can do for them – and that's never a bad thing to hear.

There's a part of me, of course, that thinks, Roddy, give it up. The dream is over. You're sixty-two years old this year and you've put more than enough strain on that old heart of yours. But then I look at Claudio Ranieri, still managing at the highest level at seventy years of age, and I think, Why not? Since I started reliving my life in the course of writing my story, I've discovered that my love for the game is as strong as it ever was, and so is my appetite.

I can pretend that I'm not going to get sucked in again, but I'd just be lying to myself. How could I *not* get involved – when under this Louis Copeland suit and this camel-hair coat beats the heart of a football manager who still thinks he could do a job for Manchester United?

Acknowledgements

First of all, I would like to thank Michael McLoughlin in Sandycove for giving me the opportunity to tell my story. Thanks to Brendan Barrington for being such a diligent and professional editor. Thanks to my agent, Faith O'Grady, for believing in the project. Thanks to Louise Farrell for her patience in organizing the publicity and media.

But mostly I want to thank Paul Howard, who I've known for more than thirty years. I've always said there was only one writer I would trust to tell the story of my life and that was Paul. I'd like to thank him for his skill as a writer and his understanding of human nature, which have made this book what it is. Over the course of a year, we worked hard and we laughed hard while putting the story together. Caroline and I can't thank him enough.

I'd like to thank my ma and da, the best-looking couple in Cabra and the best mother and father in the world. They were loving and caring and always there when we needed them. My da was strong and dependable. My ma was easygoing and full of love and forgiveness. I'd love to think they gave some of those special qualities to me.

I want to thank my big brother, Mick, for being just that – my big brother. He was the star of the show when I was growing up and he still is today. I want to thank my little brother, Stephen, for being himself and for bringing our family so much joy. I know my da was watching and he was so proud. Thanks to my sister Collette for being the kindest, most unselfish person I've ever met. Thanks to my sister Audrey for her strength, honesty and devotion. Thanks to my little brother, Paschal, who lost his father when he was very young but overcame that loss to become the wonderful human being he is today. I can't say enough good things about him. As my da would say – a man.

I would like to thank my 'other' family, the Hanneys. Thanks especially to Caroline's ma and da, Ellen and Billy. They were the strongest, most caring and most united parents you could dream of. They accepted me into their home (once I got rid of the leather coat) and treated me not as their daughter's boyfriend or future son-in-law but as one of their own.

I owe huge thanks to Caroline's sister Ellen and her husband Oliver, who've always been there for me with their wisdom. Thank you to Liam and Mammy Rose for the miracle that is Lauren. Thank you to Sandra and Alan and to Joaney and Robbie for always being there for me and Caroline. Thank you to Martina and Mick, the most considerate people I've ever met. Thanks to Bernadette and Jimmy 'Mr Whippy' Martin for all the babysitting you did for us and the ice creams. Thanks to Christopher for being Christopher. And to my best pal, Mikey, and his wife, Mary, thank you for everything.

If you've read my story, you'll know that I've been blessed with the best friends in the world. Thanks are owed in particular to Stevie Spicer – The Driver, as we call him. He's always been there for me. Thanks to Shaun Edwards and Mags. It's been a privilege to have you as a friend, Shaun, through good times and bad. You've thrown some of the best parties I've ever been to: 'A free bar – and chip butties for everyone!' To Vinnie Jones and the much loved and much missed Tanya, thank you for all the generosity and kindness you've shown me and my family over the years.

Thank you to Joe Webb and Tommy Miles, the first two people who identified that I could play football. They steered me in the direction of Jimmy Brannigan, a great football man, who gave me the confidence to think I had a future in the game. Thanks to Turlough O'Connor, who always took a punt on me. He bought me and sold me three times and helped put me in the Bohemians job. He has been one of the biggest influences on me, not just as a player and manager but as a man.

I'd like to thank Wilson Matthews, who gave me my first opportunity to become a manager at Bangor. He and his beautiful wife Darinda took me into their home and showed me so much kindness and hospitality.

Thanks to Tony O'Connell, who made the bravest (and some said maddest) decision in Irish football by putting me in the Bohs job and sticking with me on numerous occasions when many others would have thrown in the towel. I can never, ever thank him enough. Thanks to Jimmy Fitzpatrick, who encouraged me, advised me and watched my back at Bohs from the time I was a player and right through my time as a manager. Thanks to Pete Mahon, without whom I never would have won the double at Bohs. Thank you, Pete – you're an absolute legend.

I want to thank John 'Bugsy' Cunningham, who dropped everything to come to Carlisle United with me. Bugsy, I love you like a brother. I want to thank Terry Eviston, a man of conviction and principles who understands the true meaning of the word loyalty. He also has the wickedest sense of humour in the world. I could never be bored in his company. Terry and Trisha, thank you for being such great friends to us.

Thanks to my dear friend Allo Kearney, a legend to me in football and in life, who persisted with me and insisted I write to every club in England looking for a trial. Allo, you will never, ever be forgotten by me.

To Aaron O'Callaghan, the most knowledgeable football coach on the island – thank you for your loyalty. When you're with someone, you're with them 100 per cent, through thick and thin, and I was so lucky to have you by my side.

I want to say a huge thank you to all my friends in the Travelling community, whose wonderful hospitality I have enjoyed over the years.

Thank you to all the nightclub door staff who watched over and guided me (sometimes home) on my many nights of celebration and commiseration. Thanks especially to Robbie Dunne from my Magnums heyday and to Tommy Broderick in Rumours and later Renards. Thanks to Robbie Fox in Renards and to Tony Hickey, who always looked after me at nightclub doors and FAI functions. Thanks to Derek McGuinness, who also looked after me at the FAI dos. Thanks to Mick O'Dowd, Patsy McCarty and Jeffrey Collins for looking after me and Caroline in Lillie's Bordello.

Special thanks are owed to Dave McManus, who urged me to keep going when no club would touch me with a bargepole. You never wavered in your belief in me and you tormented me to commit my story to paper. Well, here it is, Dave – and it would not have happened without you.

Thanks to my uncles, John, Terry, James and Dixie, and all my cousins on the Collins side. You are never far from my thoughts and always in my heart. The same is true of my O'Rourke aunts and uncles – Roddy, Paddy, Jack, Sheila, Mary – and cousins. Thanks to my nanny Annie and my grandad James and my nanny Sheila and grandad Breff.

Thank you to every footballer who played with me and for me over the years. Thank you for the memories. Thanks especially to Nevy Chamberlain for making me feel so welcome and comfortable at Mansfield Town and thanks to Tony Lowery and David 'Logie' Logan for doing the same. To big Paul 'Willo' Williams for all the craic we had at Newport – I'll never forget you, pal. Thanks to Noel King, who taught me so much about football. It was a privilege to play for you. Thanks to Tommer Conway for always having my back as a player and a players' union man. Thanks to big Kirk Hunter – a Crusaders legend – for making me feel so welcome and at ease in what would otherwise have been an alien environment. I'm lucky to have you as a friend.

Thanks to Ray McGuinness at Bangor for standing shoulder to shoulder with me and for having my back. Thanks to Mick and Niall Shelly for being so brilliant to me at Bohs. Thanks to Freddie Davis for almost making me split my sides with laughter and Tommy Kelly for this piece of invaluable advice: never drink in the club bar. And I never did. Thanks to Austin Brady, who insisted I eat the food in Portugal, the reason I ran for ninety minutes, non-stop. Thanks to John Noonan, who looked after me at Shamrock Rovers – a club stalwart of the best kind.

I owe a huge debt of gratitude to all those who stuck with me during my battles with John Delaney and the FAI, especially Fran Rooney, Caoimhghín Ó Caoláin, Robert Kidd and Ger Colleran. Thanks to all my friends in the media, especially Gavin Becton, Des Gibson, Mark McCadden and Paul Lennon of the *Irish Daily Star* for giving me space to share my thoughts on the game. Thanks to Tony O'Donoghue and Ryle Nugent of RTE and their colleague Con Murphy, an absolute gentleman who gave me great guidance in the early part of my TV career.

Thank you to the woman who had a word with Willie Power about giving me an apprenticeship when I was a kid. I've forgotten your name but not what you did for me. Thanks to John Kerrigan, who had the patience of a saint to put up with me. Thanks to Derry McPhillips, John Prunty and Martin Dunne, who all employed me at various times, nurtured me – and always paid on time!

Thanks to Louis Copeland for making me look good – and also for being a brilliant friend and confidant.

And now to my team of star players – my family. I want to thank my wonderful daughter Sinéad and tell her how proud I am of her. We gave her a rough start in life. She lived in seven homes in three different countries while I chased my dream. She is always there to help her siblings with their problems – we call her the Terminator. Caroline and I are so proud of you, Sinéad, for all your achievements but mostly for the person you are today. Thank you to Niamh, the twinkle of her daddy's eye, a kind-hearted, easygoing soul whose outlook on life I love. Thank you to Rod Junior – The Messiah, as his sisters call him – who I love for his strength of character, his honesty and the courage he shows in just being himself. Thank you to Rod Junior's partner, Katie Fox, for loving him so much. Thank you to Padraig, a big, cuddly bear of a man, who can go a week without talking but doesn't go a minute without thinking. His thoughts are always for others and never for himself. He is full of love – until you step into a boxing ring with him. I love you, champ. Thank you to Lauren – Lorrie Bops – the strongest, most thoughtful and givish person I know. We love you so much, Lauren, and we can never express in words how much joy and happiness you have brought to our lives. Thank you to Donnacha, our first grandchild, who lived with us for the first ten years of his life, and who I love like a son.

I want to thank Alan Byrne for being a great husband to Sinéad and a great father to their beautiful daughters, Fiadh and Grace.

Thank you to Warren Keogh for being such a great partner to Niamh and for giving us a beautiful grandson in Sonny.

But above all else, I want to thank Caroline. We met for the first time when we were fifteen years old. I fell in love that day. Forty-seven years later, I love her forty-seven years more. Caroline has given me the best moments of my life. She gave me five beautiful children. She directed them, advised them, loved them and nurtured them to help them become the wonderful people they are today. She gave us all the best of herself. She filled us all with the belief to think we could overcome any obstacle that confronted us. She is the most selfless person that God ever put on this planet. She puts everyone else first and herself last. She brought out the best in all of us. Caroline, as we say to each other every night – I love you, pal.

Index

C · E · A · C · E · T

Numerical
factor